GALATIANS

A Supernatural Justification

Exegetical Sermons on Galatians

GALATIANS

A Supernatural Justification

Exegetical Sermons on Galatians

Douglas Van Dorn

Waters of Creation Publishing
1614 Westin Drive, Erie, Colorado 80516

Unless otherwise noted, references are from the *English Standard Version* (ESV) of the Bible.

Cover Design by Stephen Van Dorn

Fonts: Titles – BatangChe and Bell MT; Scripture – Tahoma and Georgia; Headings – Garamond, Janson, Janson SSi; Text and Notes– Bembo Book MT Pro.

ISBN: 978-0-9862376-1-4

Also by Douglas Van Dorn through Amazon.com

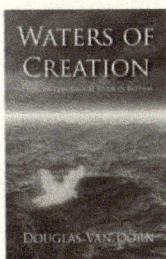

Waters of Creation: A Biblical Theology of Baptism
This ground-breaking study gives a Reformed Baptist argument for baptism from the continuity of Scripture via covenant theology. It shows the OT roots of baptism, along with a detailed analysis of how baptism fits into every OT covenant. Helpful charts included.

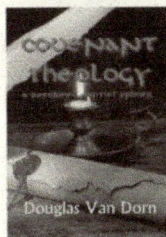

Covenant Theology: A Reformed Baptist Primer
Originally a series of Sunday evening lessons, this turned into a primer, my attempt to give an overview of covenant theology as a Reformed Baptist. All of the major covenants of the Bible are presented in historical order. A section on application ends the book.

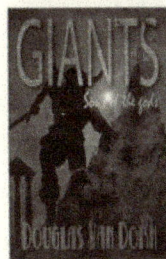

Giants: Sons of the Gods
An Amazon bestseller for the genre. *Giants* is a biblical theology on a topic that many wrongly believe is exhausted in the person of Goliath. This book is a worldview changer. It includes a semi-technical *Introduction* on the "son of God" from Gen 6:1-4 and several Appendices on extra-biblical literature and giants in the Americas.

Coming Soon...

From the Shadows to the Savior: Christ in the Old Testament
Originally a series of blogs for the Decablog, this book looks at the vital question of how Christ is in the Old Testament through things such as prophecy, typology, law, and numerous words that personify Him such as the Word, Glory, Wisdom, Son, and Name.

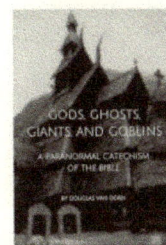

Gods, Ghosts, Giants, and Goblins
This book may be the first catechism on the paranormal or supernatural things in the Bible. It is written in a simple question and answer format, and as a story. It begins with God, deals with Satan, gods, idols, demons, giants, and eschatology. With Scripture proofs. A two volume commentary will eventually accompany it.

Table of Contents

Preface

This book contains twenty sermons I preached from Galatians between May – October 2011. As such, they are meant to teach, feed, and edify those sitting in my congregation on a weekly basis.

Through this study I came to realize that Paul tackles the power of the cross from two perspectives. One is the earthly human perspective of which many are familiar. From this vista, much of what you see here is a defense of the traditional Protestant view of justification by faith alone and other important matters of salvation.

The other perspective is not often caught by interpreters of this letter (or many other NT books). It is a heavenly perspective. Much of what you will read here discusses heavenly creatures and strange invisible things that will captivate and fascinate, all while showing that the power of Christ extends not only to mankind, but to the entirety of creation. He is truly the Lord of heaven and earth. His cross has conquered all of his enemies.

As you will discover when reading, I love footnotes. I mostly have them for my own sake, so that I can remember where I read something, so I can reference it in a later work, or so I can remember some thought I had about a particular passage. I have found it helpful to be thorough in my notations when preparing sermons. Consider these notes excursions into things I think about when writing a sermon.

I hope and pray you will find the material herein beneficial for our soul, helpful for your faith, and expansive for your brain as you come to know the Savior better and worship him with greater passion.

For Christ's sake and his kingdom,

Doug Van Dorn

Galatians

Bagpipes from Heaven

A Letter to Ancient Celts, Otherwise Known as Galatians

[1] Paul, an apostle--not from men nor through man, but through Jesus Christ and God the Father, who raised him from the dead-- [2] and all the brothers who are with me, To the churches of Galatia: [3] Grace to you and peace from God our Father and the Lord Jesus Christ, [4] who gave himself for our sins to deliver us from the present evil age, according to the will of our God and Father, [5] to whom be the glory forever and ever. Amen.

Galatians 1:1-5

Parody of Galatians

EXCLUSIVE: IN AN EXCITING EXAMPLE of scholarly cross-collaboration and interdisciplinary research, textual critics and archaeologists have just published a translation of a recently discovered first-century letter, apparently authentic, written to the Apostle Paul himself. Scholars believe it was likely written in the late AD 40s or early 50s. The parchment was remarkably well preserved in a jar buried in a cave on the island of Satiricus. It is surmised that the author of the letter, Parodios, was an elder who had met Paul on one of his missionary journeys. The translation, published here for the first time, reads as follows:

Parodios, a servant of the Lord Jesus Christ, to our brother Paulos.

Grace to you and peace from God our Father and the Lord Jesus Christ.

Our church recently received a copy of the letter that you sent to the church of Galatia. We hope you will not mind hearing our humble concerns. In the past we have noticed you are more interested in confronting people rather than conversing with them, but we hope you will receive this letter as an invitation to further dialogue.

First of all, we are uncomfortable with your tone throughout the correspondence. We know it is difficult sometimes to discern tone of voice from written communication, but you should keep this in mind as well. One could gather from your careless use of words that you are losing your temper. You certainly sound angry. This is unbecoming a spokesperson for the faith. As you say yourself, one of the manifest fruit of God's Spirit is gentleness.

Aren't you being a hypocrite to preach grace but not show it to our Judaizer brothers? They may not worship as you do or emphasize the same teachings you do, but our Lord has "sheep not of this fold," and there is certainly room within the broader Way for these brothers. Their methodology may differ from yours, but certainly their hearts are in the right place.

You yourself know that our Lord required personal contact when we have a grievance against another. Have you personally contacted any of these men? Have you sat down to reason with them personally? Have you issued a personal invitation? Some of them may even reconsider their viewpoints if you had taken a different tack. We know that your position is likely that public teaching is open to public criticism, but we can do better than what is expected, can't we?

In one portion of your letter, you indicate you don't even know these persons! "Whoever he is," you write. Our dear Paulos, how can you rightly criticize them when you don't know them? It's clear you haven't even read their material, because you never quote them. We implore you to see that they are plainly within the tradition of Moses and of the Prophets. They understand the context of the covenant in ways you appear deaf to.

Similarly, we find your tone and resorting to harsh language not in keeping with the love of Christ. "Foolish Galatians." "Let him be accursed." "Emasculate themselves." Really? Can you not hear yourself? You think this is Christlike? Does this sound like something our Lord would say? Do you think this flippant, outrageous, personal, vindictive manner of speech speaks well of God's love or the church? It is clear you are taking this way too personally. Indeed, you ask the Galatians if you are now their enemy. Does everything have to be so black and white to you?

Paulos, what will unbelievers think when they read this letter? Do you think this will commend the gospel to them? This kind of harsh language just makes us look like a bunch of angry people. They see we can't even love each other, and over what? Circumcision? This is a terrible advertisement for God's love to an unbelieving world. You have given plenty of people permission now to disregard Jesus, if this is what his mouthpieces sound like.

We hope you will reconsider your approach. We know that you catch much more flies with honey than with vinegar. We are concerned that your ill-worded letter signals a divisiveness that threatens to fracture the church. We beg you to reconsider how important these minor issues are, and how in the future you may speak in ways that better reflect God's love.

The grace—and the love!—of our Lord Jesus Christ be with your spirit, brother.

Perhaps this could have been written by an elder in a Galatian church. We do not know what kind of temperament these people had, but we do know that the original churches did not last long in this part of the world. Such a response would have sped their demise even as it is speeding many today. However, this letter is not ancient. It is a piece of satire was written by Justin Taylor (and Jared Wilson) and was published on his blog on March 25, 2011.[1] It cleverly points out the sorry state of Evangelicalism today, which is more concerned with "being nice" than with protecting the good news of Jesus Christ so that people might actually be "delivered from the present evil age" (Gal 1:4).

The Gospel

In some places, "being nice" has become the new gospel. Where this is so, the gospel is by definition, no longer the gospel. Today we begin a

---

[1] Justin Taylor, "A Recently Discovered Letter of Critique Written to the Apostle Paul," http://thegospelcoalition.org/blogs/justintaylor/2011/03/25/a-recently-discovered-letter-of-critique-written-to-the-apostle-paul/.

study of the book of Galatians. Perhaps more than any other book of the Bible, Galatians is concerned with getting this good news <u>right</u>. This is the most important thing you can ever know, because when you believe it, you are saved and when you do not (whether it is because you do not believe it, have never heard it, or are hearing something that replaces it) you cannot be saved.

"Good news" translates the Greek word *euaggelion* (Gal 1:6, 7, 11, 2:2, 5, 7, 14), from which we get the word "Evangelical." An Evangelical was, historically, someone who held to and proclaimed the "good news" that Jesus Christ had been crucified and died because of our sins and was raised from the dead for our justification (Rom 4:25). The good news is therefore an announcement, not a way you treat one another. It is gospel, not law.

The gospel is the primary topic at the beginning of the body of this letter. Galatians is a letter; that is its genre. Typical letters of that day followed a standardized formula: *salutation, thanksgiving, body, paraenesis* (i.e. moral exhortations), *final greetings*, and *benediction*. Galatians, however, has no thanksgiving. Instead, it unleashes a quick volley of shots off the bow of those who are so quickly turning away from the gospel that has been proclaimed to them. There is shock ("I am astonished;" 1:6) and anathema ("let him be accursed;" 1:8, 9) followed by autobiography, example, allegory, satiric rebuke, and exhortation all aimed at bringing the audience back to its senses. These churches have been duped, "bewitched" (Gal 3:1) is the term, a word that signifies Satanic delusion which is causing them to turn away from the gospel that they were taught. This gospel is a gospel of free grace, freedom in Christ, justification from sin, faith alone to salvation. But they have turned it into its opposite, a "gospel" of law-keeping, slavery, and works-based acceptance from God. The stakes could not be higher: heaven vs. hell. Therefore, there is no time for cordial niceties. These people must see the grave danger that they are in, before they turn away altogether and perish for eternity.

Beloved of God, see here that in having no thanksgiving because of these things, God is telling you that you must get this story straight. To have any hope at all in this life, and especially the life to come, you must know and believe God's gospel. He greatly desires this for you. Therefore, you must heed the words of this letter. You must take it to heart, consider your own soul, think on your attitude about this good news: are you in love with it; are you complacent about it; do you long for something different than it? These are the questions you must ask yourself.

When reading this kind of genre, it is always helpful to figure out the thesis. You remember back in grammar school, when they taught you how to write a letter, and they told you to put a thesis statement at the end of your first paragraph? The thesis is the "big idea" of the paper. It is the argument that is being proved. The thesis of this letter is found in vv. 11-12,[2] "For I would have you know, brothers, that the gospel that was preached by me is not man's gospel. For I did not receive it from any man, nor was I taught it, but I received it through a revelation of Jesus Christ."

Notice that the thesis is about the gospel, but also about the origin of the gospel. This is very important to keep in mind as we go throughout this letter. The origin of the good news is in heaven. This heavenly or supernatural origin of the good news has an opposite throughout the letter. It is the supernatural origin of the tendency to disbelieve, confuse, obscure, or deny the good news. In other words, there are satanic forces aligned against God who greatly desire that you turn away from the truth. So, you read about the following supernatural terms: evil angels (1:8-9), good angels (3:19); gods (4:9); principalities (*stoicheia*; 4:3); witchcraft/basilisks (*baskaino*—"to bewitch;" 3:1), heavenly cities (4:14), and the present evil age (1:4). This emphasis is not often given its due, but I want to help rectify that in this series.

It is also important to keep in your mind when you have doubts about the truth or when your friends do and you are called to give them an answer for the hope that is within you. The point is, the letter is written to prove to these people where the gospel originates and why you can therefore trust it! Everything else revolves around this question of origin, and the answer ought to give you great comfort.

---

[2] It is difficult to find commentaries that will talk about the "thesis" of Galatians. But this is the view put forward by Robert K. Rapa, "Romans-Galatians," *Expositors Bible Commentary* revised edition, ed. Tremper Longman II and David E. Garland (Grand Rapids, MI: Zondervan, 2005), p. 568. Also Frank J. Matera, *Galatians* (Collegeville, MN: Liturgical Press, 2007), 78.

Author

This morning I want to look at the first five verses, which are the introduction or salutation of the letter. The author begins by identifying himself as "*Paulos Apostolos*" (Gal 1:1). "Apostolos" is not his last name, but his title. His name in English is just "Paul," but we know that before he was called this his name was "Saul." Actually, *Easton's Bible Dictionary* points out, "His circumcision-name was Saul, and probably the name Paul was also given to him in infancy 'For use in the Gentile world,' as Saul would be his Hebrew home-name."[3] We first meet Saul in the book of Acts, presiding over the stoning of Stephen the Deacon, receiving the robes of the witnesses who killed him (Acts 7:58). He is first referred to as Paul in Acts 13:9 where it says that he was "filled with the Holy Spirit" opposing a demonically inspired magician who was himself opposed to preaching about Jesus. Obviously, something radical had to happened to Saul. Curiously, Paul means "little," just like Mordecai in Esther, and like Mordecai, Paul is from the tribe of Benjamin. God loves to use the little things of this world to shame the big, the foolish things to shame the wise, so that he can gain all the glory for his mercy and grace.

We read about Paul's dramatic change in Acts 9. But we also read about it later on in chapter 1 of Galatians. Therefore, when we come to that portion, we will spend some time looking at what happened to this man who wrote more of the NT than anyone else. For now, it is enough to mention that Paul delves into this autobiography in order to convince his audience that his words are to be trusted as true and having come from God himself.

This leads to his title: Apostle. Apostle "connotes personal, delegated authority; it speaks of being commissioned to represent another."[4] To put it more briefly, the word refers to someone sent by another person, an envoy or a "messenger." This last word is curious, given Paul's reference to "angels" just a few verses later. For the word "angel" also means

---

[3] M.G. Easton, *Easton's Bible Dictionary* (Oak Harbor, WA: Logos Research Systems, Inc., 1996).
[4] Richard N. Longenecker, vol. 41, *Word Biblical Commentary : Galatians*, Word Biblical Commentary (Dallas: Word, Incorporated, 2002), 2.

"messenger."[5] The difference? Apostles refer only to human messengers,[6] while angels can also refer to heavenly messengers.[7] For now, just keep in mind that both apostle and angel mean "messenger."

The Bible uses the word apostle broadly and narrowly. Broadly it can refer to anyone sent by another (cf. John 13:16). It can refer to any Christian brother sent out from a church for a mission, be it tied to official duties or just sending letters (Rom 16:7; 2 Cor 8:23; Php 2:25 etc). Used in this way, it is arguable that a woman could be considered an apostle (see Rom 16:7's "Junias"). Used in the narrow sense, however, only men are Apostles, and here it refers only to a very select few men. In other words, contrary to the movie starring Robert Duval ("The Apostle"), you can't just appoint yourself an Apostle (in fact, that contradicts the meaning of the word). Apostles are sent, not self appointed messengers. This small band of men was given special functions, tasks, and powers and was each called by name personally by Jesus himself.[8]

The function of these men was to proclaim the gospel to all the world using uncommon supernatural gifting of the Holy Spirit and the "keys of the kingdom," to organize the church, giving her the inspired apostolic tradition (doctrine). The rules here for who was an Apostle in this sense are gathered from Scripture. All had with their own eyes seen Jesus and his resurrection. All were called personally to that office by Christ *by name*. All could perform miracles, real miracles, not the stuff you see Benny Hinn do. These were given for the special purpose of attesting at that time to the truth of their preaching, the origin of their gospel, and the authority of their ministry (Mark 16:20; Acts 2:43; 1 Cor 12:8–11). All were infallibly inspired in the public teaching (whether by word or writing; John 14:26; 16:13; 1 Thess 2:13; 2 Pet 3:2 etc), though they were sinners and as we will see when Paul talks about Peter, could some-

---

[5] For example, see the translation of the seven "angels" in Revelation (cf. Rev 2:1 etc) as "messengers" (Tyndale New Testament, Young's Literal Translation). The Hebrew word *ml'k* derives from *l'k* which means "send" (*Dictionary of Deities and Demons in the Bible*, "Angel"), p. 45.

[6] Jesus is once referred to as an "apostle" in Heb 3:1. Here he is being compared to Moses rather than angels as previous to this.

[7] The word *ml'k/aggelos* can refer to humans (cf. 1 Sam 11:4; 1 Kgs 19:2; Luke 7:24; James 2:25 etc).

[8] This is probably why Paul seems almost to replace Matthias in the Scripture. For, while Matthias was with Jesus from the beginning, we are never told that Jesus called him personally as we are with Saul/Paul.

times slip into gross hypocrisy. Therefore, these Apostles could have no successors. That includes anything from a Pentecostal self-called apostle to the Bishop of Rome to me or you. These are the only infallibly authoritative teachers of Christian doctrine. These 12 become the foundation of the church of Jesus Christ.

Origin of Apostolic Authority

Therefore, to question the message or authority of one of these 12 men, as these people were doing to Paul, was to question God the Father and Jesus Christ too. It was an incredibly serious sin which is at the very heart of this letter. While people today cannot commit this sin in the same way, that is all of the Apostles have died and so you can't question them personally, it is still very easy to commit this sin by not believing what the Apostle's wrote down for us which God has preserved in his word for us to believe. This is something that happens all the time as people question their message, their authority, their authorship, and just about anything else they can think of to question. So, Paul's message to them applies to us as well. Do not let anyone, even if it be an angel from heaven teach you a different gospel than the one found here, for this is God's good news.

Thus, the very next words out of Paul's mouth are, "not from men nor through man, but through Jesus Christ and God the Father, who raised him from the dead." What Paul says about his Apostleship fits right in with the thesis of the book (that the gospel is not of human origin). He is not an Apostle because some person made him one or some group in Jerusalem voted him into "the club," but because God made him one when Jesus Christ personally appointed him on the road to Damascus. At his conversion Jesus told him, "I have appeared to you for this purpose, to appoint you as a servant and witness to the things in which you have seen me and to those in which I will appear to you, delivering you from your people and from the Gentiles--to whom I am sending you" (Act 26:16-17). This was confirmed to Ananias when Jesus told him, "He is a chosen instrument of mine to carry my name before the Gentiles and kings and the children of Israel" (Acts 9:15).

Perhaps "on the testimony of two or three witnesses," Paul refers to both Jesus and the Father as two persons who made him an Apostle. To this he adds even more authority, that this Father "raised Jesus from the dead." This is a sly way of telling these people, "Look, not only did Jesus call me to this position, but this is the same Jesus who was raised from the dead. Oh, and by the way, the Father who raised him also called me to this position." Like these early Christians, it is important to tell you that those who deny the truth of the Scripture must deal honestly with these very first words of this letter. From the very first, you are faced with the fact that Jesus was said to be raised historically from the grave by someone claiming to have been called by this very Jesus to teach this truth to you! What has the resurrection of Jesus from the dead done to your faith lately? It ought to spur you on to righteousness and boldness in the face of any opposition. But before any of that, it ought to generate faith in your heart, for this is what you need to do anything. You need faith that Jesus Christ has truly been raised, in his body, from the dead.

The resurrection is a supernatural occurrence. The resurrection of Jesus is always at the very forefront of the NT books. It is the central point of the gospel. It is the singular event in history. It is the fulfillment of prophecies as old as man himself (see Gen 3:15). It is the heart and soul of Christianity. It is the single most important reason to even be a Christian, for as Paul says in 1 Cor 15:14, "If Christ has not been raised, then our preaching is useless, and so is your faith" (NIV). Either he rose from the dead which changes everything, or he didn't and the Bible is the most untrustworthy book in existence. If he did not, then do not pretend that he did, but if he did, stop living your life as if he did not. There can be no middle ground, for that is a lukewarm place, vile and repugnant and good for nothing.

Now, apparently, Paul was not alone when he wrote this letter. There were many "brothers" with him (Gal 1:2). This is important. In most of Paul's letters, he only identifies himself. Sometimes he identifies Timothy (Col 1:2, 1 Thess 1:1, 2 Thess 1:1) and in a few others also Silvanus (1 Thess 1:1, 2 Thess 1:1). But here, you get the impression that there are a host of brothers that are looking over Paul's shoulder as he writes. This means that Galatians is not the mad ravings of an Internet flamer. Have you ever received a flaming email from someone? They are always written by one person, usually off the cuff, and are never anything but emotional outbursts. Instead you get the impression that Paul has been in deep discussions with these others over what to do about these

Galatians

people. They are all deeply concerned. Their counsel was for Paul to write a letter from them all.

Recipients

This leads to who the letter was written to: "The churches of Galatia." I want to give a slightly detailed explanation of who this is. It needs to be addressed in two separate parts. First, Paul is breaking his normal custom and writing to many churches rather than just one. Of Paul's 13 letters,[9] eight were written to a single church and four were written to individuals. Now, all of these letters would circulate throughout the Christian churches (c. 1 Cor 1:2; Col 4:16; 1 Thess 5:27). They would then copy the letter and this is eventually how we came to have them in our Bibles. But Galatians is the only Pauline letter written to more than one person/group. This means that the things he is saying here were widespread. They were not just the problem of one isolated church. Whole groups of churches were headed down the same dangerous road, which implies to some degree that unlike other churches, what Galatians says is probably more important to understand than any other letter, because what it speaks against is apparently easier to fall into than other problems. Their main problem seems to have been a particularly gullible spirit that would listen to religious teachers that would contradict the essential parts of the gospel. They were easily swayed, willingly led astray, quick to have their ears tickled, fast to believe whoever came into their midst. Does this sound familiar to our contemporary world?

Second, these churches were all in a place called Galatia. Galatia lies in the middle of what the NT calls Asia Minor or what we today know as Turkey. But where in Galatia are these churches? This is actually an important question for people concerned with fixing a date for the writing of the letter (and in turn for how you interpret certain events in the letter, such as Paul's rebuke of Peter). There are two possibilities. The first is northern Galatia, up in the mountains. The second is southern Galatia.

---

[9] Romans, 1 and 2 Corinthians, Galatians, Ephesians, Philippians, Colossians, 1 and 2 Thessalonians, 1 and 2 Timothy, Titus, Philemon (not including Hebrews, which I think was written by Luke).

The problem lies in understanding exactly what Paul means by "Galatians" (Gal 1:2; 3:1).

"Galatia" can be an ethnic term or a territorial term, like Cheyenne or Dakota which are both places and people. That is, it may refer to a people group or to a province of Rome. If it is being used ethnically, then it refers to the original inhabitants of this region known as the Celts,[10] and its probable audience is central and northern Galatia.[11] You may be surprised by this, because we normally think of the Celts as living in Britain or Ireland ("Boston Celtics" whose logo is a leprechaun) or if you really know your history, the ancient land of France (Gaul).

The history of these Celts is obscured by the ancient mists of time. Josephus stated that Gomer the son of Japheth the son of Noah settled in Galatia. "Gomer founded those whom the Greeks now call Galatians (Galls) [hence Gaul = France], but were then called Gomerites."[12] The name Gomer in Akkadian is Gimirru (they called them Gimmerai). Europeans called them Cimmerians or Cimbri.

As Josephus said, Galatia takes its name from the Gauls (Celts). "Gaul" is thought by some to derive from a word meaning "powerful."[13] Others suggest that "Celt" and "Gaul" have the same meaning, something like "potent" and "valiant men."[14] It comes from a Greek word (*gala*) meaning "milk." For example, think of our galaxy which comes from *galaktos*. When you look at the center of the galaxy you see the "Milky Way." Thus, Galatia means something like "she who is milk-white." Why? Because the Celts were the very tall, extremely strong, white skinned blonde peoples of ancient times. I will come back to the ethnicity of these Galatians later on in the letter. For now, it is enough to say that if Paul is using this term this way, then he is referring to northern Galatia.

---

[10] David Noel Freedman, Allen C. Myers and Astrid B. Beck, "Galatia," in *Eerdmans Dictionary of the Bible* (Grand Rapids, Mich.: W.B. Eerdmans, 2000), 476.

[11] Hans Dieter Betz, *Galatians: A Commentary on Paul's Letter to the Churches in Galatia*, Hermeneia--a critical and historical commentary on the Bible (Philadelphia: Fortress Press, 1979), 5, 9-13.

[12] Josephus, *Antiquities* 1.123.

[13] See Helmut Birkhan, *The Celts* (Vienna, 1997), 48.

[14] Paul Pezron, *The Antiquities of Nations; More Particularly of the Celtæ or Gauls*, Mr. D. Jones, translator (London: R. Janeway, publisher, 1706), 276.

It is important to note, however, that we are not told specifically that Paul ever went here on his missionary journeys. If he did (there is room for this interpretation in Acts 16:6 and 18:23),[15] then the date of the book is sometime after his first missionary journey (circa 46-48 AD) and the council of Jerusalem (*circa* 50 AD).[16] Liberals love this later date, because it allows them to see contradictions in Paul's story of Peter and the issue of circumcision as it played out in Acts 15. Again, I will have more to say about this at the appropriate time.

As Carson-Moo-Morris put it, "It is much simpler to accept [Acts and Galatians]" together, rather than throwing one or the other out as mistaken.[17] This means you read the term "Galatians" geographically, which means that Paul is writing to the churches that he planted in Pisidian Antioch, Iconium, Lystra, and Derbe (Acts 13:1-14:28) on his first missionary journey. Thus, the letter of Galatians is viewed by southern-Galatian scholars as having been written prior to his second journey and before the Council of Jerusalem, in perhaps 48-49 AD.[18] All of this will have more relevance as we move through the letter.

There is a lot wrapped up in the identification of these people. Their history and mythology comes into play later in the letter. Their calling Paul an "angel" is related to their Celtic worldview. The question of Paul's incident with Peter is related to who these Galatians are. Most importantly, however, and this does not depend upon either theory, the primary audience of this book is *Gentile* Christians.[19] This is important because none of them had been circumcised. Thus, this issue would have been painfully important to them, considering that some group of people were in their midst forcing them to undergo this ancient Jewish covenantal

---

[15] Cf., Carson, Moo, Morris, *Introduction to the NT*, p. 292.

[16] A conservative dating of Paul's life can be found here with the appropriate times of the missionary journeys.http://www.biblestudy.org/apostlepaul/timeline-life-of-paul-from-first-missionary-journey-to-death.html. The point here is that Acts 16:6 falls in Paul's second journey, which occurs after the Council of Jerusalem.

[17] C-M-M, p. 294.

[18] See F. F. Bruce, *The Epistle to the Galatians : A Commentary on the Greek Text* (Grand Rapids, Mich.: W.B. Eerdmans Pub. Co., 1982), 3-18 and the Chronology Table p. 475.

[19] Of course, there were Jews here. Timothy, who appears to have come from Derba or Lystra in Galatia, had a Gentile father and a Jewish mother (Acts 16:1).

rite in order to be considered "true Christians."[20]   There are a lot of problems that these people have. Thus, you could really think of this whole letter as a kind of music to these ancient Celts, bagpipes calling them from distant places to pick up their swords and come join God's war against the spiritual forces aligned against them.

Salutations

This leads us into vv. 3-5. In typical salutation form, Paul greets the churches with "grace and peace" from God our Father and the Lord Jesus Christ (vs. 3). As we say in our own liturgy (order of worship) each week, God is among his people because he is alive and covenants to be with them. Therefore, you are greeted by God when you come together in worship so that a blessing may be upon you and so that you may know with certainty that God is really in your midst. In our case as in Paul's, the idea is that grace would be extended to you and peace be given to you by God.

These two words are important to reflect upon. As Martin Luther says, "Grace and peace comprehend in them whatever belongs to Christianity. Grace releases sin, and peace makes the conscience quiet. The two fiends that torment us are sin and conscience. But Christ has vanquished these two monsters, and trodden them underfoot, both in this world, and in that which is to come ... Only Christians have this kind of doctrine and are exercised and armed with it to get victory against sin, despair, and everlasting death. It is a kind of doctrine neither proceeding from free will, nor invented by the reason or wisdom of man, but given from above."[21] This again shows us the origin of the gospel. Grace and peace are not given by men, but by God. He gives both to those who trust in Christ by faith alone to deliver them from the present evil age.

When you compare vs. 1 with vs. 3 you see that both the Father and Jesus are mentioned, but in reverse order. Here, grace and peace come *from*

---

[20] As hinted at above, it also means they would have come out of a very pagan non-Jewish background. Their supernatural worldview would have been much more Greek or Assyrian than Jewish. This will explain some of the more curious supernatural references in the letter that cannot be understood from a Jewish perspective. For example, when Paul chides these people for "observing days and months and seasons and years," is this a rip on OT Jewish days or pagan holidays that they may still celebrate in honor of the gods?

[21] Martin Luther, *Commentary on Galatians* (Grand Rapids, MI: Fleming H. Revell, 1988), 31.

God the Father first, *and also* from the Lord Jesus. But in the first, Paul's Apostleship is *from* the Lord Jesus *and also* from God our Father. Why the difference? The Father is the ultimate source of grace, peace, and the Apostolic calling. But Jesus is the instrument through which any of these are made manifest to human beings. The two persons are inextricably entwined as persons in the Godhead. While not saying that Jesus is God, it is clear that he must be, because he is doing the exact same things as the Father. No angel or man or beast has such power or authority. So, from the very beginning, Paul wants the Galatians to know that if they are going to disagree with him, that they have to take it up with the Father and the Son, who even at the present moment are filling them with grace and peace! The confidence that comes from knowing where all of this comes from in an objective sense should greatly benefit your faith. For this is not the babbling of children, the ranting of lunatics, but the very speech of God.

Now, of Jesus one more thing is said, even as one more thing is also said of the Father. Paul tells us that Jesus "gave himself for our sins to deliver us from the present evil age." He did this because it was the will of our God and Father.[22] Here you have the primary reason for the death of Jesus. He gave himself *to deliver us*. His delivering us was because of our sins and thus he became a sin offering to take away our sins.[23] But what kind of a taking away is this? How has Jesus delivered us? It is not the removal of but the rescue from the power of the present evil age.[24] The rescue is now; the removal is later.

But what is the present evil age? This is the only time Paul uses the adjective "evil" (*ponērou*) to describe this age, though he implies it in other

---

[22] It is curious to me that three different times Paul refers to the Father as "God" (1. "God the Father," vs. 1; "God our Father," vs. 3; "God and Father," vs. 4). Jesus, on the other hand is referred to as "Lord" (vs. 3). I believe Jesus is not referred to as "God" here because what is in mind is not theology proper but functional distinctions within the Godhead (see above). But there are other times that Paul does refer to Jesus as God (Rom 9:5; Php 2:5-6; Col 2:9-10; Titus 2:13).

[23] Hence, "for our sins" is *huper* ("on behalf of") or *peri* ("to take away;" "atone"), depending upon the manuscript evidence. William Arndt, Frederick W. Danker and Walter Bauer, *A Greek-English Lexicon of the New Testament and Other Early Christian Literature*, 3rd ed. (Chicago: University of Chicago Press, 2000), 798.

[24] Richard N. Longenecker, vol. 41, *Word Biblical Commentary : Galatians*, Word Biblical Commentary (Dallas: Word, Incorporated, 2002), 8.

places.[25] Again, we have supernatural things in mind. People in ancient times understood it this way: that Satan was the god of this world, a world fallen into sin. He rules as the prince of this world. He has free reign, is unbound, and able to deceive and create much evil in the lives of men.[26] One of the alternate endings of Mark 16:14, clearly a 2nd or 3rd century addition, gives a good commentary on this: "And they excused themselves, saying, 'This age of lawlessness and unbelief is under Satan, who does not allow the truth and power of God to prevail over the unclean things of the spirits.' "[27] A more cryptic but reliable idea is the Lord's Prayer: "Deliver us from evil." Evil actually has the article ("the"). So, some translations say, "Deliver us from *the* Evil One." The idea is that in this present evil age, you cannot separate the work of Satan from the evil that exists here, even if we are fully culpable for everything we do (think of Adam, Eve, and the temptation of the Serpent). He is the god of this world and he has blinded the minds of those who live in darkness.

Sometimes we refer to the present evil age as "the world, the flesh, and the devil" (see my notes on Galatians Supernatural Worldview). God has not promised to take us out of this present evil age, but to deliver us from its power. This, then, is the great hope of the resurrection. Satan no longer has hold upon us, especially Gentiles, because Christ conquered him and removed his authority at his resurrection. To submit to his legalistic rules or to indulge in fleshly desires, is therefore contrary to your calling as Christians, because both of these things belong to the order and kingdom of Satan, of darkness, of sin, of evil, of the flesh. But those who have been redeemed belong to the age to come, the kingdom of Christ, the realm of the spirit, to that which is eternal and lasting.

---

[25] Rom 12:2; 1 Cor 1:20.

[26] Cf. 4 Ezra 5:55: "[The present age has] "already grown old, ... already past the strength of youth." 7:12-13: "The ways of this world ... became narrow and sorrowful and painful, and full of perils coupled with great toils ... but the ways of the future world are broad and safe, and yield the fruit of immortality." 7:50: "The Most High has made not one age but two." 14:20: "The world lies in darkness, and the dwellers therein are without light." 1 QpHab 5:7-8 (of the Dead Sea Scrolls): "The Epoch of Wickedness" is ruled by Belial who opposes the will of God and has free rein.

[27] Codex Washingtonianus. See Bruce Manning Metzger and United Bible Societies, *A Textual Commentary on the Greek New Testament, Second Edition a Companion Volume to the United Bible Societies' Greek New Testament (4th Rev. Ed.)* (London; New York: United Bible Societies, 1994), 104.

This is "the will of God the Father" that such a state be true of all Christians. Notice, we do not deliver ourselves, nor does Christ deliver us through *our will*. There is no freewill here, not as most people understand it. It is the will *of God* the Father that all whom he has given to Christ should come to him by faith alone. Who can thwart God's will? If it is his will to deliver us through Christ, who can turn back his hand? We will learn much about faith in this book (it occurs 23 times in Galatians), for faith is the hinge upon which the gospel turns.

Also, the will of God here is directed particularly at the work of Christ. Christ came to do his Father's will. Part of the Father's will was that Jesus should lose none that the Father has given him (John 6:39-40). But in order to accomplish this, the Father's will also included that Jesus be led to the cross. He was pleasing his Father for our sake. That means, nothing that Christ underwent was accidental or out of control. Rather, it was perfectly planned by God, for this speaks of God's inscrutable, hidden, and mysterious will known as predestination, by which all things move in their foreordained order.

Therefore, even though we have not hit the heart of the letter today, you have been exposed to a great deal of theology or right thinking about God. As I said, this whole letter is about getting the gospel right! You have seen the founders of the church, the Apostles, that were called personally by Jesus. You have seen that this Jesus has been raised from the dead. God who did this gives grace and peace to those that trust in the Son. This son died for your sins. He did this to deliver you from the present evil age; not for you to deliver yourself, but that he would deliver you making your deliverance certain. God did this because it was his will and it pleased him to do so.

Most of all, the last words of the salutation are appropriate. God does this to receive glory in his church. "To whom be the glory forever and ever." As with Paul, these things ought to lead you to doxology—praise! God has done all of these things for his people so that they might praise him and so that he might be glorified in their midst. To have glory is to have a weightiness, a heaviness attached to your praise. This is serious business we are embarking upon. These things have cost God a great deal. But they are yours as a free gift of grace in Christ. Trust in them and you will know grace and peace. They belong to anyone that believes God has done this to remove their sins and to transfer them to the kingdom of light. Therefore believe upon this God today. Then, come and learn all about this good news that is powerful to deliver even a dead man from the grave.

To God be the glory forever and ever. Amen.

Galatians

Another Gospel

A Curse Upon False Teachers

[6] I am astonished that you are so quickly deserting him who called you in the grace of Christ and are turning to a different gospel-- [7] not that there is another one, but there are some who trouble you and want to distort the gospel of Christ. [8] But even if we or an angel from heaven should preach to you a gospel contrary to the one we preached to you, let him be accursed. [9] As we have said before, so now I say again: If anyone is preaching to you a gospel contrary to the one you received, let him be accursed.

Galatians 1:6-9

The Rapture was Last Night

"ANOTHER GOSPEL." THAT IS PAUL'S LANGUAGE in the text today. I want to give you two examples of another gospel in our own day before moving into the passage. The first example eclipses the gospel through deflection. It may be there, but it doesn't really matter. First, it needs a little caveat, since I am writing this the week prior to the events said to unfold below.

To whom it may concern.

If, by chance, you have found this sermon just laying there on my printer and can't figure out where I am, I have been raptured. Please disregard the following sermon. I was wrong. But now I am in heaven and you are not, so maybe you can still get something out of it after all.

Sincerely,
Doug Van Dorn.

Now that I have that out of the way, on to the story. On Tuesday Sept. 6, 1994, dozens of believers gathered inside Alameda's Veterans Memorial Building just south of Oakland, CA. For two years they had been preparing for this moment. Dressed in their Sunday best (it did not matter that it was not a Sunday because they were told years earlier that anyone who continued to stay in a church was under the curse of God) their Bibles open-faced toward heaven, they listened to their modern prophet, Harold Camping, tell them how in just a few more hours Jesus would take them home to keep them from the hell on earth that was going to be unleashed from heaven the following day. But the day came and went with nothing unusual—much less supernatural—occurring. Camping had miscalculated! He promised that he would return quickly to his magical abacus to discern where his computations had gone wrong.

Then he discovered the problem. He had not been taking Noah's flood into account nearly as much as he should have. The flood, he now reasoned, occurred in 4990 B.C., a date that he arrived at by looking at carbon dating, tree rings, and other data. The Bible says that Noah's flood came on the "17th day of the second month." As he was pondering what this could all mean for our future, it occurred to him that "a thousand years is a like a day." He remembered that history is only a total of 7,000 years long. So he crunched the numbers again. When taken into account the fact that there is no year "0," he was stunned to learn that his previous prediction was 16 years and some nine-odd months off.

Two days ago (as I preach on Sunday, assuming I'm still here), on Friday May 20, 2011, the gospel according to Family Bible Radio and several clone prophets of Camping was the gospel of personal escapism: You still have time to be taken up in the Rapture of the church so that you will not have to suffer God's five months of judgment upon planet earth followed by the obliteration of the entire universe on Oct 21, 2011. Camping's "good news" has taken the world by storm … again. All of the major news networks covered the story.

Then, last night, Saturday May 21, 2011, at precisely 6:00 pm (I assume it was Jerusalem Standard Time), just as predicted, the Rapture occurred. Unfortunately for you and I, we missed it! So much for the good news! Now we will have to suffer God's wrath with everyone else on earth. But perhaps even worse, Camping and his followers missed it too, because this morning they are still here. In fact, Jesus didn't take anyone up with him in the Rapture. Apparently, he is so angry with everyone on earth, that he didn't want to take anyone with him. This shouldn't surprise Mr. Camping, since he himself told us that the church age has been over since the late 1980s and that no one remaining in a church after that time can be Raptured. Apparently, God considered Family Bible Radio more of a "church" than he was willing to admit.

All sarcasm aside, the continuous blatant end-run around the explicit words of Christ that "no one knows the day or the hour" of his return shows that some people will say and believe just about anything except that which matters most. Unfortunately, sometimes the things they believe end up ruining their lives here on earth, and potentially also in heaven. Some of the people who were not taken up last night are going to have to come to grips with the stark reality that today all of their worldly assets are now in the corporate holdings of Family Bible Radio which has no plans on giving them back. They will have to start all over, and this time what do you suppose their attitude will be towards Christ and the Bible?

The second example of another gospel occurred between 1545 and 1563. In this example, the gospel is not obscured, but effaced. I am referring to the Council of Trent, an "ecumenical" council (even though the Eastern and Northern European churches were nowhere to be seen) where the Church of Rome shot itself in the foot, leading to a gangrenous poison that she is not able to extract in any who affirm her official position. On January 13, 1547, the council fathers presented to the world the following official Church canons about justification, in response to the Protestants who were creating colossal rifts in the church (Trent, Session 6):

- "If any one saith, that by faith alone the impious is justified; in such wise as to mean, that nothing else is required to co-operate in order to the obtaining the grace of Justification, and that it is not in any way necessary, that he be prepared and disposed by the movement of his own will; let him be anathema." *Canon 9*

- "If any one saith, that men are justified, either by the sole imputation of the justice of Christ, or by the sole remission of sins, to the exclusion of the grace and the charity which is poured forth in their hearts by the Holy Ghost, and is inherent in them; or even that the grace, whereby we are justified, is only the favour of God; let him be anathema." *Canon 11.*

- "If any one saith, that justifying faith is nothing else but confidence in the divine mercy which remits sins for Christ's sake; or, that this confidence alone is that whereby we are justified; let him be anathema." *Canon 12.*

These canons strike at the heart of justification, which the Reformers believed was the heart of the gospel. As such, they reflect a newly minted "gospel" of Roman retaliation, one she had never officially stated or bound her people to until now. As one person has summed it up, "The 'gospel' of Rome is [now] faith plus works, grace plus merit, Christ plus the church, baptismal regeneration, penance, masses, the rosary, indulgences, Mary, the pains of Purgatory, and so on."[1]

To date, Rome has never overturned these canons, though it should be said that at Vatican II, in its *Decrees on Ecumenism* paragraph 2 we read, "The children who are born into [schismatic communities] and who grow up believing in Christ cannot be accused of the sin involved in the [Protestant] separation, and the Catholic Church <u>embraces upon them as brothers</u>, with respect and affection." This is a nice sentiment, but it creates a logical contradiction for Rome. She has placed anathema upon anyone who believes in salvation by faith alone, through grace alone, because of Christ alone. Protestants are supposed to believe this. Yet, Rome considers such persons "separated brethren." How does this make any sense? The contradiction comes in the use of the word "anathema," which also happens to lead me straight into the text today.

Another Gospel

---

[1] This nice little summary is, I believe, faithful to the position of Rome. It is found at: http://www.justforcatholics.org/ecumenism.htm and was written by a Reformed Baptist named Joseph Mizzi on the Island of Malta.

Galatians 1:6-9 is about "a different gospel" (and there are MANY today), and about the anathema that the Apostle places upon those who teach one. By the end of this sermon you will understand good and well what "anathema" actually means. After the salutation, Paul dives straight to the purpose of his letter, bypassing any kind of thanksgiving for these churches. "I am astonished," he says, "that you are so quickly deserting him who called you in the grace of Christ and are turning to a different gospel" (Gal 1:6).

First thing after the salutation, Paul expresses astonishment or bewilderment over the present situation, one of which we know nothing about yet. His astonishment occurs because it has only been a few months or perhaps just a year or two since he first preached to them. To think of how soon these troubles have come upon these people, let alone their inability to withstand strong winds of false teaching, causes Paul and his cohorts no end of puzzlement. Yet, as Luther points out, he does not immediately blast the Galatians saying something like "A plague on your apostasy! I am ashamed of you. Your ingratitude wounds me. I am angry with you."[2] This is true.

Nevertheless, Luther is too kind when he says that Paul shows "maternal affection" and speaks "gently" to them. Paul's next words explain the reason for his astonishment, "You are so quickly deserting him who called you in the grace of Christ" and "are turning to a different gospel." This is the opposite process as repentance, which is a turning away *from* sin *towards* God. This is a turning away *from* God *towards* Satan *through* acceptance and embracing "a different gospel." Other "gospels" lead to destruction, just as The Gospel leads to life.

Desert, Desert

The word he uses for "deserting" could mean simply "turning away from." But there is precedent in classical Greek for it to refer to something much more sinister. Diogenes Laertius was a 3rd century biographer of Greek philosophers. He relates the story of one Dionysius of Heracleia

---

[2] Martin Luther, vol. 26, *Luther's Works, Vol. 26 : Lectures on Galatians, 1535, Chapters 1-4*, ed. Jaroslav Jan Pelikan, Hilton C. Oswald and Helmut T. Lehmann, Luther's Works (Saint Louis: Concordia Publishing House, 1999), Gal 1:6.

who was a philosopher of the Stoic school and left it to become a member of the rival Epicurean school. He is referred to by Diogenes as "Dionysius the Turncoat" (*Ha Metathemenos*).[3] This is *not* a title of endearment. This is the same word Paul uses to describe the Galatians (*metatithesthe*).[4] In military use, it refers to soldiers in an army who revolt or desert and this is very much the way the word is used here by Paul. Thus, referring to the Galatians as ancient times Benedict Arnolds, traitors of Christ, is not exactly a maternal gentle scolding.

Now, tuck what I am about to say for later. I find it interesting that the English word "to desert" (vb.) is related to the word "desert" (n.). One means "to forsake or abandon." The other is "an abandoned and forsaken place."[5] There are a lot of strange word associations with this in Scripture. For example, I found it curious that an OT word "to desert" is *n–ph–l* (*naphal*), which is used to describe the "fallen gibborim" in Ezek 32:27, "And they are laid with the <u>giants</u> that <u>fell</u> of old, who went down to Hades with their weapons of war" (LXX).[6] Or take this one. The NT word for a desert is *eremos*, a word possibly borrowed from Mt. Hermon at the base of which was the worship of Pan the son of Hermes. *Eremos*, Hermon, and Hermes are all related etymologically. In a few minutes, you will see why I bring this up. It is actually quite relevant to Paul's argument. For now, just remember that we are talking about people deserting.

Who are they turning from and who are they turning to? They are deserting "him who called you in the grace of Christ." Here, Paul still says that they are under God's grace. He does not call them apostate, but rather they are in the process of apostatizing. But why would they want to? God has called them. Paul does not say that he called them, but that

---

[3] Diogenes Laertius, *Lives of the Philosophers* VII.

[4] So John Stott, *The Message of Galatians* (Downer's Grove, IL: IVP, 1986), 21-22; Ronald Y. K. Fung, *The Epistle to the Galatians*, The New International Commentary on the New Testament (Grand Rapids, MI: Wm. B. Eerdmans Publishing Co., 1988), 43-44; Hans Dieter Betz, *Galatians : A Commentary on Paul's Letter to the Churches in Galatia*, Hermeneia (Philadelphia: Fortress Press, 1979), 47 n. 41.

[5] Compare their etymologies: http://www.etymonline.com/index.php?term=desert

[6] Some think "the giants that fell" could be translated "nephilim warriors." Most lexicons think that *n–ph–l* is the root word for the nephilim of Genesis 6:4 and Num 13:33, but Michael Heiser, following Herman Gunkel (*Genesis* [Göttingen 1910]), has demonstrated that nephilim is actually a word meaning "giant" not "fallen ones." *DDD*, "Nephilim," p. 619 also mentions this possibility. Thus, the text refers to the fallen giants as the LXX correctly has it. *Naphal* is a word play on the older word nephilim that is not in this passage, but which is hinted at in the word *gibborim* (giants).

God did. This is a supernatural calling. Paul does not say that those effectually called will turn away, because he is not interested in the theology of effectual calling, which is clear in other places. Rather, he is trying to get them to see that this call comes from above, just as Paul's own calling to be an Apostle comes from above, just as the gospel itself comes from above. If that is true, why would they want to turn away?

This is truer when considering that this gospel brings "grace." They have received what they have not deserved. They have been granted a reprieve of doom, forgiveness of sins, eternal life in Christ. Why then would they ever want to give it up? That's the great question for all people who would rather be justified by their works, isn't it? Here, grace is already being set apart from works of the law, which is in fact the very thing that the Galatians are turning towards. God's grace is utterly free. It is not something they have earned, merited, or worked for. It is simply God's gift to them for turning to Christ, who is the author of this gift.[7] To desert such grace is to turn your back on God himself.

How Many Gospels Are There?

It is to turn to "a different gospel." This last phrase in Gal 1:6 has caused many people to wonder if there is more than one gospel. Dispensationalists and Liberals make strange bedfellows here. Dispensationalists have insisted for a long time that "the gospel of grace" was not preached on planet earth until Christ revealed this gospel to Paul. This was a gospel for "the church" which is the great parenthesis and mystery hidden until Pentecost. But Jesus preached another gospel which they call "the gospel of the kingdom." This gospel was given to Israelites.[8] Liberals follow a similar line of thinking. They come to Galatians 2:7 and insist that Paul preached "a gospel of uncircumcision" while Peter and others preached a "gospel of circumcision."[9] These are contradictory and created quite a stir in the early church until one won out over the other.

---

[7] The Textual Committee (see Metzger, Textual Commentary on the Greek New Testament) gives grace "of Christ" a "C" rating. The other alternatives are "of Jesus Christ" or "of God," which are less certain. This follows both Jerome, but Luther and Erasmus preferred "of God."

[8] Cf. Miles Stanford, The Dispensational Gospels, http://withchrist.org/mjs/gospels.htm; Bob Hill, The Big Difference Between the Two Gospels (Biblical Answers Ministries, 1999).

[9] Betz, Galatians, 48; also Rudolf Meyer, TDNT VI: 83.

Both views are extremely strange, since in the very next breath Paul says, "Not that there is another [gospel]" (Gal 1:7). Seems pretty clear! One liberal scholar says about this, "The apostle seems to deny here the existence of 'another gospel,'" but then goes on to say that "Paul goes on to mention another gospel in 2:7!"[10] This is what you call letting your theological bias color your exegesis. Is this really so difficult to understand? There is no other gospel, not really, though there is news that masquerades as the good news. Paul is being facetious. Or, as Luther says, he is speaking ironically as if saying, "Now you Galatians have different evangelists and a different gospel. You despise my Gospel now, and it has lost your respect." Luther goes on to imagine what the false teachers were telling the Galatians, "To be sure, Paul made a good start. But a good start is not enough, for there are more sublime things to follow." Those "things" are Jewish laws like circumcision which he concludes are "tantamount to saying that Christ is a good workman who has begun a building but has not completed it, and that Moses must complete it."[11]

Luther referred to the schismatics of his own day, who were accusing him of virtually the same thing saying, "Luther's gospel is a good start, with a return to Christ and faith and all that. But we need to have more." Ironically, these sectarians end up returning to the same kind of law keeping that Luther left behind in Rome, but they did so apparently, with a most hostile attitude, referring to the Lutherans as "cowards" who "do not speak the truth frankly." Luther returns the favor referring to them as "perverse and satanic men," rightly bringing the supernatural back into the discussion, as Paul himself does shortly.

Before that, he says that there are "some who trouble you" who "want to distort the gospel of Christ" (Gal 1:7). Here Paul switches the blame from the Galatians who are becoming traitors to the false teachers that are tempting them. He calls them "certain ones" or "some." He uses an indefinite pronoun (*tines*) as one scholar (the liberal above) rightly says

---

[10] Betz, 49.

[11] Martin Luther, vol. 26, *Luther's Works, Vol. 26 : Lectures on Galatians, 1535, Chapters 1-4*, ed. Jaroslav Jan Pelikan, Hilton C. Oswald and Helmut T. Lehmann, Luther's Works (Saint Louis: Concordia Publishing House, 1999), Ge 1:6.

"avoiding the use of names and the providing of free publicity."[12] The Apostolic father Ignatius gives a reason why he would not mention names and perhaps he is speaking for Paul, "since they are unbelievers, I have decided not to write [them] down, but may I not even remember them until they repent about Christ's suffering, which is our resurrection" (Smyrnaeans 5:3). These people are not even worth mentioning!

In one way, it would have been helpful for Paul to give them a label, so that we could know exactly what the situation was he was so angry about. But in another way, leaving them anonymous gives them a sort of timeless quality, meaning that they can represent any kind of teacher that perverts the gospel of Jesus, turning it into works righteousness. This means it is not wrong to apply the letter to cults or false teachers in churches today that do similar things, even if the exact issue (like circumcision) is not on their agenda.

You see, anyone who puts new laws before you to follow *in order to gain God's forgiveness and receive justification*, is in the category of these false teachers. It doesn't matter if they tell you to become Jewish or Roman or Mormon or Muslim in order to do it. If they pervert the free grace of God in Christ, and tell you that your deeds make your righteous, they distort the gospel. It matters not if those works are circumcision laws or Sabbath laws, blue laws or fundamentalist rules. It doesn't matter if they are religious or secular, Arminian or Calvinist, Protestant or Roman Catholic, Christian or Buddhist. Anyone who proclaims a message of grace that is not grace, a gospel that is not good news, is distorting the truth. That includes the good news of a rapture, if that good news is allowed to eclipse Christ's teaching and his first coming.

There are a lot of errors that people can have which do not strike a fatal blow at the gospel. There are weaker and stronger brother issues. There are questions over lawsuits or marriage or speaking in tongues or suffering for Christ. There are doctrinal questions and ethical questions, questions about eschatology and soteriology. People can be seriously messed up in all sorts of ways. Their thinking can be bizarre, illogical, contradictory. But none of these receives the Apostolic rebuke the way

---

[12] Betz, 49 n. 65.

changing the gospel does, telling people that in order to be saved, they must do certain things.

My heart wants to give Rome the benefit of the doubt here, for she has proven herself to be extremely confused on this point. She believes that the Lutheran and Calvinist doctrine of faith alone is a faith *that is alone*. Along with many Protestant semi-Pelagians, she claims we are antinomian, that we hate the law, and that we want to disobey God in all things in order to magnify grace. They are utterly mistaken. Like so many others in Church history, they cannot believe that God could declare a person righteous on the basis of someone else's righteousness, let alone give them a desire to obey God that is not out of merit. As Charles Finney so aptly put it, that would be a "legal fiction." They think that good works must earn justification.

But this is exactly why the good news is GOOD news, because they cannot. Once justified, we believe the gospel creates a new heart that desires to obey God out of gratitude rather than merit. But the gospel is that God justifies sinners, not the righteous, his enemies rather than his friends. It is not about me, but God. It is not about works, but grace. Do not let anyone take away this precious pearl of Christian comfort, or you will know no end of psychological and emotional misery that accompanies those who believe they must win their Father's approval.

False Teachers

As I said a moment ago, Luther turns this into a supernatural issue. Gal 1:8-9 do the same thing. These two verses are parallel. Vs. 8 describes two very specific examples of potential false teachers. These are *real* possibilities, though we are not told that either one has actually occurred here. Vs. 9 is a restatement that moves from the specific to the general. Both verses are followed by that word I brought up earlier: Anathema. Let's look at these verses.

Verse 8 gives an example of a false teacher from earth. It then gives an example of a false teacher from heaven. Neither is a dark, evil figure. They are the least likely candidates to commit such a grave sin. In this way, Paul encompasses every possibility he can think of. Both examples seem at first to be highly improbable. But are they?

The first example is "we." "If we ... should preach to you a gospel contrary to the one we preached to you, let him be anathema." The "we" here must include all of Paul's entourage, including probably Mark, Luke, Barnabas and others, those whom he mentioned in vs. 2. We do not know if in fact one or more of those teachers who initially came to Galatia left Paul, stayed behind, and started preaching something different, or if these false teachers rose up from the midst of the people themselves, or if they came in afterward, as if intentionally following Paul around on his missionary journeys in order to counteract everything he was teaching once he left.

It is curious that Paul had more than one of his companions turn on him. He tells us that Hymanaeus, Philetus, and Alexander had swerved from the truth and shipwrecked their faith (1 Tim 1:20; 2 Tim 2:17-18). More curious still, at least two of these were teaching something very similar to Harold Camping. They taught that the resurrection had already occurred. While Camping has not done this yet, cults like the Jehovah's Witnesses which made identical date-setting claims for the return of Christ a hundred years ago, would not repent, but instead claimed that Jesus did come back ... spiritually.[13] This kind of date setting begs for apostasy, because it is so difficult to admit sin and deception. That is why I felt it was both timely and advisable to mention it in this sermon.

Continuing on, Paul mentions that another man named Demas was in love with the present age (which God has rescued us from; Gal 1:5) and had "deserted" him (2 Tim 4:10). He uses a softer Greek word than the deserting of Gal 1:6 for Demas, but the point remains. Combine these examples from his own real-life ministry and almost anything is possible. Paul knows himself to be the "chief of sinners," and therefore quite capable apart from God's grace of perverting the very gospel he has been preaching.

Because the first example is a possibility, so is the second, and this is important to grasp. "If an angel ... should preach to you a gospel contrary to the one we preached to you, let him be anathema." The word "angel" means "messenger." Since angels can be human or heavenly mes-

---

[13] See Ruth Tucker, *Another Gospel* (Grand Rapids, MI: Zondervan, 1989), 139-41.

sengers, Paul clarifies which one he has in mind by adding the preposi-
tional phrase "from heaven." Paul is considering the fact that real angels
can come down to earth and proclaim false teachings that lead people
astray. Many Christians do not have a supernatural worldview capable of
handling the truth of this teaching, and so they dismiss it as hyperbole.
But you should not be so inclined as to think that Paul's example here
could never occur in this world.

Consider the following verses. "Now the Spirit expressly says that
in later times some will depart from the faith by devoting themselves to
deceitful spirits and teachings of demons" (1 Tim 4:1). He says regarding
incorrect practice and belief of the Lord's Supper that he does not want us
"to be participants with demons" (1 Cor 10:20). He refers to an "angel of
Satan" sent to buffet him – to keep him from exalting himself (2 Cor
12:7). Paul uses Satan's temptation in the Garden of Eden as a present example, "I am afraid that as the serpent deceived Eve by his cunning, your
thoughts will be led astray from a sincere and pure devotion to Christ" (2
Cor 11:3). Then he compares "false apostles, deceitful workmen" who
"disguise themselves as apostles of Christ" adding the important part,
"even Satan disguises himself as an angel of light" (2 Cor 11:13-14). Even
in Galatians he refers to the law being "put into effect by angels" (Gal
3:19). The point is, not only *can* demonic and angelic beings teach evil
things ... THEY DO!

Simply put, this was the worldview of the ancients. We have a
wealth of material from antiquity that makes it virtually certain that Paul
has in mind actual cases of "angelic revelations."[14] This gets weirder and
weirder the more you look into it, but it is important to look into it here,
if you want to really understand what is going on here as well as later on
in the letter. In Gal 4:14 Paul says to the Galatians, "Though my condition was a trial to you, you did not scorn or despise me, but received me as
an angel of God." In my mind, this almost certainly refers back to Acts
14:11-12 when, in Lystra, a city in southern Galatia, we read, "When the
crowds saw what Paul had done, they lifted up their voices, saying in Ly-

---

[14] Betz, 53 citing Walter Grundmann *et al.* "ἄγγελος," *TDNT* 1.74–76; Johann Michl, "Engel," *RAC* 5.53ff.
(pagan), 60ff. (Jewish), 97ff. (gnostic), 109ff. (Christian).

caonian, 'The gods have come down to us in the likeness of men!' Barnabas they called Zeus, and Paul, Hermes."

Who is this Hermes? In pagan thought, as is similar in biblical thought, angels are messengers sent to men by the gods. TDNT says, "'The earthly sacral *aggelos* is the prototype of the heavenly *aggeloi*.' The heavenly *aggelos* in the strict sense is Hermes."[15] Socrates says, "This name 'Hermes' seems to me to have to do with speech; he is an interpreter and a messenger" (Plato, *Cratylus* 407e). And Homer tells the story of Zeus addressing Hermes, "forasmuch as even in all else thou art our herald" (Homer, *Odyssey* 5, 29). Hermes is an incredibly important figure. He is the god of speech and writing as well as healing and magic. From him we get the words "hermeneutic" as well as "hermit," a solitary desert dweller. As the god of writing, he has a parallel in 1 Enoch in a being called Penemue, one of the *gregori* or watchers who descended upon Mt. Hermon in the days of Jared.[16] Whether they are remembering the same being or not, the point is, in calling Paul "Hermes", the Galatians were echoing their worldview that angels can and have descended from heaven to teach human beings. Paul does not say this is impossible, but actually implies the opposite! That is quite a frightening thought!

Anathema!

With this in mind, we come to the climax of these two verses and of the text today. Whether it is himself, his companions, or an angel from heaven, he then says that if they preach another gospel, "let them be anathema." Some scholars believe the word signifies excommunication. One writes that this passage, "Is the first instance of Christian excommunication."[17] However, as Herman Ridderbos and others point out, this cannot be true in an ecclesiastical sense, because angels do not belong as members of churches.[18] That seems reasonable.

[15] Walter Grundmann, "Aggelos," *Theological Dictionary of the New Testament* vol. 1, ed. Gerhard Kittel, Geoffrey W. Bromiley and Gerhard Friedrich, electronic ed. (Grand Rapids, MI: Eerdmans, 1964-), 75.
[16] 1 Enoch 69:8-9; 6:6.
[17] Betz, 54.
[18] Herman N. Ridderbos, *The Epistle of Paul to the Churches of Galatia*, The New International Commentary on the Old and New Testament (Grand Rapids, MI: Wm. B. Eerdmans Publishing Co., 1953), p. 49 n. 18; Fung, *Galatians*, 47.

Galatians

Some translations focus on the eternal rather than temporal curse, rendering it as something like "eternally condemned" (NIV). In other words, this is an excommunication all right, an excommunication to hell. This fits with the idea of church discipline, binding and loosing, and the keys of the kingdom. This is obviously a much more serious kind of thing than merely being kicked out of a church, though the two have been related throughout Israel and church history until very recently. If one is out of the community, one is condemned to damnation. Think about the Hebrew who was kicked out of the camp in the wilderness. This signifies exclusion from participation with God and his people. The church represents and is in a very real sense, heaven on earth. But to find the real significance of this word, you need to go looking in the OT. Hang onto your hats!

As Jerome long ago noticed, this word is "properly a word of the Jews."[19] The LXX translates the Hebrew word ḥ-r-m (*kherem*). Here is where things get fascinating. You find the same root word, for instance, in Mt. Hermon (ḥ-r-m-n).[20] Mt. Hermon, as I said earlier, was where Hermes' son Pan was worshipped. But of course, I just mentioned that these Galatians called Paul—Hermes! It gets better.

Ḥ-r-m is translated in English as "devoted to destruction."[21] In other words, this is the word used for the famous "ban" spoken of throughout the conquest of Canaan. The first persons ever put under the ban, according to the Jews, were the Watchers who placed themselves under *kherem* in 1 Enoch when they descended upon Mt. Hermon. Enoch

---

[19] In Luther, Lectures on Galatians 1:9 (*Works* vol. 27).

[20] Heiser (The Myth That Is True) writes, "The very word *kherem* is connected to the Genesis 6 incident and the Nephilim. The relationship would have been readily apparent to an Aramaic or Hebrew speaker. Recalling that Hebrew originally had no vowels, *kherem* is spelled with three Hebrew consonants, transliterated for our purposes as *kh-r-m*. The "kh" in our transliteration is actually transliterated in academic literature more accurately as an "h" with a dot under it—but the pronunciation is basically the "kh" sound. There is an ancient geographic place name with these exact same consonants—plus a final "n" consonant typically used in geographic place names names: *kh-r-m-n*.123 The place name *kh-r-m-n* is spelled "Hermon" in English—Mount Hermon, the mountain where, according to the intertestamental Jewish book of *1 Enoch*, the sons of God (the "Watchers") descended from heaven and subsequently cohabited with human women. According to *1 Enoch*, the mountain got its name because the Watchers were cursed (*kharam*) for what they had done." On the word play between Hermon and the curse see Nicklesburg, *1 Enoch*, Hermeneia, 177.

[21] Hermon is "anathema." So Luther, *Lectures on Romans* (Louisville: Westminster John Knox Press, 2006), 261. He has similar ideas in his comments on Galatians 1:8-9.

reads, "They were in all two hundred; who descended in the days of Jared on the summit of Mount Hermon, and they called it Mount <u>Hermon</u>, because they had sworn and bound themselves with a <u>curse</u> upon it" (1 Enoch 6:6). So Hermon and *kherem* provide a nice wordplay in the passage.

This word *kherem* can be used of anything devoted to God. But it is only used in a positive sense on rare occasions (i.e. Lev 27:28). The vast majority of the time it refers to something delivered up and devoted to the judicial wrath of God.[22] It is to be thought of as a sacrifice, an object for religious devotion as in "devote to destruction." When the Israelites went into the city of Jericho, everything in the city except for Rahab was placed under the ban (Josh 6:17-18). But Achan took some of the spoil for himself (Josh 7:1, 11-13) and because of it, brought the anathema of God upon the community and Achan was eventually killed for his treason.

Here is where it gets crazy. Very specifically, the word is used almost exclusively in the OT to refer to the people or spoils of the land of Canaan; that is to the Canaanites, Hittites, Amorites, Perizzites, Hivites, Jebusites and other giant clans that were on the earth in those days.[23] Jericho was one of these places (in ancient times it was called "the city of giants"[24]). I believe one of the specific examples of this ban is actually in the forefront of Paul's mind as he writes this. Deuteronomy 13:13-18 explains, "If you hear in one of your cities, which the LORD your God is giving you to live in [that is to the cities of the giants], anyone saying that some worthless men (lit. beliyyaal; "children of Belial" [KJV] or Satan)[25] have gone out from among you and have <u>seduced</u> the inhabitants of their city, saying, 'Let us go and serve other gods' (whom you have not

---

[22] Fung, *Galatians*, 47.

[23] See Num 21:1-3; Deut 7:26; 13:16, 18; 20:17; Josh 6:17, 18; 7:1, 11, 12, 13; 1 Chron 2:7.

[24] *Jewish Encyclopedia*, Vol. 5 (New York: KTAV Publishing House, 1901), p. 659. Joshua mentions the "valiant warriors" of Jericho (Josh 6:2). These are the same gibborim translated by the LXX as "giants" in Gen 6:4 and other places.

[25] This word is transliterated 8 times by the Vulgate (here [Deut 13:13], Jdg 19:22; 1 Sam 1:16; 2:12; 10:27; 25:17; 2 Sam 16:7; Nah 1:15) and once it translates it as "diabolus" (devil). It is used by Paul to refer to Satan (2 Cor 6:15) and is used often in the DSS in a similar manner. The word has been understood variously as meaning "those who had thrown off the yoke of heaven" (b. Sanh. 111b) by ancient Rabbis or as "those wicked who do not ascend from the underworld" or as more commonly "worthless." At any rate, the supernatural flavor of the word is obvious.

Galatians

known)" (ESV) … "You shall utterly destroy all the dwellers in that land with the edge of the sword; you shall solemnly curse (anathema) it and all things in it. And all its spoils you shall gather into its public ways, and you shall burn the city with fire, and all its spoils publicly before the Lord your God; and it shall be uninhabited forever [i.e., a desert], it shall not be built again. And there shall nothing of the cursed (anathema) thing cleave to your hand, that the Lord may turn from his fierce anger and show you mercy and pity you" (LXX). In this passage you have, quite literally, a child of Belial proclaiming a message to worship other gods.

This is remarkable given the fact that Paul has just spoken of angels preaching another gospel and placing the ban upon even one of them if they should be so bold. Recall finally that these Galatians are the ancient Celts of old, that they have referred to Paul himself as Hermes and an angel from heaven, and you start to see these two verses in a whole different light! Here is the point of this little detour. I believe what Paul is doing here is placing any teacher, be it human or angelic, of earthly origin or human origin, in the same category as the notorious and nefarious nephilim and their fathers of elder days. In fact, I think he is saying that such a teacher is actually following this ancient example which caused God to place them under a curse in the first place. Their message is a resurrection of a Luciferian message perpetrated upon men since ancient times. It slaps Christ in the face while exalting evil beings who fell from heaven and propping up wicked men on the earth. Simply by looking at the anger that God had against the inhabitants of Canaan and the contempt the Israelites were to have against everything associated with them, including utter and complete destruction of them, their animals, and their possessions, and you begin to get at the seriousness of this anathema from Paul. I wonder, do you think of counterfeit gospels as a spiritual counterfeit, a satanic deception, a message from elder times? Or do you just tend to think that men innocently disagree with God and find their own new message to promote? Have you been deceived as to the seriousness of all this? This ought to cause you to consider the supernatural origin of Paul's message as well as that of his opponents and recognize that before you is a spiritual battle for the eternal souls of men and women, including yourself.

The Apostle is not messing around here. In fact, I know of no other place in the Bible where a curse is actually repeated immediately after it has just been spoken. Vs. 9 summarizes vs. 8. "As I have said before, so now I say again." Most commentators think that Paul refers here in vs. 9 not to vs. 8 but to some previous warning that he gave to these people in their presence.[26] Galatians 5:21 for instance "repeats" a list of sins that have not in fact been spoken of in this letter.[27] The idea is then that Paul saw the seeds of this very thing even when he was with them in person. Now those seeds are beginning to sprout.

Thus he says, "If anyone is preaching to you a gospel contrary to the one you received, let him be anathema." Let the ban be on him. May he be devoted to destruction. May he and all his belongings perish with him. May he be cast into the very pit of hell with those Satanic forerunners who taught similar lies and led men into the worship of gods and demons, rather than the only true God who is forever praised.

I began today with examples of rapture fever and Roman anathema against the Protestant gospel. The first virtually eclipses the gospel through fanatic obsession with the second coming and perfect disregard for Christ's own words on the matter. The latter actually places the ban upon anyone who believes that we are justified by faith apart from works. It teaches that ours is a lie from hell itself. I am actually thankful that both groups contradict themselves on these matters, for it allows their followers the ability to not be finally taken over by their deception. Nevertheless, they both demonstrate that the gospel is under attack on many fronts and in many ways.

Through the mud and confusion, through the lies and deception, you must listen to and believe only in the grace of God that comes in Jesus Christ alone. You must place your hope in his death, burial, and resurrection. If you do, God will impute to you a perfect righteousness because he loves to show grace. Do not be led astray by the false teachers that appeal to your carnal senses, prey upon your fears, tickle your ears, promise you

---

[26] See Ridderbos, p. 50, n. 21; Betz p 45, 50 (the reference is to an earlier occasion); D. C. Arichea, Jr., and E. A. Nida, *A Translator's Handbook on Paul's Letter to the Galatians* (Helps for Translators 18; Stuttgart, 1976), p. 14; Fung, p. 47.

[27] See also 2 Cor 13:2; 1 Thess 4:6.

the world, or get you to focus on yourself. God will deal with them, but he will hold you accountable as well. The anathema remains upon anyone who preaches a different gospel. But the warning goes out to those who hear it and believe it too. So trust in Christ alone and be satisfied in him as you wait for God to take you home in his good time.

Personal Testimony

¹⁰ For am I now seeking the approval of man, or of God? Or am I trying to please man? If I were still trying to please man, I would not be a servant of Christ. ¹¹ For I would have you know, brothers, that the gospel that was preached by me is not man's gospel. ¹² For I did not receive it from any man, nor was I taught it, but I received it through a revelation of Jesus Christ. ¹³ For you have heard of my former life in Judaism, how I persecuted the church of God violently and tried to destroy it. ¹⁴ And I was advancing in Judaism beyond many of my own age among my people, so extremely zealous was I for the traditions of my fathers. ¹⁵ But when he who had set me apart before I was born, and who called me by his grace, ¹⁶ was pleased to reveal his Son to me, in order that I might preach him among the Gentiles, I did not immediately consult with anyone; ¹⁷ nor did I go up to Jerusalem to those who were apostles before me, but I went away into Arabia, and returned again to Damascus. ¹⁸ Then after three years I went up to Jerusalem to visit Cephas and remained with him fifteen days. ¹⁹ But I saw none of the other apostles except James the Lord's brother. ²⁰ (In what I am writing to you, before God, I do not lie!) ²¹ Then I went into the regions of Syria and Cilicia. ²² And I was still unknown in person to the churches of Judea that are in Christ. ²³ They only were hearing it said, "He who used to persecute us is now preaching the faith he once tried to destroy." ²⁴ And they glorified God because of me.

Galatians 1:10-24

Worshipping Paul

I BEGAN THIS SERIES WITH A SATIRE which was said to have been written by one Parodios on the island of Satiricus to the Apostle Paul because of his harsh tone against the Galatians. When that satire was put on Justin Taylor's blog (see Bagpipes from Heaven), I linked my Facebook to it.

Immediately, one of my old acquaintances from college wrote, "If this is truly a letter to Paul then it should be considered carefully. The apology presented at the end of this article was poorly written and conceived. The indictment of Paul written by [Parodios] was in my mind on point and exceedingly wise." He said this not only believing the letter to be genuine, but also that Paul is often wrong, fallible, and just plain mean. He then told me that "Paul would turn in his grave if he knew how he is worshiped." Apparently, if you believe that Galatians is infallible, then you are worshiping Paul. He said, "Many Evangelicals treat Paul like Catholics treat Mary."

This strange reaction to the Apostle Paul gives me a good introduction to the passage today. Who was Paul? How did we come to have so many of his books in the NT? Why are some people so taken aback by what he says?

The Apostle speaks forthrightly in Galatians 1:10, "For am I now seeking the approval of man, or of God? Or am I trying to please man? If I were still trying to please man, I would not be a servant of Christ." This is the introductory statement of the autobiographical part of Galatians, which also happens to be the longest autobiography in the entire NT and maybe even the Bible. From Galatians 1:11-2:14 (that's 28 verses), Paul tells us all about his life as a zealous Pharisee, his conversion, his early life as a Christian, how he came to be in the company of the Disciples, and even gives us a story about him and Peter. He tells us all of this for one simple reason: It is proof that the gospel he is preaching is not something he derived from anyone but Jesus Christ through personal revelation. In other words, he is building a case for the authenticity of his gospel. Today we will only look at the early "silent" years of Paul's life before he ever met with the other Disciples to be sent out as a missionary by them. We will look at the impact his early life had upon the Christians whom he had never met. Throughout, I will talk about some specific things that I hope will help you understand Paul and our present culture better. Most of all, I hope to show you where the focus of such a "personal testimony" should be.

The Approval of Men

First, why does Paul bring up this whole thing about seeking the approval of men or of God? Let's consider what he has just said. He believed himself to be an Apostle called by Jesus Christ and God the Father alone (Gal 1:1). His authority and ministry came directly from God. He then immediately lampoons the Galatians for being so quick to despise this authority and so eagerly long to give up the message he preached to them, effectively deserting God. Finally, he places the ban—the utter devotion to destruction, an anathema—upon anyone who preaches a different gospel from the one he preached, even if that be himself or an angel from heaven.

Obviously, this kind of language is not popular. You could not get any more politically incorrect than what he has said in these first few sentences. He realizes the harshness of his tone and rebuke of his message, and so he lets these people know up front that he isn't writing this letter to win brownie points with them. In effect, vs. 10 says, "Maybe some of you are hearing stories that I go around from town to town trying to win the approval of men, that my gospel is soft, even something I made up. So let me ask you, do people like that generally go around condemning people to hell?"

It is easy to think of people in our own day who care much more of the accolades and praise of men than they do of God. These people go on nationally syndicated television shows and when asked direct questions about things like hell or the exclusivity of Jesus Christ squirm, smirk, hedge, fudge, and even lie about either what the Bible says or what they actually believe. They do it because they want to be liked. They enjoy the attention, the applause, having their name in lights. They like being patted on the back, called "uniters" or "ecumenical" or "culturally sensitive."

You get absolutely none of this in Paul's letter here or in any other letter. This is one of the reasons why it is so baffling to me that my friend would say that people worship Paul like they worship Mary. It is rare to find someone who speaks so harshly to his own people being worshiped. On the other hand, it is pretty easy to see why he doesn't like Paul.

A Servant of Christ

In the second half of vs. 10 he adds, "If I were still trying to please man, I would not be a servant of Christ." In other words, Christ pleasers are by definition *not* man-pleasers, for sometimes they have to rebuke, correct, and discipline their own people. Christian parents could learn a lesson from this, just as pastors could. Too many parents think that they need to please and cater to their children's sinful actions and words. They feel like if they don't, then the child will end up hating them for not giving them everything they want or for coming down hard on them.

So let me say this. God did not create you as parents to be your child's "best friend," but their parent. You can be their best friend when they grow up! For now, you have a job to train them in the way they should go (Prov 22:6). The biblical ideal is to train them in correct theology and right behavior and love of Christ and his church. If they get out of line, it is your obligation and responsibility to discipline them, not to be liked by them. But people-pleasers hear this very message to really mean, "You should do everything in your power to not be liked by your children, to be mean, to lord your authority over them, to beat them mercilessly, and to generally make sure that you have no personal interaction with them other than authoritarian." This bizarre reaction occurs because they have never been disciplined in love themselves and cannot therefore personally relate to what discipline is supposed to do. Discipline is not pure punishment, but a setting straight of the mind. When a child sees her parent doing what she knows he is supposed to do, she may not like the immediate punishment, but she loves the fact that he loves her enough to not let her get away with sin. Biblical discipline actually creates a bond of love between parents and children, and when handled properly (both before and after), increases the affection between the two, for the parent does not enjoy disciplining, anymore than the child likes to receive it. Paul is disciplining his children in Galatians 1.

This is another reason why it baffles me that anyone would say that Paul is worshiped by most Christians today. This man does not care what people think of him. He cares about what they think of Jesus.

Paul thinks nothing of himself. He isn't holding himself up here as God. On the contrary, as William Hendriksen paraphrases this part of the verse, Paul is saying, "If, *in spite of* my claim that I am Christ's servant, I were *still,* or *nevertheless,* attempting to please men, my claim would be false."[1] "So don't listen to me!" Generally, it is people who speak of themselves as the root of all goodness, their ideas as the root of all truth that are never possibly wrong that end up being worshiped. Think about politicians who claim that their brand of "change" can only and always be for the better, that they alone know how to fix all bad things. How does this not inspire worship among the followers? These are the people that create a following for … themselves! The Apostle here does the exact opposite.

Origin of the Gospel

Thus, he moves into perhaps the most important claim in Galatians 1. "I would have you know, brothers, that the gospel that that was preached by me is not man's gospel. For I did not receive it from any man, nor was I taught it, but I received it through a revelation of Jesus Christ" (Gal 1:11-12). There are two things I want you to notice in these two verses. First, the gospel is not of human origin. There are so many things I could say about this.

The main thing I will say is that this means that the gospel is an objective thing, it has its origin not only outside of you, but outside of all people in the mind of God carried out through the obedience of Jesus Christ. People go astray here in a couple of ways. One way is the liberal way, to think that the gospel is actually a subjective thing that has its origin inside of you. Freidrich Schleiermacher (1768-1834) was the father of modern liberalism. Born a pastor's kid in the German Reformed Church, he was later sent away to a Moravian center for piety and faith. But from there he came away quite tainted by objective religion. In a letter to his father in 1787 he wrote, "I cannot believe that He, who called himself the Son of Man, was the true, eternal God: I cannot believe that His death was a vicarious atonement, because He never expressly said so Himself: and I cannot believe it to have been necessary, because God, who evidently did not create men for perfection, but for the pursuit of it, cannot possibly

---

[1] William Hendriksen and Simon J. Kistemaker, vol. 8, *New Testament Commentary : Exposition of Galatians*, New Testament Commentary (Grand Rapids: Baker Book House, 1953-2001), 44.

intend to punish them eternally, because they have not attained it."[2] This is the objective religion that Schleiermacher did not "feel" was correct. Instead, he asserted that religion is primarily a matter of feeling, intuition and experience.[3] But Paul did not get the gospel from what he felt was right (as we will see he felt just the opposite!), nor from his personal experience which was to torture and murder the followers of Jesus of Nazareth.

The other way people go astray here is by confusing the gospel with that which is inside of you already. This may sound the same, but I mean something different. I'm speaking specifically about the old Protestant distinction between the law and the gospel. The law is in you by nature, because you were created in God's image. But it is not subjective. This is how it differs from your feelings and intuition. God gives people a conscience which confirms that they are doing right or wrong. This confirmation tells you that there are moral absolutes that are outside of you, even if they are also written on your heart at birth.

The implication of this is that one way you can recognize if what you are hearing is the gospel or not is if this is something you do not have in your conscience or memory by nature. Is the "good news" you are being told something that you already knew? Are you being told to accept a feeling or to be a better person or to live life however you feel like living it? If so, then you know it is not the gospel, because that is something you could have made up yourself. Nobody could have made up the message of the gospel. Nobody would want to!

Receiving the Gospel

That leads to the second part of these two verses. The gospel is received only through a supernatural means of God. Paul says that he received the gospel through a revelation of Jesus Christ. The word "revelation" is the word *apokalupsis*. This word means an "unveiling, uncovering,

---

[2] Friedrich Schleiermacher, *Life of Schleiermacher*, trans. F. Rowan, vol. 1 (London: Smith, Elder, and so., 1860), pp 46-47.
[3] See Iain H. Murray, *Evangelicalism Divided* (Carlisle, PA: Banner of Truth, 2000), p. 5.

or making someone or something known."[4] It generally occurs in the context of some kind of a supernatural vision like the book of Revelation which is called the Apocalypse. This is the way that Paul means it as well.

Paul is talking about his conversion on the road to Damascus. Luke tells the story three different times (Acts 9, 22, 26). What he tells us is that as Paul was approaching the ancient city in Syria where Abraham sojourned, suddenly a light from heaven flashed around him. He fell to the ground and heard the voice of Jesus. He mentions an important fact that the men who traveled with him stood there speechless, hearing the same voice, but seeing no one (9:7). Later he mentions that they also saw the light, but did not understand the voice that they heard (22:9).

I need to say something directly to you about this. You need to receive the gospel through a revelation of Jesus Christ too, for you are not capable of accepting the good news of Jesus apart from hearing the voice of Jesus call you by name. Yet, your "revelation" is not like that of Paul's. I am not saying that you need to see a vision that makes you go blind. I'm not speaking about an apocalypse in that sense. But you do need an unveiling of the truth before your spiritual eyes. Your calling comes from the Holy Spirit who is Jesus' personally sent witness, but you need not see Jesus personally as the Disciples did. In fact, if you do, I would tend to be extremely cautious.

The Holy Spirit's calling is misunderstood by many people. This is not a verbal audio soundtrack in your ears, but a deeply felt knowledge in your heart that the words you are hearing about Jesus are in fact true. It is subjective, but it is not *only* subjective. It becomes personal, but its origin is outside of you. This is what the calling of the Holy Spirit is: an inward confirmation in the soul of your being that what you are hearing *about Jesus' death and resurrection* is the truth. It has Jesus' work on your behalf as its object. You do not know that Jesus lives "because he lives within your heart." That is sentimental subjective liberalism. You know that Jesus lives because he rose from the dead and the Holy Spirit testifies to your heart that this is the truth. And there are plenty of objective reasons he

---

[4] Walter A. Elwell and Barry J. Beitzel, *Baker Encyclopedia of the Bible* (Grand Rapids, Mich.: Baker Book House, 1988), 1844.

also gives you as confirmation, such as he was seen by many people, he predicted it before it happened, they never found the body, the disciples all became martyrs because of it, etc. If you have this inward confirmation, then you have been called by God even as Paul was. If you sense that this is in fact true, then call upon Christ, repent of your sins, and trust him by faith.

This brings me to yet another reason why what my friend said about Paul is absurd. By reading and studying Paul's letters together, we are not worshiping Paul. We are worshiping Jesus, because Paul was an Apostle of Jesus, his personally appointed messenger to the Gentiles. Messengers do not speak their own message, but another's. This is the claim Paul makes here. His message comes straight from God and no man. But now he has to prove this point and this is where he launches into his full blown auto-biography. What we will look at today occurs in three stages of Paul's life:

1. His life before conversion.
2. His conversion.
3. His life immediately after his conversion.

Paul's "Personal Testimony"

This brings me to an interesting point. You could call this Paul's "testimony." Today, the personal testimony has often become the gospel itself. It is "The Gospel of My Personal Testimony." People say, "Look at what God did for me. I was a drunk, and now I'm not. He can do that for you too if you trust in Jesus." The more amazing the testimony, the more of an antithesis you can find in your testimony between what you were and what you now are, the better. This is why we kids growing up who trusted in Christ at age 5 always felt like our testimonies were lame and we didn't want to get up and share them, especially after the ex-prostitute turned millionaire WNBA superstar has just gone before us.

If anyone had a testimony of great change, it was Paul. So, it is not bad to have a testimony of dramatic change in your life. In fact, it shows God's amazing grace as people rightly understand. The point is, Paul does not use his testimony *as the gospel*. So many people who give their testimony never actually get around to talking about Jesus and what he did.

Paul is not telling the Galatians about his amazing change in life *in order to say that they can have the same kind of change* if they will believe in Jesus. No. It isn't about "change" (like politicians say), it is about God. He is giving it only for the purpose of demonstrating that there is no possible way, given the kind of person that he was, that he could have or would have made up the gospel that he preached to them. The purpose of the testimony is to point at the reliability of the MESSAGE that he preached to them about the death and resurrection of Christ, how a person is only saved by believing this message is true, and how God is glorified because of it.

Paul's Former Life

Here is how he does it. First he talks about his former life. "For you have heard of my former life in Judaism, how I persecuted the church of God violently and tried to destroy it" (Gal 1:13). "And I was advancing in Judaism beyond many of my own age among my people, so extremely zealous was I for the traditions of my fathers." There is more potential for danger here, if you glamorize Judaism as many Christians do today. What kind of Judaism is Paul talking about?

He does not have in mind biblical Judaism, the OT revelation which centers upon and converges upon Jesus' birth, life, death, and resurrection. This is true Judaism. That is not what Paul was talking about.

He is talking about the kind of Judaism that elevated legalistic obedience to Jewish traditions above that of the Law of God, and turned a life of faith in the promises to one of merit for salvation. This kind of Judaism is very much like Islam. He speaks of "the traditions of my fathers." This is the oral law that Jesus destroys in his Sermon on the Mount. For instance, the law said, "Love your neighbor as yourself," but Judaism said, "Love your neighbor and hate your enemy" (Matt 5:43).

What this Judaism stirred up in Paul was intense violent hatred for Jesus and all of his followers. People don't often think legalism that way. This is what he points out directly saying that he persecuted the church and tried to destroy it! In fact he says of this that it was at THIS time that he was trying to please men. Notice, he said, "If I were *still trying* to please man, I would not be a servant of Christ." Those who persecute Christ and his church do so because they are trying to please men. It's an interesting thought, isn't it?'

We actually know quite a bit about this, because both Luke and Paul spoke often about it. Paul describes himself as persecuting "this Way unto death" (Acts 22:4). He says that he was "exceedingly mad" against the saints (Acts 26:11). Right before the conversion on the road Luke says that he was "breathing murderous threats against the disciples of the Lord" (Acts 9:1). This is what they did to our fathers in the faith. They (the Jews now, not the Romans), put them in chains, imprisoned them, urged them to blaspheme, and put them to death. One example of this is James the brother of our Lord, who is mentioned in vs. 20.

According to tradition, the Jews took him to the top of the temple (just as Satan did to Jesus) and threw him off the highest point. Incredibly, he did not die. So they went down and beat him to death with clubs.[5] Though Paul was already converted at this time, it is clear that he would have eagerly participated in this kind of action, even as he did when he presided over the stoning of Stephen (Acts 7:58). This is how he was advancing in Judaism, as if chopping ahead and hewing out a path through a forest and destroying every obstacle in order to advance in their religion.[6] This is the kind of violence that some false religions actually incite and stir up, including false forms of Christianity. It is because the false religion is not one of grace, but of keeping laws that someone has made up. It is directly opposed to the grace of God.

Paul's Conversion

It was in this altered state of consciousness, this raving lunacy of blind hatred against the church that Jesus called Paul. I've told you a little about that conversion and how it came about through a miraculous apocalypse from our Lord Himself. All Paul seems to want to tell of it here is God's electing love and effectual calling by grace. He says, "But when he who had set me apart before I was born, and who called me by his grace, was pleased to reveal his Son to me, in order that I might preach him

---

[5] Eusebius, *Ecclesiastical History* 2.1.
[6] See Hendriksen, *Galatians*, 51.

among the Gentiles ..." (Gal 1:15-16). Here there are two precious pearls of Christian comfort for you to hold tightly to.

The first is God's electing love. Paul was "set apart before he was born." This is an incredible thing to say given what he has just said about what he was doing against Christ. It gets at the heart of personal election, a doctrine that is so precious to us Reformed Christians and so sadly misunderstood by many outside of our tradition. Some admit that election is in the Bible, but that it is always corporate election (of groups) and only a general kind of election to service. But Paul, almost directly quoting Jeremiah's personal testimony ("Before I formed you in the womb I knew you," Jer 1:5) says that he (the individual) was set apart from birth. This is an incredible thing to say. It speaks of the personal electing love of God set directly against his own consuming hatred of this very same God. Why would God do that to someone who hates him so? Paul told the Roman Christians why, "If when we were God's enemies we were reconciled to him through the death of his son." The point is, God did not choose anyone because he foresaw what good they would do. Rather, he chose those who were his enemies who hated him.

The only word for this is grace. Do you see how in this testimony, he is not bragging about himself, but God? There is no reason in Paul, you, or me that made God choose us. There is no good work that he knew you would do, nor a good choice that he foresaw. Don't even try to go looking for a reason in yourself as to why God would choose you and not another. You cannot find one. For we were all like Paul and nothing save the effectual calling of God could ever turn us from our murderous path against him. This is why the gospel is *good* news. It is because God chooses horrible people to save and to set his love upon. And the good news is that God did this before we were ever born. Election takes place in eternity past. This too is why it is good news. For it means that all who come to faith in Christ may rest assured that they did so because God came after them, having loved them before the foundation of the world. No one who is not chosen ever has saving faith, for it is the gift of God.

But this eternal choosing becomes effectual in real time through a call. Paul, scared and frightened on the road by the beatific vision of Jesus Christ, heard the call and immediately was converted by the power of the omnipotent sovereign enthroned king of heaven and earth. Just by speaking to him Paul was converted, and I trust in the same power of the preached word to you. God's power called him and converted him and he willingly changed his mind against him from that moment on. He was given new affections, set free from his slavery to the devil, and his desire was now to follow his new master. Such is the power of the Holy Spirit in salvation, and he uses this power every time a sinner is made to hear this good news and turn to Christ. Do you hear the call? Have you believed upon Christ and been baptized?

The last part of this verse is that Christ called him so that he might preach him among the Gentiles. So there are two parts of this calling and election. One is to salvation. The other *is* to service. But God never chooses people to serve him without also bringing them to him. That is absurd. Likewise, God does not call Christians without also giving them a purpose in life. The two go hand in hand.

The Reformers spoke of "vocation" rather than "work" or a "job." Vocation comes from from a Latin word (*vocatus*) meaning "a calling." Christians are to view their work as a calling from God. All (lawful) work is good work. All (lawful) work can be a spiritual calling. You don't have to become a missionary, like God called Paul to become. But you do have to glorify God in what you do, praising him for your calling, doing that work to the best of your ability, and being free in your mind to know that you are in God's sovereign will.

God does call some to specifically serve the body of Christ, and this is what he did with the Apostle(s). Notice again that this is part of his personal testimony. But he does not use it the way celebrities so often use their work (as a means to convert people through their fame), again making the testimony be the good news. Rather, Paul uses this to point again to the good news. God called him to preach among the Gentiles (that is the Galatians) and that is why he came to them with this gospel that was not from him. Everything in this testimony is there to make the gospel shine, not himself.

Paul's Immediate Life After Conversion

This leads to the third stage of the testimony, Paul's immediate choices after conversion. First he tells us, "I did not immediately consult with anyone" (Gal 1:16). Saying this advances the argument by showing that he did not go running to any person to tell them what had happened to him. This was a very sobering event in his life, and besides, he probably feared what the Christians might do to him. Why should they ever believe him? The point of this is to introduce the idea that once he was converted by Christ, the message of Christ really was from Christ, because Paul was not talking to other people about Christ yet!

But what about Ananias? Didn't the Jesus come to Ananias in a vision and command him to meet with Paul, lay his hands upon him, restore his sight, and baptize him (Acts 9:10-17)? Wouldn't we consider this a "consultation"? Not really. Ananias sought Paul. Paul did not seek Ananias. Furthermore, Jesus did this so that Paul might know in an objective way that what happened to him was real. How could Ananias know about it unless he was told by Christ himself? Finally, Ananias was only a convert in Damascus. He was not an Apostle. Perhaps he was a pastor there, but his visit served to initiate Paul into the new covenant priestly ministry through baptism.

Next he says, "... nor did I go up to Jerusalem to those who were apostles before me, but I went away into Arabia, and returned again to Damascus" (Gal 1:17). When you read Acts, it might seem like Paul went to Jerusalem fairly quickly. Luke says he did this "many days" later. But Paul tells us he went from Damascus down to Arabia, which is probably the Nabataean empire in today's Jordan, Saudi Arabia, and Sinai Peninsula. Petra was one of the main cities at that time, in the ancient land of Edom. The point is, he went down there to preach the gospel and still has not consulted with any human about what that Gospel is! Because he's proving that he didn't learn it from a man, but from Christ.

I want to make one brief point to foreshadow a major theme later in the letter. Notice back in vs. 16 that God "was pleased to reveal his Son to me." The title of Jesus as God's Son is important. Luke tells us only this about Paul's message in those days, "For some days he was with the disciples at Damascus. And immediately he proclaimed Jesus in the synagogues, saying, 'He is the Son of God'" (Act 9:19-20). Both accounts match as to the title of Christ and his message. Tuck this information away, because I will explain it in more detail in the coming weeks.

In the next verse, we learn that it was actually three years until he finally went to Jerusalem. He went there to visit Cephas (Peter) and stayed there fifteen days (Gal 1:18). He saw none of the other apostles except for James, the Lord's brother (Gal 1:19). This is James who wrote the book of James and who I told you of how he was killed earlier. He died in 62 AD according to Josephus. We know that James did not believe Jesus while he was alive. But in a most incredible act of grace, our Lord appeared to him in a vision just as he did to Paul, after he had ascended (1 Cor 15:7). Perhaps the two of them meeting was mutual confirmation and help about the visions they had both seen of the resurrected Christ. I'm sure it would have been fascinating to have been there when they first spoke. In Acts 15, he is clearly the most important person in the church of Jerusalem.

Why is this detail here? Paul is making the point that the church had not even officially accepted him yet. He was busy with his missionary work to the Gentiles. They were busy in Jerusalem. Probably Paul wanted to meet with Peter in order to get some kind of idea about the larger organization developing there. But he apparently has no intent of joining them.

We could ask all kinds of questions about the legitimacy of Paul's actions. Shouldn't he have gone to them sooner? Isn't it better to be part of the church than do your work apart from it? This may explain why he says, "In what I am writing to you, before God, I do not lie!" (Gal 1:20). Whether he was ashamed of his lone-ranger actions or not, he is telling them the truth about what happened. He isn't making it up in order to gain any of the Galatians' favor.

He continues to pour it on. After this, he went north to Syria and farther north to Cilicia (Gal 1:21), which is where his home in Tarsus was located (today's Turkey), which is not very far from Galatia actually. If he is acting according to what we know of Paul during this entire time of his life, he was witnessing to the truth of Christ to Jews and Gentiles in these places far away from Israel.

He actually explains his point, now saying, "I was still unknown in person to the churches of Judea that are in Christ" (Gal 1:22). The only thing they knew about him was hearsay, "He who used to persecute us is now preaching the faith he once tried to destroy" (Gal 1:23). He was gaining a good reputation among the churches, even while he was being persecuted in the places he was evangelizing. Even more, "they glorified God because of me" (Gal 1:24). It mentions "the faith" here. What faith is that?

It is the SAME Faith, the gospel known to all Christians. And that is the climax of this section. Paul has the same gospel as the other Apostles, but he has never talked to any of them about it! There is only one gospel that he has ever preached and that they have preached. There is only one good news yesterday, today, and forever. Paul received the same life changing message of the death and resurrection of the God man that they did, but that he did not receive it from them. How can you account for this other than direct revelation from Jesus himself?

Going back to my earlier comments on testimonies, and this phantom worship of Paul that I have never heard anyone in the real world engaging in, notice again that they are not glorifying God, not Paul. They are worshiping God, not Paul. And they are doing so because God changed this man who is now promoting the same Faith that they are.

What a remarkable story and an important piece of autobiography, not because it glorifies a man, not because the testimony is the good news, but because of how it is used, to point us to the only truth that can ever save us from our sins. You can trust what this man says, because only the sovereign work of God could have done these things and brought this information about Jesus to these Galatians, and all these years later, to you. Take confidence in the power of God's word to convert and to save, to be powerful in the lives of men, and to bring glory to God. That is why he gives it, so that you might praise him for his marvelous grace shown to terrible sinners like you and me.

Galatians

The Gospel That We Preach

Paul and the Jerusalem Council

[1] Then after fourteen years I went up again to Jerusalem with Barnabas, taking Titus along with me. [2] I went up because of a revelation and set before them (though privately before those who seemed influential) the gospel that I preach among the Gentiles, in order to make sure I was not running or had not run in vain. [3] But even Titus, who was with me, was not forced to be circumcised, though he was a Greek. [4] Yet because of false brothers secretly brought in--who slipped in to spy out our freedom that we have in Christ Jesus, so that they might bring us into slavery-- [5] to them we did not yield in submission even for a moment, so that the truth of the gospel might be preserved for you. [6] And from those who seemed to be influential (what they were makes no difference to me; God shows no partiality)--those, I say, who seemed influential added nothing to me. [7] On the contrary, when they saw that I had been entrusted with the gospel to the uncircumcised, just as Peter had been entrusted with the gospel to the circumcised [8] (for he who worked through Peter for his apostolic ministry to the circumcised worked also through me for mine to the Gentiles), [9] and when James and Cephas and John, who seemed to be pillars, perceived the grace that was given to me, they gave the right hand of fellowship to Barnabas and me, that we should go to the Gentiles and they to the circumcised. [10] Only, they asked us to remember the poor, the very thing I was eager to do.

Galatians 2:1-10

Why Do We Preach?

Galatians

WHAT IS THE MISSION OF A PREACHER? What is the content of his message? Why is it that he stands up week after week to speak to you? Why do you come, and what do you come to hear him say? What makes his words different from those you might hear at a seminar, during halftime in a football locker room, on a television or radio talk show? What is the default message that people want to hear? What temptations do they have when they approach the text? What do they tend to make it do?

Let me offer some brief suggestions. The mission of the preacher is to preach Christ. Sounds good, but which Christ are we talking about? That is one of the temptations people face, to create a Christ in their image. The content of his message is the passage which is before him. This also sounds good, but this likewise has a temptation, to make the text say something other than what it says because it isn't interesting enough, pragmatic enough, exciting enough for our fancy. Why does he stand there week after week preaching? Because this is the spiritual food that keeps you alive. But this too has a temptation, to preach only fun passages, to feed the people only steak or candy, but never broccoli and spinach. Yuk! What makes his words different from those heard other places? Obviously, there are a lot of places you can go to hear someone say something. Generally people go to seminars to get tips, hints, helps, aids, techniques, programs, formulas for better living. At halftime, the boys hear a motivational speech. Depending on the circumstances, it can be full of anger or emotion. People listen to talk radio often to hear political talking heads or to enter into some new or ongoing "conversation." Is this why the preacher preaches? Not really. You may get some of that, depending upon the circumstances and the particular text. But preaching is something altogether different than all of that. He preaches a message others do not even know, unless they are believers too, and even then, their message is generally not going to overlap with the message of a preacher, for theirs is a different calling. As we are going to see, Paul is quite concerned in Galatians that the other Christians know that he is preaching the same message that they are preaching, even though he has never even really talked to any of them personally.

What is the default message that people want to hear? This is easier. We want to hear things about us. Let's be honest. We like to hear about ourselves. We like to know how we can become better people. We like the preacher to take our tired eyes and awaken them by propping up our chins with his kind words. Or, masochistically, I think there is a tendency in all of us to sometimes want to have the preacher beat us upside the head in order to reinforce in public how we already feel about ourselves in private. Either way, it's still about us, isn't it? What about the temptations we have in approaching the text? This too is easier. We always seem to want to make the text tell us how to do something. Again, it's about us. We like ourselves. Even if the Apostle is giving us his own autobiography for the purpose of extolling Christ, we want to hear, not about him, but about us. How does his story apply to me!

In and of itself, it is not a bad thing to want to find yourself in the Bible's story. This is actually a very good thing! The temptation comes, not in wanting to find yourself in its story, but in making it your story. That is why the great trend is to make every passage we read be about law! Even if there isn't a command within five chapters, we always seem to wish there would be one, because—we come to church expecting to hear about ... us! We feel like if we don't come away being told to do something, that we haven't really gotten our money's worth. So command us pastor, give us our marching orders, tell us what to do! The saddest thing of all is when Reformed Christians think like this, for they above all people are supposed to know that no matter what they are told to do, they can't do it perfectly anyway, which is why they need Christ, need to hear about him, need to feast upon him! But that's too much like the old spinach sometimes, isn't it?

This, in my opinion, is exactly where the Galatians find themselves now. The Apostle has come to them, preaching a message of absolute freedom in Christ. They, naturally, take this to mean freedom from obedience rather than freedom to serve, because it is so very difficult to understand what freedom in Christ apart from law could possibly mean. It doesn't strike them as right. It is too freeing, too easy, too something. This is why, when the opponents of the Apostle came to them they were so eager to abandon the gospel. And for what? For the law! Like so many people today they said, "The gospel is for the unconverted. But the law is for the Christian." I will have much more to say about this particular temptation in chapter 3.

Galatians

Today we get a bit more specific about the nature of this legalistic temptation, the temptation to turn away from grace back to the law. The temptation is to say, "Christ isn't enough. Christ isn't practical. Give us something to do. Tell us what we have to do, Mr. Apostle. Give us something to do. We want to be good little Christians. We want to make God happy with us." The most incredible thing about the particular temptation in view today, is that the people (prior to the advent of appendage numbing medications) were actually being tempted by it.

What was this temptation? These were Gentiles. The temptation was that they had to be circumcised in order to be "good" Christians. That is, they had to do some law, and a biblical law at that, if they really wanted to reach the higher life and be victorious in their Christian walk. But this particular law was incredibly painful to obey, and I'm quite sure, not a small bit embarrassing. It is tempting to think that maybe it was the women who were being tempted more than the men by these false teachers, since they didn't have anything to lose, literally. It's always easier to follow the law if it is your friend who has to do it instead of you. But that's just a guess. Maybe these men were masochistic!

Off To Jerusalem

What we have before us, then, is the story of the Apostle Paul travelling to Jerusalem some 14 years after he first met Peter there in order to "make sure I was not running or had not run in vain" (Gal 2:2). What in the world is going on here? Up to this point we have seen a completely God-centered Paul prove that 1. His calling and election was from God, not his own freewill. 2. His calling to be an Apostle was from a direct summons from the personal risen Jesus. 3. His message was revealed to him (literally apocalypse: unveiling) through the teaching of this same risen Lord. In other words, Paul wasn't looking for Christ, he wasn't seeking Christ, he wasn't in this to make money; he was trying to kill Christians. In short, there is nothing about his personal experience that made him want to proclaim this message to anyone. It was only by the grace of God in showing him the message that he came to this conviction.

That leads me to an interesting application. It was when he understood the message that he wanted to *tell* the message. A lot of people have a basic understanding of the message, and it causes them to want to turn, but they never get around to telling anyone else about it. Partly this is due to fear. But fear is very often overcome *by learning the message better*. A lot of times the fear people have is not of rejection, but of confidence in knowing what to say. But how can they ever know what to say if they are never told about this message again after they are "saved?" This is why it is astonishing to me that so few preachers preach the gospel message to Christians. But you, dear Christians, like the Galatians, need to hear the message and you need to believe it.

Belief is not a one-time event in the past, and maybe that is part of the problem some have when they are told to believe. They say, "I've already believed, so now what do I do?" But this is to see salvation as an Arminian and faith as something like walking an aisle and raising your hand. If you do that, you're in. My answer to the question is you believe. Belief is ongoing, like a race to use Paul's metaphor here. You don't stop believing. You press on in faith. You do all of your running through trust in the good news. You understand that any willing or working or running that you do is always through faith in Christ. Belief and understanding is what opens your mouth and moves your feet. If you are having problems obeying, it is because you are having problems believing and have in one way or another turned away from the good news to the temptation of works. You are not looking at the good news and really understanding how good it is, how freeing, how comforting. If you did, those good works would *necessarily* follow, for they are what Christ predestined beforehand that you would do.

But here is an interesting thing. Even in my application, this is still to a large degree about … you! This isn't the altruistic goal of simply hearing about Christ for Christ's sake. I pray all of God's people would reach that goal. How blessed would any church be when all who came wanted to hear a message about Jesus and learn what he has done simply so that they could leave saying "Glory be to God in heaven! Praise be to his Son for his salvation wrought in history and in us!" That should be our highest desire, for it is the chief end for which we were created. Everything else, the things about us, is icing on the cake, part of God's magnificent beneficence towards those whom he loves. The fact that we are able to enter into this story personally is by the sheer grace of God.

What Paul is doing then is putting forth a very powerful argument that the gospel not only comes from God, it is independent of man's evaluation. Think about this. Paul went the first 17 years after his conversion[1] preaching from Jordan to Turkey and everywhere in between, facing taunting, mocking, ridicule, whips, stones, imprisonment … and all without ever having met with the group of Apostles whom Jesus called during his earthly ministry to consult with them about it.

What he tells us is that 14 years after meeting with Peter he went back to Jerusalem with Barnabas and Titus. Barnabas is the "son of encouragement," and a great figure of personal faith in the Bible, though he is a sinner as is even mentioned in this chapter. Titus is a young Gentile helper of Paul's who even has one of the NT letters named after him. He will come up again in a moment. Paul says that he went to Jerusalem because of a revelation and "set before them the gospel." That is, he spoke to the church in Jerusalem, filled with Apostles and leading men of prominence, men like James the brother of Jesus. He spoke to them about his gospel. This is all Paul really even seems to want to talk about, because he loves it so much!

I will take the minority position in this sermon that the time frame of this coincides with the so-called "Jerusalem council" of Acts 15, sometime around 50 AD. Some scholars think this refers to a much earlier episode (in Acts 11:27-30, 12:25), but this would put it somewhere around 44 AD (the death of Herod Agrippa I in Acts 12). As William Hendriksen convincingly argues, this date seems impossible for this reason. Seventeen years prior to 44 AD—that is, the time Saul was converted on the road to Damascus—would be 27 AD, at or even before the ministry of Jesus even begins. So it looks like we have the Jerusalem council in mind. Therefore, I'll have to say a little something about it during our study of Galatians 2.

---

[1] Many commentaries say that the "14 years" is after his conversion just as the "3 years" were after his conversion. This must be done to justify their claim that Galatians 2 refers to Paul's earlier trip to Jerusalem (Acts 11:30, 12:25) rather than to the Jerusalem council (Acts 15), see below. The natural way to read this, however, is that Paul went to Jerusalem to meet with Peter (circa 35 AD) and then, *fourteen years after that*, came back to Jerusalem (around 49-50 AD). The biggest objection to this reading is that it appears that Paul is skipping a trip to Jerusalem which occurred around 44-46 AD (Acts 11:30). Hendriksen (Galatians, n. 45 point #7, p. 71) responds to this objection by noting that there is nothing in Galatians 2:1 that necessitates that these were Paul's only two trips to the city.

Let me finally answer the question. What does it mean that he tells the gospel to the church in Jerusalem to make sure he was not running in vain? What he does not mean is that he sought the stamp of approval of the Jerusalem church. That would undermine his entire argument. Rather, he knows that there is a growing rift in the church over the issue of the place of the law. He goes down to Jerusalem to make sure that they know that he is not responsible for this rift and to confirm publically that Jerusalem and Paul are in one accord.

You see, Paul and Barnabas had been in Antioch north of Israel when this issue erupted in the church up there. After a long discussion, they were sent down to Jerusalem to the apostles and the elders to discuss this question (Acts 15:1-2).[2] They were warmly welcomed by the church there and began discussing all the things God had done through them for the Gentiles (15:4). Paul seems to have met with a small group of prominent men prior to the larger public meeting (Gal 2:2). But once they were out in the open, the same group of legalists in Antioch were present here too. This was an epidemic that threatened to destroy the church! It was a very serious matter.

Council on Circumcision

Thus, the first church council was called over this issue of circumcising Gentile Christians. What is frightening about this today is how easy it is to say, "Circumcision? That issue is dead and buried. We are no longer tempted like they were, so what is the point of a passage like this?" Such is the subtlety of the devil. He makes you look at the issue rather than the principle of the thing. The principle before us is, when all is said and done, is basically this. Is Christ enough? Is it enough to hear about him and what he has done, or do we need more? It is the reason for the first 10 minutes of this sermon. We are utterly tempted to turn away from Christ to the best of things, taking our eyes off of him and putting them, no matter how secretly and deceptively even to ourselves, upon us.

---

[2] Gal 2:2 says Paul and Barnabas went down because of a revelation. This revelation need not be seen as mutually exclusive to the sending by the Antiochian church.

Some might be tempted to say, "Well, the issue was about how a person gets saved. It was about justification. Obviously, we are not saved by our works." But this response completely misunderstands the issue. Who is being tempted here, non-Christians or Christians? Who are these Galatians? When Paul says later in this letter, "Do we begin with the Spirit and finish with the law," is he referring to how we get saved or what we do after we are saved? Again, I'll have more to say about this in Chapter 3.

Let me get back to the issue. Titus was mentioned because he serves as a case study. As a Gentile, he was not circumcised. But he became a Christian. He had the option to become circumcised, but he opted out (remember, Timothy was later circumcised by Paul as he left Jerusalem and went to the Gentile cities to give them the verdict of the Jerusalem council and he did it because there were so many law abiding Jews there; Acts 16:3). "He was not forced." None of this would have been a problem, except that "false brothers" were "brought in secretly" to spy out Christian freedom. It is difficult to know exactly what this means. It probably refers to a deliberate attempt to put on a Christian façade, join the fellowship, and then begin to create havoc once they were respected and had some measure of authority. In other letters, this kind of person is called a wolf who breaks into the sheep pen and guess what he wants to do? This raises the ugly problem of how some people actually want to be part of churches in order to destroy the truth of her message. It is a sobering thought that demands much wisdom and discernment. God allows this to test his church, to see if she will really stay true to him. Do you see how deep the temptations run and how important they are to get right?

Paul raises the issue of "freedom in Christ" (Gal 2:5) and puts it in direct opposition to the mission of these false brothers. What is freedom in Christ? Again, Paul will address this in great detail later in the letter. Nevertheless, freedom in Christ is freedom from the tyranny of law keeping for salvation. Calvin called it a necessary appendage of justification. This gets to be a difficult subject very quickly, but Peter put it like this in the Jerusalem council, "You are putting God to the test by placing a yoke on the neck of the disciples that neither our fathers nor we have been able to bear" (Acts 15:10). He then puts it positively, "We believe that we will be saved through the grace of the Lord Jesus, just as they will" (vs. 11).

In other words, freedom in Christ is salvation (and I mean that beginning with justification, moving through sanctification, all the way through glorification) by grace alone and not by keeping the law. No part of our salvation is by law keeping. No part! So were people in the OT saved by keeping the law? Well, those who looked to God in faith—faith in the promises of the Coming One, were always saved by faith. But those who did not were under the covenant of works, and so they *were* in fact bound up as slaves to law-keeping to merit their salvation. And the same is true to this day. If you will not be under grace, then God will judge you by the law. Is that what you want for him to do with you? That is exactly Peter's point. It was an impossible yoke to be under. No one could do it. They could have been saved, hypothetically, but no one was, because no one was perfect (from the get-go they were born in original sin).

This is James' point in Acts 15 as well. After agreeing with Peter's verdict, the brother of Jesus in the flesh said, "My judgment is that we should not trouble those of the Gentiles who turn to God (with circumcision), but should write to them to abstain from the things polluted by idols, and from sexual immorality, and from what has been strangled, and from blood" (Acts 15:19-20). At first glance, it appears that James is hopelessly contradictory, saying that we should not place Gentiles under the law, but that we should. What James is saying, however, is that the laws governing both Jew and Gentile proselytes in the OT apply today in order that the two groups can get along at the same table (i.e., communion).[3] James does not have in mind salvation here, but the freedom of a Christian to place himself under the law for the sake of not offending weaker brothers. This is about someone else, not oneself. The Jews were, in fact, no more under the law than Gentiles were, but the NT allows for Christian liberty in areas like meat sacrificed to idols, etc.[4]

---

[3] These laws are found in Leviticus 17-18. The four laws James gives are repeated in Acts 15:29 but are actually put into a different order than found in vs. 20. Importantly, this is the order they are found in the Levitical code (sacrificed to idols; Lev 17:8; blood; Lev 17:10-14; what is strangled; Lev 17:15; unchastity (Lev 18:6-30). It is this fact, that these laws in the OT pertained to Gentiles who came into the community that accounts for Acts 15:21 where James says that Moses has been read in synagogues in Gentiles cities for long periods of time, meaning, that they are fully aware of the Mosaic regulations on these matters already.

[4] The issue of sexual immorality seems out of place for matters of indifference, since it is an immoral activity(ies). There are two possible answers to this. First, the kind of immorality in mind may be related to the others in that it refers specifically to pagan temple worship. Several scholars have offered this solution. While

The entire problem at the Jerusalem council, then, was that there were people teaching that legalistic obedience to the law is what got a person saved and what kept them in God's good graces. If they were not circumcised, how could they really take seriously the Law of Moses? This is the issue then, and it is so often the issue today. "But pastor, I need to keep the law. Tell me how to keep the law. Tell me what to do!" Me, me, me. "I want to put myself back under tyranny. I just can't live with all this grace and freedom in Christ (again, as if freedom in Christ is the desire to disobey)."

The point for Paul is that he did not waver in the midst of this public attack by certain people in Antioch or in Jerusalem. He stood firm his ground on the good news and he did it "so that the truth of the gospel might be preserved for you" (Gal 2:5). When he got to Jerusalem, he was prepared even if the apostles themselves should have compromised on this point, not to waver on this, harkening back to the anathemas of chapter 1. He said, "Those who seemed influential ... added nothing to me" (vs. 6).

But of course, what he found was that he was preaching the very same thing that Peter was preaching. Galatians 2:7 is one of the more badly distorted verses in this letter. "On the contrary, when they saw that I had been entrusted with the gospel to the uncircumcised, just as Peter had been entrusted with the gospel to the circumcised ..." They take this to mean that Paul had his gospel and Peter has his. Some dispensationalists will say that Paul's gospel was "uncircumcision" and Peter's gospel was "circumcision." The Greek literally reads, "gospel uncircumcision" and "gospel circumcision" and we have to supply the preposition. The two words for circumcision are in the Greek case called the Genitive. There are at least 14 different ways to translate the genitive![5] You can translate it with the words: "of," "from," "for," "during," "belonging to," "that is"

James does not seem to restrict his word to this with an adjective, the context of the other three prohibitions may. In fact, the context of Leviticus 18 is "do not do as they do in the land of Canaan"). The other answer is that even sexual immorality is not the measure of salvation. A person is not saved because they keep themselves pure, rather they keep themselves pure because they are saved by faith alone. It is an act of gratitude not obligation. James is clearly not saying that these are the four things that will get Gentiles to heaven.

[5] Genitive of possession, genitive of relationship, subjective genitive, objective genitive, genitive absolute, Genitive of Direct Object, Genitive of material or contents, descriptive genitive, genitive of apposition, genitive of comparison, genitive of time, genitive of measure, genitive of source. See David Alan Black, *It's Still Greek to Me* (Grand Rapids, MI: Baker Books, 1998), 48-51.

and others. It can get a little bewildering. Again, some Dispensationalists interpret it to mean something like "the gospel, that is circumcision" (a genitive of apposition). In other words, "circumcision" identifies the content of the gospel.[6] This is a bizarre thing to see two gospels here, seeing that Paul has already said that anyone who preaches another gospel is to be damned to hell.

Instead, it is better to translate it as John MacArthur (who is himself a Dispensationalist) and all Reformed Christians do (as the ESV takes it), as an objective genitive, where the genitive receives the action. As MacArthur says, "the gospel to the circumcision ... it is not 'of' in terms of definition; it is 'to' in terms of direction. Same gospel. Paul gave it to the Gentiles; Peter gave it to the Jews, that's all. Same gospel. Just one gospel."[7]

Why was Paul preaching the same thing that Peter was preaching? Why did they have the same gospel? Because Jesus personally delivered it to the both of them. This is what Paul says in vs. 8, "For he [Jesus] who worked through Peter for his apostolic ministry to the circumcised worked also through me for mine <u>to the Gentiles</u>" (Note how this verse helps interpret vs. 7).[8] Let me back up again.

What was the content of Paul's sermons? The good news. What was the content of Peter's sermons? The good news. They preached the same good news. This good news was the relentless message—in the face of great opposition to turn from this message to the law—that Jesus Christ died on the cross for our sins and was raised to life for our justification. It was a message about Jesus. The message of the legalists was about them. Not *Soli Deo Gloria*, but *Soli Homini Gloria*, to man alone the glory!

That does not mean the only thing Peter and Paul talked about was the crucifixion or the resurrection. No, they spoke of Christ in all of Scripture. But the focus of their preaching to the unconverted and the converted was Christ and what he has done. But that isn't enough for le-

---

[6] Some may see it as a genitive of possession: "the gospel belonging to the circumcision." This can be better, but if they use this to say there are two gospels, it is no better.
[7] John MacArthur, comments on Gal 2:7. http://www.gty.org/Resources/Sermons/1654
[8] While the phrase "to the circumcised" is the same genitive, the phrase "to the gentiles" uses the preposition eis "to," making it clear that this is a gospel going <u>to</u> the gentiles, not a gospel <u>of</u> uncircumcision.

galists. They want to turn from Christ to something more. Christ is a good person to have on the first leg of the relay, to be sure, but he is a bad anchor man to finish the race. For that we need our own effort, because it makes us feel good, it makes us feel like we are contributing, it makes the whole thing seem relevant and practical. But it switches true religion on its head. It snuffs out grace with the greatest of intentions and the best of motivations. Because isn't doing good, isn't keeping the law a good thing? Yes it is! But only when it is kept in its proper place.

Paul is not finished. He adds that when he had finished talking to the group that James, Peter (Cephas) and John perceived the grace that was given to him (vs. 9). I think "grace" here is deliberately contrasted with law, even though the law is not mentioned. Paul was a Pharisee of Pharisees, a law-keeper *par excellence* in his previous life. But now he is proclaiming salvation through Christ and not the law. Something has changed. What has changed is his knowledge of the gospel. It has sunk into his head that he is not saved or kept by what he does, but by grace. And God has given him grace to see this grace, to preach this grace, to hold fast to this grace against all odds.

When the "pillars" of the church perceived this, they extended "the right hand of fellowship to Barnabas and Paul." This meeting served its purpose. Paul would not be accused of teaching legalism in the churches, and he would not accuse them of the same. They were of one Spirit, one accord. The church would not be split in half over this issue. They would hold their ground in their own territories, but it would be a united front.

The "right hand of fellowship" is a technical term for acceptance among the brothers through a binding mutual agreement or oath. The oath was concluded with a handshake—a symbol of mutual agreement, acknowledgement, and fellowship (*koinonia*). It is a binding sign of both friendship *and a covenant*. We do it today just as Parthians, Persians, Hebrews, and Greeks (2 Kings 10:15; 1 Chron 29:24; Ezra 10:19; Lam 5:6; Ezek 17:18) did it back then. 1 Macc 6:58 explains, "Now then let us give the right hand to these men, and make peace with them." Xenophon of Athens (430 – 354 BC), a Greek historian, soldier, and mercenary, gives you a pagan equivalent, "I know that both of us have taken oaths and given right hands [pledges]" (Xenophon, *Anabasis* II. V. 3).[9]

The point is not that their acceptance legitimizes his gospel, but that his gospel generates their acceptance and creates an intimate bond of love between them. This is really the purpose of church membership, which is a similar formal agreement between two parties. Far from disagreeing with him, as is so common to see in NT studies these days where Paul and Luke and James and Peter are all hopelessly contradictory and at odds with one another, the three great pillars of the church enthusiastically approve of Paul and Barnabas. They acknowledge that Paul's gospel is their gospel and that their gospel is Paul's gospel.

Not only this, they then send them back out with their blessing and with a sign to all the Gentiles that the church is not divided on this issue. The text adds one final important verse for us today. I've been telling you over and over of the message of the gospel, the reason why we gather, the content of what you are supposed to hear. I hope through this passage today, that I have delivered this message once again to you today, and that through it you have been encouraged to worship God for the incredible sovereignty he has demonstrated in the church. Were it not for God's actions in Jerusalem, God's actions in the lives of the apostles James, Peter, and John, God's actions in the lives of Barnabas, Titus, and Paul, God's actions in giving the same gospel, God's actions in preserving it in the midst of hostile wolves, and so many other things, you dear people and I would not be here today. Instead, we would be worshipping Thor or Zeus or Gaia; we would be neck deep in gross immorality with no escape because this is what our religion insists upon; we would be worshiping demons and continue to be bound in shackles by Satan the prince of this world, just as all of our ancestors were before this same gospel came to them and set them free. Have you thanked God for this today? Do you think this an impractical thing to your Christian life, to worship God and fulfill your chief end? I pray to God that the power of the gospel would so grip each one of you that never would such a thought enter into your

---

[9] William Hendriksen and Simon J. Kistemaker, vol. 8, *New Testament Commentary: Exposition of Galatians*, New Testament Commentary (Grand Rapids: Baker Book House, 1953-2001).

Galatians

minds. That you would see the good news for what it is, the power of God and so give him glory. That this would open your mouths to speak forth the word to others, and that it would open your hearts and control your tongues and move your feet to do good to all people.

It is curious to me that the Apostles and leaders of Jerusalem would tell Barnabas "remember the poor" (Gal 1:10). I can see James' footprints all over this remark, for this dear brother wrote his own letter to the churches about this very thing. He knew his brother's tenderness (that is Jesus) towards others and saw this as the necessary outworking of the gospel. What I want to remind you of is that remembering the poor, Paul says, "was the very thing he was eager to do." In fact, he had been making this a point of his ministry since the earliest days! Indeed, the last time they were in Jerusalem we read, "The disciples determined, everyone according to his ability, to send relief to the brothers living in Judea. And they did so, sending it to the elders by the hand of Barnabas and Saul" (Acts 11:29-30).

You see, far from making the law irrelevant, the gospel frees you for the first time to actually care about … others. Legalism is almost always focused upon yourself, or at least upon others only in the sense that *they* had better do what is right. But the gospel causes you to look outward. How can it not? How can someone who has been saved and understood such grace not think outwardly? How can they not see the actions of their own Lord, and the compassion that he had upon the suffering and not do something about it? The gospel gives feet to the law, because it frees you from its shackles and creates a desire to love and fear God. This is what we preach. This is why we come. This is what we desire. This is what we love.

May he who has an ear, hear.

Hypocrisy and the Gospel

Even the Apostles Continued to Need the Good News

[11] But when Cephas came to Antioch, I opposed him to his face, because he stood condemned. [12] For before certain men came from James, he was eating with the Gentiles; but when they came he drew back and separated himself, fearing the circumcision party.

[13] And the rest of the Jews acted hypocritically along with him, so that even Barnabas was led astray by their hypocrisy. [14] But when I saw that their conduct was not in step with the truth of the gospel, I said to Cephas before them all, "If you, though a Jew, live like a Gentile and not like a Jew, how can you force the Gentiles to live like Jews?" [15] We ourselves are Jews by birth and not Gentile sinners (sarcasm); [16] yet we know that a person is not justified by works of the law but through faith in Jesus Christ, so we also have believed in Christ Jesus, in order to be justified by faith in Christ and not by works of the law, because by works of the law no one will be justified.

Galatians 2:11-16

___

Hypocrisy

HYPOCRISY. IT MEANS, "The state of pretending to have beliefs, opinions, virtues, feelings, qualities, or standards that one does not actually have." A pompous deacon was endeavoring to impress upon a class of boys the importance of living the Christian life. "Why do people call me a Christian?" the man asked. After a moment's pause, one youngster said, "Maybe it's because they don't know you." Hypocrisy!

A recent survey of adults who do not attend church, not even on holidays, found that 72% thought the church 'is full of hypocrites,' but that 78% would 'be willing to listen' to someone who wanted to share their beliefs about Christianity.[1] How bizarre is that? Why do you think so many people think the church is full of hypocrites? The answer is, because it is!

Two Types of Hypocrisy and One Assumed Type That is Not		
Hypocrite #1	**Hypocrite #2**	**Non-Hypocrite (but still not good)**
Claims people, including himself, are basically good, but acts totally depraved.	Claims people are free, then forces others to live in bondage to the law.	Claims people are totally depraved, and then acts like it.
The Good News: *"Live the Christian life."*	The Good News: *"You are free in Christ, but …"*	The Good News: *"Christ saves wicked sinners."*

In the story of the boy to the deacon, the hypocrisy is set against the backdrop of a certain kind of "gospel," which is really no gospel at all. The "gospel" here is "Live the Christian life. Christians are good people." So many people have this as their gospel. It really encapsulates what most Americans, including professing Christians, think the central Christian message is: "Jesus died as an example of how you should live your life" and you can enlist him as your life-coach to help you do it. The problem is, the Bible says that there are no good people, no not one.

I think you should realize something here. Though it is not a good thing, those who teach total depravity of themselves and others cannot, by definition, be hypocrites. If you teach total depravity, and then act totally depraved, you may be a dirty rotten sinner, but hypocrisy is not one of those sins! If you are not a good person, but tell everyone else that they should be, you are a hypocrite. No wonder the kid was keen to it and

---

[1] *Tuscaloosa News*, USA, Jan 19, 2008. http://www.religionnewsblog.com/20397/survey

pointed out the man's hypocrisy. This is the "gospel" of works righteousness. It is the gospel of many of the Jews in the book of Romans.

In Romans, Paul is speaking to a kind of Jew who "brags about his relationship to God," is proud that he is a "guide for the blind" and a "teacher of infants," because he "relies on the law" which for him is "the embodiment of knowledge and truth" (Rom 2:17-20). In other words, God approves of him because he does so many good things. So Paul asks his man, "You then, who teach others, do you not teach yourself? You who preach against stealing, do you steal? You who say that people should not commit adultery, do you commit adultery? You who abhor idols, do you rob temples? You who brag about the law, do you dishonor God by breaking the law?" (Rom 2:21-23). Paul's sarcasm could not be any thicker.

Unbelievers use the same kind of sarcasm today for this kind of hypocrisy in the church. It results in mocking jokes such as this, "As a result of high-level talks many years ago, the Roman Catholics had finally decided to eat meat on Fridays, the Jews came back with their own 'high-level' conference and decided that they would finally accept Jesus the Christ as the Messiah, the Baptists huddled for several weeks to try to come up with an appropriate response and after half-a-dozen closed-door conferences that reportedly almost ended in fist-fights, the Baptists finally emerged with the following statement: *Henceforth, the Southern Baptist Conference will agree that Baptists will agree to smoke, drink, cuss, dance, play cards, go to movies and start ADMITTING it openly.*" Again, this hypocrisy comes from a works-oriented gospel (works of laws that aren't even in the Bible nonetheless), the gospel so common in our culture today, and the "gospel" that Paul says causes men to blaspheme God because of it (Rom 2:24).

Today's passage has hypocrisy front and center, and from a most unsuspecting source. This man taught total depravity and yet was still a hypocrite. How can that be? It is not because he taught total depravity and then acted totally depraved (which he did). This was not his hypocrisy. His hypocrisy was of a sort that has not been touched upon yet. This hypocrisy is not about getting saved, but more about staying saved. It's not about being accepted by Christ at the first moment of salvation, but more about staying acceptable to Christ afterwards. It is not really about justification, but sanctification. It is a kind of hypocrisy that many people would never think is even possible, and yet many Christians engage in it. I want to remedy this situation for you today, so that you will be able to see his hypocrisy for what it is and leave here taking seriously the vital importance of not engaging in it.

The hypocrisy I'm referring to cannot be committed by an unbeliever. This in itself is frightening, and thus this message is relevant only to a group of Christians. This hypocrisy presupposes a correct gospel at the start, a true belief in its teaching, and a true delight and love for it and especially the freedom that stems from it. Freedom in Christ will become a major theme later in this letter. This is because freedom in Christ is at the heart of this kind of hypocrisy.

This hypocrisy knows Christian liberty for itself, but when peer pressure or temptation comes, it shirks back from freedom and forces others to live under bondage to the law. Do you hear what this kind of hypocrisy does? The first hypocrisy knows nothing of freedom; the second does. The first hypocrisy is about being good from the start; the second begins with good news but ends with bad.

This is a difficult concept to understand. In order for me to be able to explain it, I must first show you what this gospel is, where it comes from, how high it is, how magnificent it is, and how it leads to Christian freedom. If this hypocrisy presupposes the true gospel, then you have to understand the gospel before you can make sense of the hypocrisy! Only then can you possibly see how serious the sin before us is.

Before explaining this gospel, I want to remind you of how high the gospel is. In Galatians 1:8-9 the Apostle says that, "Even if we or an angel from heaven should preach to you a gospel contrary to the one we preached to you, let him be anathema. As we have said before, so now I say again: If anyone is preaching to you a gospel contrary to the one you received, let him be accursed."

Other than God himself, the author and creator of the gospel, there is nothing higher than that gospel.[2] The gospel is over everything like the

---

[2] Do not think that God and the good news are the same. God is higher than the gospel. John Piper has a book out called, "God is the Gospel." The book is about seeking God through Jesus Christ and Piper expounds this very nicely; but as the title stands *by itself*, it is really misleading. God is not "good news" in his bare essence. This is the very problem of all world religions which think they can climb up to gain a glimpse of God through

sun is over the day. In these verses, angels are not higher than the gospel. The Apostles are not higher than the gospel. By implication, the church is not higher than the gospel. The Pope is not higher than the gospel. Rome is not higher. Orthodoxy is not higher. "Holy Tradition" is not higher. Calvin and Luther are not higher. Reformed churches are not higher. Technology is not higher. Cultures are not higher. Missions are not higher. Relevancy is not higher. Nothing is higher than the gospel. If not for the gospel, these others would not exist. The gospel creates the church, not the other way around. The gospel makes the church relevant, not the other way around. All is subordinated to the gospel. Thus, it is of the upmost importance that we get the gospel right and keep it that way.

What is The Gospel?

So what is this gospel? It is an announcement. What is this announcement? In the middle of our text today it says, "We know that a person is not justified by works of the law but through faith in Jesus Christ … by works of the law no one will be justified" (Gal 2:16). In the middle it says, "We have believed in Christ Jesus, in order to be justified by faith in Christ and not by works of the law." The word "justified," this is the gospel. If you do not have justification, you do not have good news.

Justification is a word that at least one professor in my seminary suggested we not use, because people can't understand it. It is too big of a word. I respond with a question, do people know how to use dictionaries? Paul apparently never got that memo, nor did Jesus. Yes, Jesus talked about justification. Paul got his gospel from Jesus! On one occasion Jesus spoke of a man "wishing to justify himself" (Luke 10:29). On another, he spoke of a man who "went down to his house justified" (Luke 18:14). The man wishing to justify himself did so through the law. He told Jesus he had obeyed the entire law. So, Jesus gave him one law he had not considered. The other man went home justified because he cried out "God, be merciful to me, a sinner!" That's all he did. He trusted in God to save

---

merit or mysticism. Anyone in hell will tell you that God in his essence is not the gospel. God is "good news" only as he is mediated to us through the person and work of Jesus Christ, through word and sacrament (audible and visible gospel), and through faith that Christ's work alone saves me from God's wrath. The gospel is an announcement of something God has done for us through Christ alone. It is not God in his bare essence.

him. But his friend said, "I thank God that I'm not like other men." "Look at me. I'm not a sinner. I obey everything." So what is justification?

Justification is a legal term. It is the verdict from a judge at his bench after he has heard the testimony of the defendant and all of the prosecution's evidence against him. What is this evidence? As Jesus pointed out time and again to people who wanted to justify themselves, the evidence against any person is plentiful. "All have sinned." This is the evidence against you.

The first kind of hypocrite (above) may think that his good deeds can outweigh his bad deeds. He does not understand that any evidence is enough to condemn him. Sometimes he will try to argue that he has no evidence against him. Other times, he might admit it, but will try to show the court that he has done many good things. Imagine O.J. telling the judge, "OK, I murdered Nicole and Ron Goldman, but I was a great running back and gave people a lot of joy, I did Hertz commercials and everyone knows car rentals help people, and I was an actor which is an honorable profession. Those three things ought to be enough to outweigh this one indiscretion." It would be absurd, but this is how people who try to justify before God act.

So in the Bible, the evidence condemns everyone. The Judge should rightly declare everyone "guilty as charged" and pronounce the death penalty as punishment. That is what justice demands. But Paul says that we are justified through faith in Jesus. The question becomes, how can God declare a person not guilty when they are guilty?

It is because of the work of Christ in obeying all of the law perfectly as a substitute. That is, God put the punishment of your sin upon him at the cross. He was given the death penalty that all people deserve. But God raised Jesus from the dead. And God decided in eternity past that this entire activity of Jesus should be done so that those who are raised from the dead through the gospel and trust in his work by faith alone might be credited with his perfection even as he credited to Jesus' account your punishment. It has been dubbed "the great exchange." Jesus gets your sin and punishment while you get his perfect status credited to you.

Thus, God has provided a way that your sin might really be punished and yet you might really be declared "not guilty." This is truly "good news." It is the only good news that matters. It is justification through faith alone and not by works of the law, because by works of the law no one will be justified. It is just not possible because your works are "filthy rags" and even the best of them deserve punishment. This good news will be discussed in greater detail in Galatians, because this particular church was giving it up.

The context of his announcement of justification is freedom. For Paul it was the freedom that Jews had now that they became Christians. For Gentiles, it is a freedom to not come under the law to be saved. He begins to explain this freedom in Gal 2:15-16a. He refers to himself and the other Apostles in the first person plural ("we"). We means "Jews." "We ourselves are Jews by birth and not Gentile sinners (I take "sinners" to be slightly sarcastic, much like Romans 2 above); yet we know that a person is not justified by works of the law but through faith in Jesus Christ."

Paul is saying that even if you could make an argument that the Jews are not Gentiles sinners because they have the law, *we* (Jewish Christians) believe that *we* are saved through faith. This proves that Jews are sinners just like Gentiles. Thus he continues, "... so we also have believed in Christ Jesus, in order to be justified by faith in Christ and not by works of the law, because by works of the law no one will be justified." You ask, "where is the freedom here?" It is implicit in the context, the context of hypocrisy in not acting like you are saved by faith alone. It goes like this.

Because this gospel comes only through faith, it provides freedom from the tyranny and rigor of the law which demands absolute perfection. Anyone trying to have life by works *must* obey the entire law without exception. But anyone trusting in Christ alone will be justified utterly apart from any law keeping or law breaking. That is freedom. If faith alone brings freedom from the law, then what sense does it make that after you are saved, this freedom should give way once more to the law? It is in this context that we find the hypocrisy of Galatians 2.

Being a Hypocrite

Let's go back to the beginning of our section today. There was a group of Christians that seemed to be following Paul around subverting his gospel on purpose. There were also Apostles that were subverting the gospel without trying to. In fact, one of them is supposedly the first Pope! The first group did it through *teaching*; the other through *example*. So let's look first at the text to see who these people are. Galatians 2:11, "When Cephas (that is Peter—1:18; 2:9) came to Antioch, I opposed him to his face, because he stood condemned." Peter belongs to the second category, those who subvert the gospel through their example. Here is what he was doing.

We learn in the next verse that Peter at one point in time was "eating with Gentiles" (Gal 2:11). This refers to table fellowship, possibly to the Lord's Supper, but certainly to the more general association of Jews eating together with Gentiles. This is obviously a significant thing, because Jewish kosher laws demanded that Jews could never eat with Gentiles, who regularly ate swine and other unclean animals. Peter did it because he was now free from such binding legal red tape. Suddenly, Peter stopped eating with the Gentiles. He backed away and separated himself, and began acting "hypocritically" (2:12-13). What does this hypocrisy entail?

It says, "Certain men came from James" (vs.12). It then refers to them as "the circumcision party." The idea is that Peter was giving in to this circumcision party, forcing the Gentiles to give up their freedom from this law. Before you go getting all high and mighty, condemning Peter for something so obviously hypocritical, something that you would never do, I want to try to lay bare the subtlety of the deception he was under. I want to go back to the date that Paul wrote this letter to make a point.

This episode is one of the stronger arguments people have given for Galatians being written prior to the Jerusalem council in Acts 15. I have taken the other view—that Galatians 2:1-10 refers to the Jerusalem council. Upon my view, the episode here with Peter would have taken place after the council (Acts 15:22ff), when Paul and Barnabas went back to Antioch to deliver the news of the council's decision to the church, or perhaps even later.

Early daters will say, "There is no way that Peter could have so boldly made the comments that he made in Jerusalem about the law being such a heavy yoke that no one can bear (Acts 15:7-11) and then so quickly turned against himself and succumbed to the circumcision party." They will also add that it seems difficult to believe that James would have sent this circumcision party to Antioch after the council, because that would be

to contradict everything he said at the council about circumcision. Therefore, the argument is made, this entire chapter takes place before the Jerusalem council. I not only think this idea is wrong, I think it destroys the
real subtlety of the sin here, which is that Christians can commit such
gross errors in practice even after coming down so boldly against the very
principle they are condemning in a different practice.

There is a major problem with the alternative date. Namely, it implies that prior to the council, James and Peter didn't really understand the
gospel and Paul did![3] The early date argument presupposes that James sent
the circumcision party from Jerusalem approving of their message, and
only later changed his mind, when Paul convinced him of the 'true gospel.' But this destroys Paul's entire argument (Gal 1:11-2:10), that he and
the Apostles always had the same gospel independently of one another.
Therefore, I think something else is going on.

First, James may not have even sent these men. Rather, coming
"from James" could be interpreted as coming from the church in Jerusalem
of which James was the leader (this takes "James" as a metonymy for "Jerusalem").[4] We use this kind of language today: Piper's church, MacArthur's church, Chantry's church, etc. Bad eggs may come from a mother
church without the pastor's knowledge, but the pastor is included as sort
of guilty by association.

Second, even if James sent them, it is important to notice that the issue here is different from the one in Acts 15. This is the subtlety. Acts 15
settles the question of salvation by faith alone, using the particular issue of
circumcision to prove it. But notice, circumcision is not the issue here
with Peter. The issue is eating with Gentiles. The principle is the same
(the free gospel of Christ), but the circumstance has changed. James himself in Acts 15 said that we should tell the Gentiles to abstain from things
(food?) polluted by idols, food that had been strangled, and from eating
food with blood in it (Acts 15:19-20). James meant this with respect to

---

[3] I was pretty shocked when I heard the guys talking about Galatians 2 vs. the Jerusalem Council on the White
Horse Inn imply this very thing, saying that at the Jerusalem council "James and Paul got on exactly the same
page" ("The Book of Galatians," 1-31-2010 minutes 17-18 of the broadcast).
[4] À la the Complete Jewish Bible, "For prior to the arrival of certain people from [the community headed by]
Ya'akov." This is the view argued by Hendrickson, *Galatians*, 93.

Galatians

Christian freedom, not salvation. He is saying that because there are so many Jews in their own churches, they should be sensitive to their Jewish friends with weaker consciences over matters of indifference. Just read the Letter of James to see how serious he was about this kind of thing.

In my mind, a group of legalists looking for a loophole could have found just such a thing in James' decision at Jerusalem. As legalists, they were not concerned at all with Christian freedom, but with salvation by merit. They were still stuck back there. They saw Gentiles doing the very things the council had told them not to do (eating such food), they saw Peter eating with them anyway, and when Peter saw them, he became fearful of what they would think and say. The problem is, these people are not weaker brothers (whom James had in mind when he gave his advice). They are Pharisees with a different gospel. Their gospel comes from Satan! The weaker brother is one who cannot himself partake in some matter of conscience. The Pharisee is one who will not allow anyone else to partake in the matter. The hypocrite is the one who acts in league with the Pharisee at one time, but will partake in the very same action at other times. That is, he uses his freedom for himself, but forces others not to use it for themselves.

If this circumcision party had taught and believed that people are saved through faith alone but would have had their own faith weakened by eating unclean food with Gentiles, then Peter would have had a leg to stand on in leaving the table. That was James' point. But these men were teaching that it is by what we do that people are saved and made good Christians. Thus, Peter's leaving the table sent contradictory messages. On one hand, he told the Gentiles they were saved by faith alone. On the other, as soon as someone teaching another gospel comes in, he quickly runs to their side so as not to offend them. What do you think these Gentile Christians would make of that? They would have thought, "He says we are saved by faith alone, but his actions are that we are saved by works of the law, the way these men teach." Do you see the hypocrisy?

Peter may have convinced himself that removing himself from the table was done in the name of keeping unity with James, but he was being a hypocrite. He did not really believe that at all, because he knew that these very men were not concerned with Christian liberty. We may think we have a superhero suit on that keeps us protected from this sin of hypocrisy, but our culture has our own issues that we justify to replace the gospel just as they did. Like Peter, we can justify almost anything, can't we? Even when we know something is wrong, we can justify it on other grounds.

Someone says, "Yes, Christians are saved by faith alone, but anyone who drinks alcohol, well, he isn't a good Christian." Sorry friend. A Christian is not good or bad because they do or do not do a law. They are "good" because Christ did all the law and God credits his goodness to them by faith. But then they say, "Yes, but if you drink alcohol around my grandma who thinks Christians should never drink alcohol, then you are not a good Christian." But this is exactly what Peter was doing. If your grandma believes this, there is a good chance that she is not a Christian. (Notice, grandma did not think that she personally should not drink, but that no one else should). We are constantly being tempted with supplanting Christ with the best of good works. Fill this in with any sin you like (be it non-biblical or biblical: dancing, playing cards, or murdering and committing adultery) it doesn't matter.

Notice, even Barnabas (vs. 13) who elsewhere is held up as the model of virtue, succumbed to the subtlety of the deceit and was led astray by the hypocrisy, joining with them against the Gentiles. These Gentiles may not have been sinless here. You can easily think of this as a mixed congregation of Jews and Gentiles. Perhaps at this moment, they weren't obeying James' instructions, and as stronger brothers were lording their freedom over the weaker Jews, but we don't know that for sure. At any rate, Paul isn't concerned with that. Weaker/stronger issues are not even in the same universe of importance to Paul as getting the gospel right. He is concerned that two of the pillars of the church were acting one way and saying one thing and then the very next moment they were acting another way, effectively destroying the gospel by their actions, all because they wanted to please those whom they knew had a different gospel.

You say, Peter would never act like that knowingly! Peter is not infallible, let alone sinless. In fact, Peter is acting out his character exactly as we see him do in the Gospels! Have you forgotten? This is the man who didn't want people to think that he was associated with Jesus, so he denied him not once, not twice, but three different times! This sin is similar. Peter seems especially prone to caring too much about what people think of him, no matter even if they are trying to kill Jesus or his message!

What you especially need to understand about Peter in this situation is that he was a believer who knew the True Gospel and loved it! He is no fundamentalist who thinks that the good news is to make sure boys don't stand too close to girls of the opposite sex in college. This is what Paul says about the hypocrisy, "I saw that the conduct was not in step with the truth of the gospel" (vs. 14). This was a matter of making a mockery of the good news of Jesus Christ.

What makes Peter's hypocrisy all the worse is his background. Peter was eating with these Gentiles because he knew the truth. Peter walked with Jesus who used to eat regularly with tax collectors and sinners. Pharisees viewed these people the same way they viewed Gentiles, and you could not eat with them. Peter also went with Jesus to Gentile nations. He certainly must have eaten with Gentiles there. There was a time, in Jesus' ministry, when he pronounced all meat clean (Mark 7:19). Later, Peter was given a dream, again not once, not twice, but three times(!), where he learned that he must regard that which is "unclean" in the law as having been cleansed by God (Acts 10:9-16). Not only did Peter have this dream, but he understood it and in Acts 10:28 (before even the early date for Galatians) went into Caesarea and preached a sermon that Jews must not call Gentiles or their food unclean (and this was prior even to the early dating of Galatians 2)! Given all of this, and probably the council of Jerusalem too, Peter knew the truth, preached the truth, and loved the truth and yet still acted like a hypocrite! If Peter could do it, don't you think you are prone to being a hypocrite as well?

Anytime you behave in such a manner that by your actions you force someone back under law and make them feel like they are only acceptable to God *when they obey him*, you make an absolute mockery of the good news. God is now our Father, and good fathers love their children no matter what they do. They may not be pleased with what they do, but they always love them the same no matter what. Beloved, we are only acceptable to God because of Christ's works. All of our good works are done because we are accepted, not to become acceptable. Have you been burdened in your relationship with your heavenly Father by you sins this week, or this hour? Perhaps you are even convicted that you have been guilty of this very hypocrisy? Then trust in Christ and come to know once more the freedom you have in a loving heavenly father who accepts you with open arms for the sake of Jesus.

Peter's words were a balm for the Gentiles. His actions were a knife! This kind of hypocrisy is just as bad as the more common kind that does not even start with the right gospel. This hypocrisy may start with it, but it does not finish with it and therefore the results are the same. It destroys the power of God in a person's life. That power is the good news that sets them free from the tyranny of self-righteous law-keeping. This is exactly how the rest of the chapter unfolds. I will only look at a couple more verses this morning and then next week we will finish the chapter.

Notice, Peter does not condemn Peter to hell, but he does rebuke him. Paul rebukes Peter in front of everyone in vs. 14. It is most commendable and is in line with what he said in 1:10, "I am not trying to please men any longer." Unlike most people in our day or his, Paul wasn't afraid to call sin "sin." That's probably why so many people don't like him even today. So he rebuked the first Pope! What unmitigated nerve! Here is what he said as sort of the heart of our passage today, and the most applicable part as far as learning some kind of duty from it.

"If you, though a Jew, live like a Gentile and not like a Jew, how can you force the Gentiles to live like Jews?" You can paraphrase it this way. "If you, though a man under the impossible yoke of the law, too heavy to bear its burden, have learned that you are saved by grace alone and now have total freedom from earning God's merit, why do you act in such a way that those who never had this yoke of ceremonial laws of Moses now come under that which you yourself won't be under?" Wow! This is an incredible warning that we must take seriously.

If you do not understand the truth about the gospel I have given you today, then pray to God to make known the freedom from the law that comes by trusting in Christ alone. Repent of your sins and pray, "God have mercy on me a sinner," and you will be justified.

If you know the truth about Jesus Christ and that you are only saved by the power of the resurrected Christ through the good news, then watch yourselves very closely. Guard your activities so that you never act in a way that is contrary to this. Do not put people back under law to gain God's favor. Do not even act in a way towards them that you make them feel as if they are not accepted in Christ unless they perform some good work. To do so is to beat an already beaten person or to stir up more rebellion in their heart than they had prior to ever hearing the gospel.

Do not do it to yourself, either. Do not think thoughts that cause you to give up your freedom in Christ in your heart. If you do, then you will have destroyed everything comforting about this gospel. You will live a life of misery, depression, and anger at yourself and others. People will see your hypocrisy and want nothing to do with your God. Sometimes your preaching the good news to others, means preaching it to yourself first. Act in such a way that you preserve for all people the comfort and freedom of the good news. Keep that good news truly good by not contradicting it with your actions.

The Cruel Slave Master

Our Relationship to the Law

¹⁷ But if, in <u>our</u> endeavor to be justified in Christ, <u>we</u> too were found to be sinners, is Christ then a servant of sin? Certainly not! ¹⁸ For if I rebuild what I tore down, I prove myself to be a transgressor. ¹⁹ For through the law I died to the law, so that I might live to God. ²⁰ I have been crucified with Christ. It is no longer I who live, but Christ who lives in me. And the life I now live in the flesh I live by faith in the Son of God, who loved me and gave himself for me. ²¹ I do not nullify the grace of God, for if righteousness were through the law, then Christ died for no purpose.

Galatians 2:17-21

The Cruel Slave-Master

THERE ONCE WAS A SLAVE OWNER who knew all that was good and right and believed that if he just told his servants what to do, that this would prove them to be good themselves. Day after day he would proclaim to his two slaves, "Pick my cotton, my apples, and my peaches (he had 10 acres of apple trees, 10 of peach trees, and 20 acres of cotton), feed my cows and my pigs, water my horses, keep my children busy and teach them all that they should know in this world (he had eight children), clean up the barn, raise new fences (he had 240 acres), feed my family our three square meals of delectable and fancy food which you butcher and pick from the farm, stitch up our tattered clothes, polish our shoes, and plant and take care of the garden (the garden was an acre of various vegetables and berries)." These things needed to be done and the owner had no time to them himself. After all, that's why he had slaves.

What a great privilege it was for them to have these rules, the thought. It proves how much I love them that I tell them what I expect. If they complied, he promised them very generous rewards: a table full of the best food, clothes unlike any other slaves, comfortable shoes, coats in the winter, and several days off during the year where they could act like freemen with some money that he would give them to spend.

But the slaves did not respond to the master's orders as he had planned. Initially they were very gung ho. But soon they began to wake late and go to bed early. They took long lunch breaks. They worked in the hot sun, sweltering humidity, torrential downpours, and blustery winter storms and it was laborious. They would take time off from their duties to talk to each other about the unreasonable demands of their owner under such harsh conditions. Two hundred people could not do everything this master wanted, let alone two.

So the owner whipped them. And he whipped them some more. Day after day he would beat them mercilessly, because they did not do their assigned tasks. One day, as he was walking out to greet his slaves with another round of whippings, he found them lying there on the ground, dead. The very master who had desired such obedience had killed his own workers.

Christ and the Law

The passage before us today is crucial for understanding the power of the law over a person's life. Most *people* have this idea that law-keeping somehow saves them (to whatever heaven and whatever god they desire) and proves that they are good people, not really all that sinful. Most *Christians* have this idea that law-keeping somehow sanctifies them, proves that now that they are saved they are good people, not really all that sinful. Neither are true and both ideas pervert the grace of God in Christ and the only power on earth to justify *and to sanctify* a person, the gospel.

As an example of this, in his commentary on Galatians, Martin Luther preserved for his posterity A Form of Monastic Absolution which the most pious among the monks used to recite. "MAY GOD SPARE YOU, BROTHER. May the merit of the suffering of our Lord Jesus Christ, of Blessed and Ever Virgin Mary, and of all the saints; the merit of your order; the burden of your order; the humility of your confession; the contrition of your heart; the good works that you have done and will do for the love of our Lord Jesus Christ—may all this be granted to you for the forgiveness of your sins, for the growth of merit and grace, and for the reward of eternal life. Amen."[1] What you will notice in this prayer is that Christ is rendered superfluous, non-essential, unnecessary. As Luther put it, "the glory and the name of Justifier and Savior are taken away from Him and attributed to monastic works." This begins to get at the idea set forth in Galatians 2:17-21, except that it is worse even than this. To a legalist, "Christ alone" apart from the law is not just a wrong thing, it is an evil thing. For legalists inherently think that if you have no law with respect to meriting God's favor, that Christ is himself a minister of sin.

Context

Let me be frank. This passage (or at least vv. 17-18) is one of the most difficult to understand in the Bible. The best way to grasp it is to think about the context. Paul has just rebuked Peter publicly for acting hypocritically. What Peter did was to sit down and eat with Gentiles, but when a group called "the circumcision party" came in the doors, he immediately jumped up, ran over to them, knowing full well what they were preaching, and gave them a great big bear hug, thereby nullifying the gospel through his actions. For, these people—who had already nullified the gospel through their teachings—were saying that unless Gentiles effectively give up trusting in Christ alone and embrace the ceremonial laws of the Jews, they could not be saved.[2] The churches of Galatia are at the present moment seriously considering doing to Paul what Peter did to the Gentiles, turning their backs on him and running eagerly into the open arms of the welcoming legalists.

---

[1] Martin Luther, vol. 26, *Luther's Works, Vol. 26 : Lectures on Galatians, 1535, Chapters 1-4*, ed. Jaroslav Jan Pelikan, Hilton C. Oswald and Helmut T. Lehmann, Luther's Works (Saint Louis: Concordia Publishing House, 1999), Ga 2:18.

[2] Cf. Acts 15:1, "Unless you are circumcised according to the custom of Moses, you cannot be saved."

Galatians

What Peter did was hypocritical because he not only knew that they taught a false gospel, but he spoke up about it in Jerusalem just a few weeks earlier, calling it "a yoke that no one can bear" (Acts 15:10). Paul, who cares only about the purity of the good news, the power of God to save, and the glory of Jesus Christ, shows that this hypocrisy (which led even Barnabas astray) was not "in step with the gospel" (Gal 2:14). The gospel says that all people in Christ are free from keeping the law as a means of salvation, but Peter's actions said otherwise, because he sided only in his actions with those who taught otherwise.

Thus, Paul rebuked Peter saying, "If you, though a Jew, live like a Gentile and not like a Jew, how can you force the Gentiles to live like Jews?" (vs. 14). At this point, your ESV puts an end to the quotation marks. The implication is that this is the end of Paul's rebuke and everything after this is said to someone else (probably the Galatians). However, there are differences of opinion as to how many more verses are spoken directly towards Peter. The NAS, for example, put the end of the quotation at the very end of the chapter, implying that everything until vs. 21 is directed at Peter. This is extremely difficult to accept because of some of the things Paul says in the rest of the passage. For example, are we to think that Peter believed that Christ was a servant of sin (vs. 17)? Was Peter somehow accusing Paul of "nullifying the grace of God" by justification by faith alone (vs. 21)? That makes no sense.

Calvin thinks that Paul is finished speaking to Peter in vs. 16 and that in vs. 17 he begins talking to the Galatians again. This is the view that I'm adopting. This means that vs. 14-16 are spoken at Peter, Barnabas and the others. Here Paul says, "We ourselves (referring to the Jews, for Paul, Peter, and Barnabas were all Jews) are Jews by birth and not Gentile sinners; yet we know that a person is not justified by works of the law but through faith in Jesus Christ, so we also have believed in Christ Jesus, in order to be justified by faith in Christ and not by works of the law, because by works of the law no one will be justified." Paul says this to them (in front of the circumcision party, which is important) by way of reminder that they have trusted in the gospel of grace, not of works. If they have done this, then it should prove to them that they are sinners just like the Gentiles are sinners. Therefore, to return to some kind of law-keeping, whether it be by conviction or through hypocrisy, proves all the more that they are law*breakers*.

Now comes vs. 17. This and the next verse are extremely complicated because we do not know what is going on in Paul's head. Maybe you have had this happen to you. Sometimes my wife will say something as if in mid-sentence. We'll be driving in the car to the mall and she will say, "… no, you were supposed to do that." I say, "Do what?" She had been thinking about something we were talking about five hours ago, and forgot that I can't hear her thoughts. She basically answered something that we left unfinished, except that until she reminds me of what "that" (the indefinite pronoun) refers to, I have absolutely no idea what she is talking about.

This is often times the way Paul is. He has all these thoughts going on in his head—things that people had been saying, telling him, preaching to others—that we are not privy to because he does not choose to share them with us. This is one of the things that makes Paul so difficult to understand (to use Peter's words; 2 Pet 3:16). It is probably the result of his brilliance, just like my wife's. That's the way smart people are. The rest of us just need to catch up.

At any rate, vs. 17 says, "But if, in our endeavor to be justified in Christ, we too were found to be sinners, is Christ then a servant of sin? Certainly not!" Read 5 commentaries on this verse and you will get 15 different interpretations. The problem is that very few of them can make sense of the whole verse. If we say that Paul is still speaking to Peter, then you have to deal with the question at the end. But what sense does it make that Peter would think that Christ is a servant of sin? On the other hand, what if Paul is now talking to the circumcision party in the room? As legalists, they certainly thought that the Christ Paul was preaching was somehow promoting sin. But what sense does it make for him to say that we are all endeavoring to be justified in Christ, when he and his opponents had such very different views of justification?

Here's how I've come to make sense of it. Vv. 17-21 are Paul's switching subjects from Peter to the Galatians. He is talking to the Galatian churches now (as is made clear in 3:1). These verses deal with three separate issues. What I want to show you is 1. (vs. 17) The true thinking and logic behind the legalist. This you need to see, because few people realize how deadly serious legalism is to the Christian faith. It is a guillotine and the gospel is the head it seeks to cut off. 2. (vs. 18) The utter hypocrisy of returning to legalism after starting with Christ alone. Anyone who does this only proves how sinful they really are and that returning to the law only increases their problems. 3. (vv. 19-21) The reason why we are able to be justified by faith alone, and how freeing such a thing actually is to those stuck in the mud of legalism.

Exegesis

Vs. 17 summarizes to the Galatians the argument that they have been hearing from the circumcision party. What Paul is saying in this verse can be restated something like this. "Galatian saints, I have been preaching to you that you are justified by faith in Christ apart from the law. We are seeking earnestly to be justified in Christ alone. But those whom you are listening to are teaching you that if you drop the law, as we have done, because the law does not justify anyone, this proves you are no better than Gentile sinners who do not have the law, and therefore because it proves that you are sinners, Christ is a servant of sin, Paul's gospel promotes sin because his Christ promotes lawlessness."

To this circumcision party, the word "sinner" means "Gentile." When you read "sinner" in vs. 17 read "Gentile." Look at vs. 15. "We ourselves are Jews by birth, and not Gentile sinners." Paul is speaking to Peter and he is being sarcastic when he calls Gentiles "sinners." Paul doesn't think that Gentiles are any more sinful than Jews, and neither does Peter. *But the circumcision party*, who is listening to this rebuke, *certainly does*. This is the way they see Gentiles. Gentiles are without law. God gave the law to Jews because he loved them. The law (and this is the key point of difference between them and Paul) shows how good they are. *The law keeps you from being considered a sinner.*[3]

---

[3] The *UBS Handbook on Galatians* puts it this way, I think correctly. "This verse is apparently an answer to the assertion of Paul's opponents that his message of being put right with God by faith in Jesus Christ amounts to making Christ a minister of sin, since those who put themselves "outside of the law" (by not obeying its demands) would be regarded by Jews as being "sinners." Daniel C. Arichea and Eugene Albert Nida, *A Handbook on Paul's Letter to the Galatians*, UBS handbook series; Helps for translators (New York: United Bible Societies, 1993), 46-47.

Let me explain the verse. If you are justified by faith alone in Christ, then you are no longer under the law. This is the first part of vs. 17 and it is a true statement. But if you are no longer under the law, you become just like the Gentiles, that is you become a "sinner." That is the second part of vs. 17 and it is a false statement, but it accurately represents the circumcision party's position. The logic of it is this: If you are just like a Gentile, then this gospel of Paul's makes Christ a servant of sin. That is, it makes Christ someone who approves of lawlessness, and allows people to act anyway they want, just like Gentiles act. And the logical result of this gospel is that people will act any way they please. In Romans 6:1ff Paul puts this wicked legalistic logic like this, "Shall we sin so that grace will increase?" That is what they were thinking his gospel does.

Notice, both in Romans 6:1 and here the answer is the same "By no means," *me genoito*, the strongest possible way of saying "No" in Greek. In other words, the logic of the legalist is insane. It does not understand the first thing about Christ at all. Friend, what you need to learn from this verse is terribly important. Legalists think and even sometimes say that if you try to be justified by faith alone that you make Christ out to be someone who serves sin. This makes God utterly unjust and Christ completely wicked. For who serves sin other than very wicked people? Legalism is not an alternative room in the castle of Christianity. It is another castle altogether. This is why you must never put up with the legalistic tendencies of people taking the name of Christ, but you must be firm and resolute, standing for grace no matter what it costs you. I highly recommend you getting Martin Luther's commentary on these verses. I don't think Luther exegeted this passage perfectly, because he didn't take the context into account well enough. He was much more concerned with his own day and the legalism of Rome and Anabaptists and that said if you want to be justified you must have Christ *and love*. But as he points out, love is the law, it is not good news. That means, if you want to be justified you must have Christ *and the law*. Their "good news" was nothing but a return to that of the circumcision party, a retreat from grace alone, and surrender of Christ alone, and the triumph of my works combined with God's to save me. Is there anything more depressing than that?

Vs. 18 now arises in answer to Paul's "may it never be." To understand this verse properly, you have to think of it this way. No longer is

Galatians

Paul giving the counterfeit gospel's view of salvation and Christ. He is not giving the Galatians the logical implications of accepting the circumcision party's beliefs after having first accepted Paul's free gospel. The verse says, "If I rebuild what I tore down, then I prove myself to be a transgressor." Paul is using a corporate "I" here and it refers to anyone, be it himself, Peter, Barnabas, the Galatian Christian, or the circumcision party (who presumably originally accepted the gospel of the disciples that one is saved by faith alone). First let me explain what I think the verse is saying, then I'll tell you what I think it means, then I'll make another point about why this verse matters.

What is this verse saying? Well, think about Peter again. He was sitting with Gentiles. Then he abandoned them, leaving them to think that unless they started doing Jewish rituals, that they could not be saved. There is a verse in Ephesians that I think gives a concrete example of what this "building up" and "tearing down" means. Paul refers to the temple. "There was an inscription on the wall of the outer courtyard of the Jerusalem temple warning *Gentiles* that they would only have themselves to blame for their death if they passed beyond it into the inner courts."[4] Notice, at the temple, Gentiles could come up to that wall, but go no farther. This wall separated the Jew from the Gentile. Jews could be holy because they could go inside the temple. Gentiles could not.

The gospel of both Peter and Paul had effectively destroyed this wall, thus destroying the separation between the two peoples. Thus, in Gal 3:28 Paul will say "In Christ there is no Jew or Gentile." This is why Peter was eating with Gentiles. But by his actions, he was effectively rebuilding the wall which he had previously torn down! Building up and tearing down. This is the language Paul uses, and it fits perfectly with the context of what Peter was doing.

What does this verse mean? Paul is reminding the Galatians, perhaps alluding to Peter's actions, that when he came to them, they accepted his gospel. That is, they tore down the dividing wall just like Peter did. If the circumcision group had at one time accepted this same gospel before com-

---

[4] Crossway Bibles, *The ESV Study Bible* (Wheaton, IL: Crossway Bibles, 2008), 2265.

ing to their legalistic doctrines, they would be included here as well. But if, having once torn down that wall, they decide to rebuild it again by accepting this devilish doctrine, then they prove themselves to be transgressors. (He does not use the word "sinner" here, because that word in the context means "like unto a Gentile". He uses "transgressor" because now he is saying that they really are sinful). Why would tearing down and rebuilding this wall of hostility make them sinful? I think it is because that, if they are right to rebuild that wall, they should never have torn it down to begin with. It they tore down something so serious as this wall, which represents the totality of God's law, and they were not supposed to, then all they have done is prove that they are sinful. But if they prove that they are sinful in returning to the law, then they are no better off than they were when they accepted Paul's false gospel of justification by faith alone, which also makes them "sinners" in the Jews' eyes. See the point? Paul's logic is brilliant. They are damned if they take the legalists' view of Paul's gospel, and they are damned if they take the legalists' gospel.

What do you need to understand from this verse? The great temptation, as I pointed out last week, is to start with Christ and finish with the law. But if you return to legalism—that is seeking to earn God's favor or be considered a "good Christian" by what you do, having once accepted Christ, then all you are doing is showing yourself to be a wicked person, a transgressor of the law, because you are effectively saying that a free gospel is wrong. You gut everything good and true from the Christian faith as if you had cut it and opened it up like a fish. This is serious business, isn't it? Not only is legalism to get saved evil, legalism to stay saved is just as evil. Take care of yourself not to become enchanted with anyone who dangles the forbidden fruit of the law before your eyes and tempts you to partake of it for life. For if you do, you will die.

Vv. 19-21 offer the only remedy to the false thinking of legalists. In these verses Paul no longer has false views in mind, but his own, his gospel, the truth. He gives us the truth about our relationship to the law. It is the truth about what brings a person to life. It is the truth about what a Christian wants to do when they are alive. And it is the truth about what God thinks of a person even when they sin after having been justified by faith in Christ alone. He is still speaking to the Galatians, and also to you and me.

First, what is the truth about our relationship to the law? "Through the law I died to the law so that I might live to God" (vs. 19). This is the truth about the law. The law put me to death. Contrary to his opponents, who thought that the law proved that they were alive, the law put me to death. This is the story I gave you at the beginning of the sermon. The master who knew all things good and right and promised such great rewards for obedience is the Law. The slaves are those who serve the law. The law's demands are impossible. As the old hymn says, "Not the labors of my hands can fulfill thy law's demands." God did not give the Jews the law because they were good; he gave it to them to show them that he did not choose them because they were good. If they knew the law and their own hearts well, they would easily see this. Just read the history of the exodus! They were a holy people because they were chosen, they were not chosen because they were holy (Deut 7:6-8). And this applies in individual election to salvation even more than it applies in corporate election to receive the promises of God (Rom 9). It is God alone who makes a person holy. This is the truth about you. Anyone who thinks that God chooses them because they are holy is severely deluded by their own arrogance.

The law shows us that we are sinful, not perfect. If you live to the law, thinking by it you have life, then you are dead to God. This is the picture of the entire world who are dead in their sins. All religions on earth, save true religion, seek to earn the god's favor by appeasing them, sacrificing to them, and doing what they bid. Not God. He does it the opposite way. The message of the gospel cannot be understood by human reason, for it erases us entirely from the picture, and this is something our reason will not allow. If you die to the law, resting only upon faith in Christ, then you live to God. First you must die, then you live. This is the picture of baptism, and it is the very answer Paul gives to the similar objection in Romans 6:3-4. "Do you not know that all of us who have been baptized into Christ Jesus were baptized into his death? We were buried therefore with him by baptism into death, in order that, just as Christ was raised from the dead by the glory of the Father, we too might walk in newness of life." This is in fact a good summary of our last two verses in Galatians, too.

The great riddle to unlock becomes, how can dying to the law bring you to life to God? What a bizarre, radical, contrary idea to nature. Life brings death. Death does not bring life. The solution is found in our mysterious union with Christ. Union with Christ is a mystery, just as the union of a husband and a wife is a mystery. The two become one flesh. They remain two. They become one. The same is true in our union with Christ.

Union with Christ in our passage is discussed in relation to the death and resurrection of Jesus. "I have been crucified with Christ" (vs. 20). What does this mean? Christ was put to death because he was treated as a lawbreaker. As it says later in Galatians, he became a curse (Gal 3:13). He was treated as a lawbreaker because he was killed for our sins. The mystical union means that, through faith, God has reckoned Christ's death as your death because you believe that Christ did this for you. That is, you were crucified with Christ. The punishment that you deserve, being cut off from God, being forsaken by God, having no more knowledge of any kind of God's love in your life … this Christ took on your behalf when he died on the cross.

But if you died with Christ, then you were also raised up in Christ, when he was raised up from the grave. It is not that you were literally there in Christ, but that because you are in Christ you are treated as if you were there. And because he lives, you will live. Here, the hope of the resurrection is that because he lives, the life you live is Christ living in you. He is the one who has been raised from the dead. Therefore, he lives his life through the believer. Paul can speak of this as the Spirit living in you or Christ living in you. The meaning is the same.

What is the implication of this? If Christ did not sin, then him living in you gives you new desires not to want to sin. Therefore, the legalists who charge that a free gospel makes people want to sin know nothing of the truth. Luther was famously asked, "If your gospel is true, then people can do whatever they want." Luther replied, "This is true. Now, what do you want?" His point is that we can do whatever we want. Nothing that we do takes away justification, because we are justified by faith and not by what we do. But because Christ lives in us, what do we want to do? We do not want to sin, that is Christ living in us does not. We sin because we still live in the flesh.

So Paul continues, "The life I now live in the flesh I live by faith in the Son of God, who loved me and gave himself for me" (vs. 20). That is, even after becoming a Christian, his life is one of faith in Christ and not of works. He does not seek to be sanctified by his works. He does good works because he has been (definitely) sanctified. God has set him apart, therefore he does good works. But he does good works because he lives a life of faith in the Son of God who died for him.

Legalists know nothing of Christ because they know nothing of the mystical union, either experientially or objectively. They can't understand that Christ could represent me on the cross. They can't understand that he could take my place. Likewise, they do not understand by experience that Christ gives people new desires. That's why a return to legalism is so deadly. The whole premise of it knows nothing of the mystical union! But if it knows nothing of the union, then it knows nothing of peace, because it is through union with Jesus that a person knows peace. Therefore, how terrible is it to return to legalism?

Finally, Paul adds one more point to this sanctification process. Recognizing that Christians continue to sin, because by living in the flesh we are not removed from the world, ourselves, or the devil, he says, "I do not nullify the grace of God." That is, even when someone like Peter or Barnabas sins in such a way, God's grace is still gracious. In fact, it becomes that much more gracious, because the more you sin, the more grace is needed to cover it. Therefore, even though Christians continue to sin and to be sinful in their actions, it does not disprove that the gospel is true. Rather, it proves that the only way a person can be saved is through the gospel.

Legalism only shows hypocrisy and sin. Christians who are not legalistic continue to sin. The difference is, the one is covered by the blood of Christ and the other is not. God's grace is not nullified by our sin, it is established and proves all the more that if righteousness were through the law, then Christ died for no purpose (vs. 21). The whole reason he came to this earth and died on the cross was because we are sinful, not him. His death is the only basis upon which God can justify you in righteousness. It establishes that the righteousness of God is justifying you through faith alone.

Therefore, beloved, be raised to the newness of life through the power of the gospel by trusting in the good news to save and to sanctify you. Never forsake this good news, but hold fast to it until your dying day. This is your only hope, but what a great and sure hope it is. Because this day Christ has been raised from the dead and he has given all those trust in him newness of life.

Galatians

The Evil Eyes

or

The Eyes of the Lord?

[1] O foolish Galatians! Who has bewitched you? It was before your eyes that Jesus Christ was publicly portrayed as crucified. [2] Let me ask you only this: Did you receive the Spirit by works of the law or by hearing with faith? [3] Are you so foolish? Having begun by the Spirit, are you now being perfected by the flesh? [4] Did you suffer so many things in vain--if indeed it was in vain? [5] Does he who supplies the Spirit to you and works miracles among you do so by works of the law, or by hearing with faith-- [6] just as Abraham "believed God, and it was counted to him as righteousness"? [7] Know then that it is those of faith who are the sons of Abraham. [8] And the Scripture, foreseeing that God would justify the Gentiles by faith, preached the gospel beforehand to Abraham, saying, "In you shall all the nations be blessed." [9] So then, those who are of faith are blessed along with Abraham, the man of faith.

Galatians 3:1-9

Medusa and the Evil Eye

THE STORY GOES THAT SHE WAS BORN from the titan Phorcys and his wife Ceto, a god and goddess of the sea. Her beauty was stunning, unsurpassed in all the world, and she knew it. She flaunted it daily, singing songs about her hair, her skin, her eyes, and her lips brazenly in the temple of Athena. One day she defiantly lay with Poseidon in the temple only to invoke the wrath of the goddess for this desecration.

Then Athena came to her and turned her into a demonic underworld monster, a hag of the sea with snakes for hair. You know her as Medusa. One direct gaze from her eye, even after beheading at the hands of Perseus, would turn anything living into stone. Was it from her demonic beauty or her hideous transformation? Or was it from the power of her evil eyes alone, eyes set on destroying the one beholding her?

This power of a single glance to destroy a person with an evil eye is shared by her two sisters, the Gorgons, as well as the Basilisk, a chimera hybrid called the king of the serpents, which was made famous in contemporary culture in *Harry Potter and the Chamber of Secrets*. Now, you say, what has this to do with Galatians? The answer is everything, though not in some detached tale of fantasy or fiction and not in some moralistic lesson.

Bewitched

We come now to Galatians 3 where Paul enters into a lengthy defense of the gospel. Thus far in his gospel defense, he has been looking at the very human source of the Galatian problem—the Jewish circumcision party that was tempting the members to give up the good news and return to a works-based justification. Suddenly, Paul reintroduces a supernatural element into the mix and later he will pick the supernatural theme up and run with it for many verses.

It is rarely understood by readers of the letter today that Paul has *anything* supernatural in mind in this letter, save God himself. This is a tragic error and results in a failure to understand vital information being discussed in the next two chapters. Why do we do this? Why do we miss it? Frankly, it is because we have all but removed the supernatural (other than God himself) from our worldview. We have been infected with Liberalism and we don't even know it. We just don't have the categories to know how to begin to think about such things. We don't know what to make of it. It makes us uncomfortable. We can't put it in a test tube and verify anything about it. Thus, modern people don't believe in such silly nonsense. We are much to evolved for that. Many conservative Christians have bought into this secular naturalism and rationalism without even realizing it.

But here it is in Galatians 3:1. "O foolish Galatians! Who has <u>bewitched</u> you?" Paul does not say, "Who has <u>fooled</u> you?" nor "My, how you have been <u>duped</u>" or "you sure are <u>gullible</u>" (by the way, did you know that "gullible" is not in the dictionary?). The word is much more ... otherworldly than this. As one translations puts it, "Who has <u>cast a spell</u> on you?" (NJB, NLT) or another "By what <u>strange powers</u> have you been tricked?" (BBE).

The word "bewitched" is *baskaino*. Does that sound like anything I've mentioned? The Basilisk! They have the same root. It means "to cast the evil eye" upon someone through magic and spells. One dictionary notes that "Superstitious people believed that great harm might result from the "evil eye" or "from being looked upon with envious and malicious stares."[1] Such superstitions continue to this day. It should be obvious, however, that Paul does not have envious or malicious staring in his mind here.[2] He is speaking about a kind of deception that has come listening to the teachings of the circumcision party. This teaching, he is saying with this word and will return to again later quite explicitly (esp. Gal 4:3-10) has a demonic, otherworldly origin.

Now, we have already seen Paul refer to this realm in the letter. In 1:4 he says that Jesus "gave himself for our sins to deliver us from the present *evil* age." This evil age includes not only the evil we commit, but that which the devil and his angels oversee. Elsewhere he calls them "The spiritual forces of evil in the heavenly places" (Eph 6:12, see Acts 26:18; Eph 2:2). Then in 1:8 he brings up that very strange idea that "an angel from heaven" can deliver another gospel. Based upon how he says that angels put the law into effect later on (3:19), I don't think he is speaking hypothetically.

This bewitching evil spell that has been cast over the congregations of ancient Turkey involves this theology: Christians are perfected by the flesh (Gal 3:3). "Flesh" here stands for the entire structure of this fallen age, including our own nature, satanic influence and rule, and world systems. Notice the subtlety here. The temptation to give up justification by

---

[1] Spiros Zodhiates, *The Complete Word Study Dictionary: New Testament*, electronic ed. (Chattanooga, TN: AMG Publishers, 2000).
[2] This is in mind in LXX Deut 28:54, 56, the only times the word is used in the Bible other than here.

faith alone, for these people, was not the typical religious idea to earn God's initial favor through good works. They knew that this was not good news. Paul asks rhetorically in 3:2, "Did you receive the Spirit by works of the law or by hearing with faith?" He knows that they know the answer is "by hearing with faith." Vs. 3 then asks, "Are you so foolish?"

This is the second time he has used the word "foolish" in three verses. You might recall that Jesus tells us not to call people "fools." Anyone who does this will be in danger of hell fire (Matt 5:22). This is not the same word that Jesus used (*raca* and *moros*). Jesus has in mind a word of disdain and hatred. This word (*anoetos*) is used only six times in the NT. Two of those are in Gal 3:1 and 3:3. Listen to another use of the word, "For we ourselves were once <u>foolish</u>, disobedient, led astray, slaves to various passions and pleasures, passing our days in malice and envy, hated by others and hating one another" (Tit 3:3). This is the language of demonic or otherworldly captivity. Paul does not hate the Galatians. He is saying that they have the inability to see that they have been led astray by Satan, away from the true God, his gospel and his righteousness (which includes keeping the law in the proper way, as those set free rather than in prison).

What makes someone foolish like this? Paul answers in other places. "You once walked, following the course of this world, <u>following the prince of the power of the air</u>, the spirit that is now at work in the sons of disobedience—among whom we all once lived in the passions of our flesh, carrying out the desires of the body and the mind" (Eph 2:2-3). That verse is relevant, but the next one is absolutely spot on with regard to our passage. "<u>The god of this world has blinded the minds of unbelievers, to keep them from seeing the light of the gospel</u> of <u>the glory</u> of Christ, who is the image of God" (2 Cor 4:4). How it is that so many Christians have failed to note these verses, not understanding that unbelievers are literally held prisoner in another kingdom by another prince, one who owns them, one who rules over them, one who makes them his slave, is a real testimony to the extraordinary power of the Evil One. He is not a being to be trifled with. He likes nothing more than when you do not believe he is even there.

But perhaps the reason so many Christians are averse to speaking and thinking about these things, is because they see the extraordinary goofiness and bizarre activities of many Christians who talk about him all the time. You've heard it and seen it. They blame the devil for everything. They see Satan under every rock. He is responsible for all the problems in the world, and it is as if humans have no real responsibility because of him. However, if you look at what the devil *does*, if you really understand his nature and those things he teaches through demons to mankind, you will have a very different view of him.

Look again. "Foolish" is a word used at the beginning of vs. 1 and the beginning of vs. 3. There is a parallel going on in the text. The "bewitching" spell is not some strange satanic superstitions, weird holy laughter, blame the devil for everything talk that we so often associate with fringe kinds of Pentecostalism (though I have no doubt that there is a lot of demonic activity going on in those circles). It is the seemingly ordinary idea that Christians are "perfected by the flesh." It is the idea that God is appeased by what we do, by works of the law. This is a teaching of Satan, a bewitching spell, but it seems so non-supernatural in its origin doesn't it?

Listen to some other verses and you will get the idea. "I imply that what pagans sacrifice they offer *to demons* and not to God. I do not want you to be participants with demons" (1 Cor 10:20). Sacrificing in this case is not human sacrifice, but the rather innocuous idea of sacrificing food. It is a religious practice performed around the world even to this day, not to God but to one of the gods. I remember the only time I saw this occurrence. We were on the Big Island of Hawaii, down by the beach approaching the flowing lava of Mauna Loa. Suddenly, these fruit baskets started popping up filled with fresh, delicious fruit. They were offerings to the goddess Pele, to appease her not to break out against their little villages of cities. They used to offer human sacrifices! This is taking place this very day in the United States of America!

Here's another verse. "Let no one disqualify you, insisting on *asceticism* and *worship of angels*, going on in detail about visions, puffed up without reason by his sensuous mind" (Col 2:18). Some angels, fallen angels, want to be worshiped! They teach you to become monastic, to whip the body, or to beat the sin out. This is a teaching of Satan.

Another one, "The Spirit expressly says that in later times, some will depart from the faith by devoting themselves to *deceitful spirits* and *teachings of demons*" (1 Tim 4:1). I think most of us read this verse thinking about

Satanists, those who have a Satanic Bible, whose rooms are filled with doodling of demons, who talk affectionately about Lucifer, people you would find in an X-Files episode. But what are these teachings of demons? They teach you to abstain from meats or marriage or other kinds of things that God created good. Have you ever thought of legalism as a teaching of Satan?

How about this? "I am afraid that as the serpent deceived Eve by his cunning, your thoughts will be led astray <u>from a sincere and pure devotion to Christ</u>" (2 Cor 11:3). Or this, "Certain people have crept in unnoticed who long ago were designated for this condemnation, ungodly people, who pervert the grace of our God into sensuality and deny our only Master and Lord, Jesus Christ" (Jude 4). These people are likened to fallen angels, "wandering stars, for whom the gloom of utter darkness has been reserved forever" (Jude 13; cf. 1 En 80:6). Did you know that all of these verses come from different books of the Bible? This is obviously a widespread problem, because it was the Gentiles' *modus operandi* for thousands of years. It is a very basic problem to this day. It is the problem is simply giving up the good news or not trusting it when it comes to you.

What you see in this is a two-pronged attack, but both attacks are against "the gospel." This is not strange, fringe, kooky-stuff. That is the key. One is a legalistic slavery to keep laws, become an ascetic, a monk, punishing the body. The other is an antinomian impulse that turns the gospel into license to sin. But both are at the heart of the bewitching. Both are *demonic* teachings. Both attack the gospel. They do not just have their origin in man, as much as that would stroke our egos to think so. These are the ways that Satan gets people not to hear the gospel. They distort it and pervert it so that it is no longer what it is. And if the gospel is the power of God to conquer Satan, his only hope is to make people think it is a different message. That is what he has become an expert at doing.

<u>Hearing is Seeing</u>

Now, with this as the background behind the bewitching, we are ready to see this power of God, this one little word that shall fell the devil. To defeat this satanic spell, Paul does not opt for some alternate magic. He simply tells them about the gospel again. That is what he does. He wanted to know nothing among them but Christ and him crucified. This is what he uses to defeat the deceptive charms of Satan, the evil eye of the underworldlings.

The first thing to notice, back in 3:1-2 is how the gospel is put in terms of seeing and hearing. This is fascinating and almost deserves a sermon unto itself. Let me put this into a little perspective. Today, the sermon has fallen on rough times. In the Protestant churches, sermons used to be expositions of Holy Scripture based upon a story of Christ the Savior. Today, they are often little more than seminars to help people make their lives more happy. If you happen to find a verse to help support the idea, all the better, but it isn't really even necessary.

The problem here is that the message has changed, though most are completely desensitized to even see it. Think about it. If you have gone to church your entire life hearing self-help techniques, you will naturally think that this is the good news. But it isn't. So, whole generations of people in churches have been duped and they don't even know it. How can you tell that the gospel is no longer present? You can tell by the forms that begin to creep into the church. This is because no other message is the power of God to save a person. So, if people are not being changed by the messages, and if people think the messages they are hearing are actually good news, then the problem must be in the delivery, in the mode of communication, in the methods.

It is because the message has been lost that the church, especially in America, began tinkering with the methods. For example, in our times the Emergent crowd experiments regularly with people painting pictures during the instruction time. Slides and movie clips are also very popular even in non-emerging churches. We now have entire pastoral job descriptions such as "pastor of worship arts" or "pastor of visual arts" or "pastor of performance arts." I could go on and on with examples. The basic idea though is that the job today is to oversee and coordinate a multi-sensory worship "experience." What people especially clamor for is images. Unlike Israel who did see God and didn't want to, they do want to *see* God. Half of their songs are taken up with this very idea. The eye is our medium of choice to mediate between God and man.

But notice what the text says. "It was before your <u>eyes</u> that Jesus Christ was <u>publicly portrayed</u> as crucified." Is Paul referring to some sacred dance performed by his paid entourage of travelling showmen, whom he would put on display as he spoke? You do realize that the Greeks LOVED drama and they would have loved for Paul to bring his gospel in such entertaining ways. Everywhere you go in the ancient Greek world you find theatres. Don't tell me Americans are unique in this. Is Paul talking about having professional painters pull out their easels, or professional sculptors begin fashioning a scene of the crucifixion out of clay while he spoke? Is this how the church "saw" Christ crucified? Frankly, the idea would have been blasphemous to a Jew who believed in the second commandment! Jews never, ever had images of persons in their synagogues.[3]

No. He tells us what he means in the next verse. "Did you receive the Spirit by works of the law or by hearing with faith?" (Gal 3:2). Did you catch it? Christ was put before the *eyes* of the people as they *heard* the sermon of Christ crucified. That is God's logic, not man's. It is utter foolishness to us, but Paul says they are foolish for not believing it any longer. There is absolutely no person on earth who would invent such a foolish idea. But that's what it says, because its origin is not with man but with God. Christ was set before their eyes as the images came into their minds through their *ears*. This is extremely profound and it is a lesson the church desperately needs to rediscover in our day of gross (though plausibly denied) idolatry in the churches.

Let's look at this a little more closely in our text. The words "publicly portrayed" is actually just one word in Greek. It is the word *prographō*. It literally means "to write before." Herodotus and others used it as "drawing" or "painting."[4] While it sometimes refers only to working with a pen, it is clear that in this case it does not. Paul is talking about preaching, not writing. He refers to the eyes as seeing Christ *crucified,* not reading about it in a book. The word often has the sense of a placard, or what we might call a billboard. It is the idea of painting a picture with

---

[3] Those (such as animals and angels) were reserved only for the temple which had the inspired command of God behind it.

[4] William Arndt, Frederick W. Danker and Walter Bauer, *A Greek-English Lexicon of the New Testament and Other Early Christian Literature*, 3rd ed. (Chicago: University of Chicago Press, 2000), 867.

words, an art form that was prevalent in America prior to the invention of the television (one thinks of old radio programs like *War of the World* which caused mass hysteria merely through words), but has now been virtually lost to the prehistoric world of the 1940s.

Do not miss what Paul is saying. He says that through the preaching of Christ, Christ was visually portrayed as crucified, as if they had driven past Calvary and the three crosses with the dead men hanging on them on the way to church that very morning. Paul does not need visual arts in church, because preaching *is* a visual art. Some are obviously better word-smiths than others. But any preacher who proclaims the death and resurrection of Christ week after week is giving the people God's movie in a form that does not tempt people to have to reach up to heaven to see it with their eyes. Yes, they can visualize it with the mind. But the eye is not doing the work here. The ear is.

This is important, because the eye is not a vessel fit to receive the good news of Christ. How can I say that? It is because the gospel is an announcement that must be heard. It is not a spectacle to be seen. You can't video him for the news. You can only report about what others have seen. When they tell you what they saw, you must process the objective logic of this announcement, not speculate about it in a subjective art form like a painting.[5]

There is another problem with the eye, especially as it surrounds multimedia, television, magazines, jumbo-trons, and the big-screen. These forms of communication create celebrity. It is what they do. Celebrity is not compatible with the gospel. The method of preaching is perfect for delivering the gospel, because it is a personal form of communication,[6] and personal communication, face-to-face communication does not

---

[5] People today argue that the motion picture is capable of sequencing objective arguments as you might hear in a lecture or sermon (which are not the same thing). To a point this is true, but motion pictures as well as any kind of drama have the unintended consequence of creating celebrity in the mind of the one watching. By the sheer fact that the person is on the screen or is performing in front of us, we tend to look at the actor as much as the one being acted out. We also iconize and celebritize them, which takes away from the story itself.

[6] There is something lost even when we hear a sermon on the radio. The celebrity status hits us even there. I can relate personally to this. I used to attend John Piper's church before he became so popular. To me, Piper was just a pastor who wrote a great book (back in those days it was only "Desiring God"). But now you hear him on the radio. You see him on the internet. If you have never been to his church, he becomes larger than life. Perhaps he succumbed just a little to this temptation himself, for in 2010 he took several months off from

lend itself naturally to the cult of celebrity, which is the sorry mess we find ourselves in today. Neither does it lend itself to shallow discipleship. It allows for personal intercommunication, interaction, catechesis, and all the rest. If you have questions about the sermon, you can actually ask someone about it. If you have joyfully received the news, you can tell someone about it.

Before turning to an explanation of the gospel, the Apostle asks a final question. "Did you suffer so many things in vain—if indeed it was in vain? Does he who supplies the Spirit to you and works miracles among you do so by works of the law, or by hearing with faith?" (Gal 3:4-5). Now, hearing is contrasted with working. To work is the opposite of to hear. The question is curious. Most translations render it as "suffering" following Chrysostom's commentary on this 1700 years ago. The problem is, we know of nothing concrete of the Galatians suffering anything. In fact, Gal 6:12 indicates that the circumcision party is preaching their false gospel so that they would not have to be persecuted, as Paul was for preaching the cross. The only person who seems to have been persecuted here is Paul.

Thus, it may be better to opt for the translation, "Did you experience so much for nothing?" (NRS). What did they experience? In vs. 5 it includes the Spirit and miracles! In this case, the idea might be similar to Simon the Sorcerer, who "experienced" the Spirit and then tried to use the power of God to make money. The Spirit showed his great power in those early days by healing people through the disciples, casting out demons and other things. Salvation was especially remarkable against the backdrop of the Gentile perversions and religious darkness that they lived in. Was all of that in vain? It will have been in vain if they turn away from the truth and embrace the very things they left behind. That is the warning. How can this spell be counteracted then? By repeating the gospel.

Faith Always Comes By Hearing and Believing the Gospel

---

preaching and writing because he had become "too prideful." I only read about this on *The Christian Post*, Mon July 11, 2011 when another pastor, C. J. Mahaney had to step down for a season for the same reasons. http://www.christianpost.com/news/cj-mahaney-takes-leave-over-charges-of-pride-hypocrisy-52127/

The gospel came to them through hearing, and hearing was combined with faith. But, you see, this is the way it has always been. And in case anyone is tempted to use the OT to prove otherwise (which is what the circumcision party was trying to do), Paul will now show them how very wrong they are. Let this be a warning to anyone who thinks that the OT provided another way of salvation that was attainable for fallen men. Yes, the legal system was always in place, and if you could have obeyed it perfectly you would have been saved. But no one did and no one could, except for Christ who took such obedience all the way to his own sacrificial death on the cross. He did this so that anyone who believes in him by faith alone might be saved.

Notice vs. 6 is about Abraham. The verse begins with "just as." This connects it to the previous verse. They heard with faith "just as Abraham" "believed God, and it was counted to him as righteousness." This remarkable verse becomes the OT proof-text for faith in Romans 4:3, Galatians 3:6, and remarkably in James 2:23.

There are, of course, many throughout church history that have sought to pit James against Paul. We saw previously in Galatians 2 that this cannot be done. Both had the same gospel. Yet, what do you do with James 2:24 that says, "You see that a person is justified by works and not by faith alone?" People will say that James preaches a salvation by works. Yet, they fail to take notice that the verse right before this was James' quotation of Genesis 15:6, the same verse Paul quotes in Gal 3:6. Calvin is worth listening to here,

They who seek to prove from this passage of James that the works of Abraham were imputed for righteousness, must necessarily confess that Scripture is perverted by him; for ... the imputation of righteousness which Moses mentions, preceded more than *thirty years* the work by which they would have Abraham to have been justified [sacrificing Isaac]. Since faith was imputed to Abraham *fifteen years* before the birth of Isaac, this could not surely have been done through the work of sacrificing him...

Why then does James say that it was fulfilled? Even because he intended to show what sort of faith that was which justified Abraham; that is, that it was not idle or evanescent, but rendered him obedient to God, as also we find in Heb. 11:8. The conclusion, which is immediately added, as it depends on this, has no other meaning. Man is not justified by faith alone, that is, by a bare and empty knowledge of God; he is justified by works, that is, his righteousness is known and proved by its fruits.[7]

Do you see how silly it is to think that James would say that Abraham was justified 15 years before Isaac was born simply by believing God and then in the very next breath (literally) say that Abraham was justified by works? It is absurd.

But what is faith? What does it do? Faith is one of the most popular words in the American vocabulary, along with prayer. But to Americans, "faith" has no object. It is just "faith," faith in faith. That is not what faith is in the Bible. In the Bible, faith rests upon the promises of God's goodwill towards us. It trusts and hopes that the promises are sure. It delights and takes comfort that they are trustworthy. In Abraham's instance, faith comes to pass prior to any promises coming to fulfillment. In our case, faith comes after receiving the message that those promises have come to fulfilment in Christ. But in both instances, faith precedes any works that come later. And all works that come later spring up from faith! We are not perfected by the flesh.

The promises of God in the gospel are conditioned only on trusting them by faith. But faith is not a work. As I said, it is resting not working. It is trusting not doing. It is hearing and believing. But, you ask, "Didn't Abraham 'do' something in order to get the promises to come true? Didn't he obey God first and then receive the promises? Didn't he set out for the Promised Land first?" I'm glad you asked. Calvin cites Hebrews 11:8, an important verse in the context of Galatians 3. "By *faith* Abraham obeyed when he was called to go out to a place that he was to receive as an inheritance. And he went out, not knowing where he was going."

---

[7] John Calvin and John Owen, *Commentaries on the Catholic Epistles* (Bellingham, WA: Logos Research Systems, Inc., 2010), 315-16.

Hebrews has in mind the very first recorded words that we have of God to Abram found in Genesis 12:1.[8] The whole segment reads, "Now the LORD said to Abram, 'Go from your country and your kindred and your father's house to the land that I will show you. And I will make of you a great nation, and I will bless you and make your name great, so that you will be a blessing. I will bless those who bless you, and him who dishonors you I will curse, and *in you all the families of the earth shall be blessed*" (Gen 12:1-3). Did you hear the gospel in this passage? It is there. Paul tells you so.

The reason why Abram "went" is because he believed ... *the gospel.* Abraham believed the gospel, isn't that remarkable? You mean, the gospel didn't start with Paul or even Jesus? No! Galatians 3:8, "The Scripture, foreseeing that God would justify the Gentiles by faith, <u>preached the gospel beforehand</u> to Abraham, saying, '*In you shall all the nations be blessed.*'" This is an interesting choice of words for Paul. He says that "the Scripture" "preached" to Abraham. We are right back to preaching. What he means is that the gospel preached to Abram was preserved for us by Moses in Genesis, in the Scripture, so that we could see that he had to believe the same things that we believe.

But of course, "Scripture" didn't "preach" to Abram. Abram didn't have anything written down to read. God preached to him personally. God came to Abram, and as Stephen says, "The God of Glory *appeared*" to him (Acts 7:2). Who is the "God of Glory?" The only seeable person in the Trinity is Jesus Christ, unless the Spirit comes in a sign like fire, a cloud, or a bird. James calls him "The Lord of glory" (James 2:1). John says, "We have seen his glory, glory as of the only begotten Son from the Father" (John 1:14). We already saw this glory today, when Paul reminded us that Satan prevents unbelievers from seeing the light of the gospel of the glory *of Christ.* The Psalmist asks, "Who *is* this King of glory?" and answers "The LORD strong and mighty, the LORD mighty in battle" (Ps 24:8 KJV). And who is that? "The LORD is a *man* of war" (Ex 15:3). But he is not a man like you or me. When Joshua saw this man,

---

[8] These were actually *not* the first words Abram received from God, as Stephen in Acts 7:2-3 (see Philo, *On Abraham* 71; Josephus *Ant.* 1.154; F. F. Bruce, Acts, *NICNT*, 134) makes clear. Stephen says that God came to him through the Angel of the LORD while he was still in Babylon, prior to coming to Haran (Gen 11:31).

he fell on his face and worshiped for he spoke and said, "I am captain of the armies of the LORD" (Josh 5:14). He is a holy angel, but an uncreated angel. For he is the LORD himself.

What did this man do in the OT? He delivered his people out of the kingdom of Egypt, out of slavery and captivity. He fought for Israel as they entered the Promised Land, seizing the strongholds of those ancient evil peoples that dwelt therein, obliterating their gods before the mighty men of Joshua and David.

In the NT, he came and delivered demonically possessed men and women from the stronghold of the devil. He bound the strongman. He obeyed God's law where Adam failed. He died to set men free. He rose from the grave to deliver them from evil. He proclaimed this message of the end of tyranny to the spirits he had cast out (1 Pet 3:19). All of this is supernatural and against the supernatural! And today, through the proclamation of his victory, this man of war wrests slaves from the captivity of Satan and thrusts them into his own glorious kingdom with one little word, his word, for he is the Word. Yes, Paul has this very thing in mind!

These people become his brothers and sisters, his church and his bride. They become, as Paul says here, "sons of Abraham" (Gal 3:7). These sons are not born of natural descent or of human will, but born of God (John 1:13). They are born by faith, through hearing and believing the message that they have been set free and delivered from the tyrannical dictatorship of Satan. No more are they under that heavy yoke and burden of slavery to the law. No more must they obey their master the devil. Their works will not avail them here, for the God of Glory has done all the work in their place so that they might be set free and brought home to dwell in a heavenly kingdom.

This is their "blessing." "Those who are of faith are <u>blessed</u> along with Abraham, the man of faith" (Gal 3:9), for the gospel was that in you shall all the nations be blessed. They are blessed through Christ who preached the gospel to Abram. This very morning he preaches to you too, though through a more moderate means of a sinful preacher who needs him, too.

Have the eyes of God penetrated your soul, not to turn you to stone, but to set you free? Or are you still under the bewitching spell of the evil one? The eyes of the Lord *are* over the righteous (1 Pet 3:12). The eyes of the LORD run to and fro throughout the whole earth, to show himself strong in the behalf of *them* whose heart *is* perfect toward him (2 Chr 16:9). Those who are perfect are those who have been justified by faith alone.

Do you clamor for excitements and entertainment? Or are you satisfied in hearing the Word who died for you? Are you still working the works of evil, attempting to appease God through what you do? Or have you received the spirit by hearing with faith? Are you now trying to be perfected by the flesh? Have you succumbed to the temptation to be religious without the power of God? Are you drowning up to your neck in a Christian life that feels burdened rather than free? Have you approached the holy city and temple of God in vain? Hear and see with a heart of faith. Believe God, and it will be counted to you as righteousness.

The Law is Not of Faith

[6] Just as Abraham "believed God, and it was counted to him as righteousness" (Gen 15:6)?[1] [7] Know then that it is those of faith who are the sons of Abraham. [8] And the Scripture, foreseeing that God would justify the Gentiles by faith, preached the gospel beforehand to Abraham, saying, "In you shall all the nations be blessed" (Gen 12:3).[2] [9] So then, those who are of faith are blessed along with Abraham, the man of faith. [10] For all who rely on works of the law are under a curse; for it is written, "Cursed be everyone who does not abide by all things written in the Book of the Law, and do them" (Deut 27:26).[3] [11] Now it is evident that no one is justified before God by the law, for "The righteous shall live by faith" (Hab 2:4).[4] [12] But the law is not of faith, rather "The one who does them shall live by them" (Lev 18:5).[5] [13] Christ redeemed us from the curse of the law by becoming a curse for us--for it is written, "Cursed is everyone who is hanged on a tree" (Deut 21:23)[6]-- [14] so that in Christ Jesus the blessing of Abraham might come to the Gentiles, so that we might receive the promised Spirit through faith..

Galatians 3:6-14

[1] And Abram believed God, and it was counted to him for righteousness. (Gen 15:6 LXA). And he believed in the Lord, and had faith in the (Memra) Word of the Lord, and He reckoned it to him for righteousness, because he parleyed not before him with words. (Gen 15:6 PJE)

[2] And I will bless those that bless thee, and curse those that curse thee, and in thee shall all the tribes of the earth be blessed. (Gen 12:3 LXA)

[3] Cursed is every man that continues not in all the words of this law to do them: and all the people shall say, So be it. (Deut 27:26 LXA)

[4] But the just shall live by my faith. (Hab 2:4 LXA)

[5] So ye shall keep all my ordinances, and all my judgments, and do them; which if a man do, he shall live in them: I *am* the Lord your God. (Lev 18:5 LXA)

[6] His body shall not remain all night upon the tree, but ye shall by all means bury it in that day; for every one that is hanged on a tree is cursed of God. (Deut 21:23 LXA)

What is Faith?

IN HIS BOOK *LOSING FAITH IN FAITH*, Dan Barker writes, "Faith is a cop-out, a defeat--an admission that the truths of religion are unknowable through evidence and reason."[7] Mr. Barker attended Azusa Pacific University in the early 1970s, served as a pastor in a Quaker congregation, an Assembly of God church, and an independent Charismatic church. He became a prominent song writer, accompanied Pat Boone and Jimmy Roberts (of the Lawrence Welk Show), and wrote two of the most popular VBS drama skits of the 1970s ("Mary Had a Little Lamb" and "His Fleece Was White As Snow"). Then, one day, Mr. Barker realized that he was an atheist.

A few paragraphs after writing this statement about faith he speaks about the gospel, thus revealing his cards on why he lost his "faith." "It was a mystery to me how anyone could be blind to the truths of the Gospel. After all, *don't we all want love, peace, happiness, hope and meaning in life?* Christ was the only answer, I believed, and I figured all non-Christians must be driven by other things, like greed, lust, evil pride, hate and jealousy." In this statement, Mr. Barker reveals the same thing exposed in the title of his book. He has absolutely no idea what the gospel is nor does he have the first clue about biblical faith. His gospel is hopelessly confused with law and his faith must therefore, ultimately, be placed in the wrong thing.

In our culture having faith is not really the problem. Atheists like Barker are in a very small minority. George Michael on the other hand sang western culture's anthem, "You *gotta* have faith." Faith is a moral imperative. But faith in what? Emily Osment recently put it this way, "Live without a doubt | All that we need is something | Alright turn it out | Live without a doubt | All that we need is something ... Gotta believe in something."[8]

---

[7] http://www.ffrf.org/legacy/books/lfif/?t=lostfaith. Barker obviously believes that faith, according to the Bible, is blind. Maybe he was reading Nietzsche who said, "Faith is not wanting to know what is true."
[8] Emily Osment, "Believe in Something," on the album *Fight or Flight*.

Barker says that "something" was "faith in faith." In George Michael's case, it is faith in me, and I tend to think this is exactly what Barker's faith was in as well, since if you confuse the gospel with the law you must put your faith in yourself to keep that law. Michael's idea is very popular. Another Michael, Michelangelo, said (taken out of context, I don't know), "Faith in oneself is the best and safest course." Paula Abdul said, "Keep the faith, don't lose your perseverance and always trust your gut instinct." Edwin Louis Cole takes this to a whole new level saying, "Have faith in God; God has faith in you." Incredibly, you are the object of God's faith!

Another popular idea is that faith is possibility thinking. Robert Schuller and Norman Vincent Peale popularized this in the church. But fifty years earlier it was William Salter, individualist anarchist, son of a Congregational minister, and friend of William James the famous Pragmatist who put it this way, "The essence of faith is to believe that [a] possibility exists." Faith, then, is "to dream the impossible dream," as Andy Williams sang it. It is personified in movies like *Field of Dreams* or *Tucker*. This pragmatic faith in human potential and reason may have made America a great world power, but it isn't what the Bible has in mind by faith.

Faith and Galatians 3

We enter today into the very heart of the Bible's teaching on salvation and on faith. How is a person saved? The short answer is that they are saved by faith and by nothing but faith. "Those of faith are the sons" (Gal 3:7). "Those of faith are blessed" (Gal 3:9). "The righteous shall live by faith" (Gal 3:11). "We receive the promised Spirit through faith" (Gal 3:14). But again, what does this mean? Today you can't just assume that people know. At the highest moment in church history you shouldn't have assumed that people know, because we are easily tempted to turn from that which we know to that which seems right in our own eyes. Recent informal surveys conducted by the White Horse Inn at Christian conventions show that most Christians give the same answers as the world (see above).[9] To counteract this creeping paganism in the church, we need to look at the text to see what it says.

The passage (Gal 3:6-14) lays out the role of faith in salvation (Gal 3:6), the content of faith (3:8), the opposite of faith (10), the result of faith (11), the reason why we need faith (12), and the grounds upon which God can justify a person by faith (13). These six ideas are tightly argued, by the Apostle, from the Old Testament. Before I get to them, I wish to ask you a question. If you had the opportunity to share your faith with someone (and by that I mean not your personal testimony, but where you get your ideas about salvation), where would you turn? Most people would turn to Paul. Perhaps many would even turn to the very passage we are looking at today. That's perfectly acceptable. In light of how so many people think that Paul created a religion out of nothing, or blatantly contradicted James or Jesus and other ideas that we have looked at (especially in Galatians 2), I want to give you something to think about. There is something you will notice about our passage today that is remarkable.

We are looking at nine verses in Galatians 3 (vv. 6-14). Six of these verses contain quotations from the Old Testament. In other words, Paul did not rely on visions or dreams or encounters with Christ that no one could confirm to demonstrate his gospel, even though he could have. He relied upon God's word. He went to the Law and the Prophets. NT religion is OT religion. It is true Judaism. It is not some Johnny-come-lately. Would you have any confidence whatsoever in proving salvation by faith alone *from the Old Testament*? It is there, you know, and it is a major theme of the Bible.

Hebrews 11 does this very thing. It tells us that Abel offered sacrifices by faith, that Enoch preached by faith, that Noah built an ark by faith, that Abraham sojourned by faith, that Isaac gave Jacob the blessing by faith, that Jacob blessed the Egyptian sons of Joseph by faith, that Joseph gave instructions about his burial by faith, that Moses left Egypt by faith, that Rahab welcomed the spies by faith, that the Judges judged Israel by faith, that David conquered and ruled by faith, that the prophets

---

[9] White Horse Inn, "What Is Faith?", 9-2-2007; "A Survey of Christian Faith and Practice", 11-8-2009.

prophesied and died by faith. These people did all of these "works" *by faith*.

But works is not faith. I was reading an article this week which was presented at an Evangelical Theological Society meeting. In the article the writer explained his view of faith. He said, "Most church doctrinal positions on faith would agree that genuine faith includes knowledge, assent, and trust. I prefer to treat "trust" as "obedience," as Paul expresses it: "the obedience of faith" (Rom 1:5; 16:26). Genuine faith must include obedience (James 2:14-26)."[10] Incredible! He couldn't get it more wrong. No longer is it "trust and obey for there's no other way." It's now, "Trust is obey." Faith and works are identical. One does not flow from the other. One is the other.

The point of Hebrews, however, is that faith preceded the things that the OT saints of God did. There was a time when all they had was faith. Then works sprang from faith as fruit springs from a living vine. In the spring there is no fruit. In the summer there is. It is the Spirit's job to produce fruit. But fruit is not faith. Paul says the same thing in our passage today when he says, "The law is not of faith" (Gal 3:12). If you think that it is, you have turned religion upside down. You have twisted it into a slithering serpent. You have tortured again the one who was tortured on the tree. There may be no more serious matter in all the world than this, because it drives a stake through the heart of salvation. Let's look at how Paul came to this.

OT Quotation #1 – The Role of Faith

Someone could, I suppose, argue that Hebrews is making all of this faith stuff up. I mean, where does it "say" that these people did any of these things "by faith?" The first quotation in our passage today provides the answer. Paul uses Abraham (called "the man of faith;" vs. 9) as his paradigm. He does this because Abraham comes before the existence of Israel, and thus to the circumcision party, it would have been terribly important for them to understand this.

---

[10] Walter D. Zorn, "The Faithfulness of Jesus the Messiah," delivered at the Midwestern Region of ETS, March 17-17, 2007, p. 9.
http://www.lincolnchristian.edu/Documents/PE.Zorn.FaithfulnessofJesus.pdf

He says, "Abraham believed God, and it was counted to him as righteousness." This comes from Genesis 15:6. This verse gives you the role of faith in salvation. The role of faith is to be the means by which God justifies a person. It was through faith, that is believing God, that he was justified. The word is "counted as righteous." This is the OT equivalent of "to justify." Listen to how this word (*chashab*) is translated in the OT: counted, calculated, considered, esteemed, imputed, reckoned, and regarded.

Notice very importantly, Abraham was not "made righteous," but rather "reckoned" or "regarded" as righteous. He was considered and declared righteous, though he was not righteous in himself. In Paul, this idea is set against the backdrop of a legal system and you could make that argument in Abraham's case as well, since the statement comes in the middle of the cutting of a covenant, a legal arrangement between a vassal and suzerain lord. God pronounced Abraham righteous through this verdict, and thereby entered into this agreement with him. Beloved, this is the very heart of the Christian religion. Christians are declared righteous though they are not righteous. Obviously, if you are not righteous, your works could not make you righteous, nor could they get God to declare you righteous. Thus, Abraham was reckoned righteous *through faith*. "Believe" and "faith" are synonyms, as we will see very shortly.

OT Quotation #2 – The Content of Faith

We see that Abraham believed God, but what about God did he believe? This is an important question. He believed that God would make him into a great nation. In other words, he believed God's promise. Not a curse, not a factoid of trivia, not doctrine, not a rebuke, not an idea, but a promise. He trusted something that God promised him. Not something he promised himself, not a dream of his own, but a promise from God. Paul next quotes Genesis 12:3, "In you shall all the nations be blessed." This is God's promise to Abraham and it is the content of his faith.

Let's think about this promise in relationship to Abraham's belief. This promise was given when Abraham was 75 years old. It was a promise not to one group of people (i.e., Jews), but to the nations (i.e., those who would later be considered Gentiles). The promise is that the nations will be blessed. As such, it is good news to them. Paul calls it "the gospel." He says that Abraham had the gospel preached to him. Amazing!

This promise implies that Abraham would have a son. In fact, this idea is later codified in a second covenant, the one in which the first citation (Gen 15:6) finds its context. What Abraham believed is that as numerous as the stars are in the heavens, so numerous would be his descendants (Gen 15:5). Yet, Abraham believed this promise *while he had no son*, and would not have Isaac, the son of promise, for at least 15 years![11] The point is that Abraham's faith preceded the birth of his son. Those who argue that Abraham was justified by what he did (i.e., sacrificing Isaac) always fail to take this into account. It just doesn't fit their system.

The context of these citations shows that those who have the faith of Abraham, that is, faith in the promises of God, are the "sons of Abraham" (Gal 3:7). This is a remarkable idea and it is tied to the birth of Isaac—Abraham's "son." In Paul's theology, Isaac represents those who have faith, because Isaac was a miraculous baby and faith is a miraculous gift from God. Remember, Abraham did have a son before Isaac. Here is another small fact about Abraham's life that those wishing to combine faith and works need to keep in mind.

After Abraham heard this promise and believed it, he was still in the dark as to how God would accomplish it. His wife, Sarah, had borne him no children. She was now old and thus *could* not bear any children! Her womb was dead. It was a physical impossibility. Thus, Sarah figured that God must have another arrangement. Since he didn't specify who the mother of this great child would be, she hatched a plan to get her maidservant Hagar pregnant. Out of this, Ishmael was born. Now, you could easily think of Ishmael as the child of Abraham's "works," because he was born (from a human perspective) entirely because of Abraham's deep bewilderment about God's promises coming to pass. His faith was genuine, but it was also confused. Does that give you any hope? Even Abraham's righteous acts were filthy rags. Abraham's "works," his attempt to make the promise of God come to pass his own way, ended up causing more

---

[11] Abraham was 75 when the first covenant (Gen 12:1ff) was given to him. The covenant in Genesis 15:1ff could have occurred anytime between this and the birth of Ishmael when he was 86 years old. Isaac was born when Abraham was 100 years old.

troubles than anyone could imagine, troubles that continue to this very day in the Middle East. This is a perfect example of what happens to anyone who thinks that their works will bring about the promises, or in a more general way, will bring about sanctification. Thus, Ishmael was born in the natural way, through human scheming and carrying out of a plan.

But Isaac is something altogether different. God came to Sarah after the birth of Ishmael and promised to give *her* a son. She could only laugh (was it out of happiness or incredulity?). Since this was not possible in any world, Isaac's birth would come to symbolize children of faith rather than works. This is why he says those of faith are sons of Abraham. Later in this letter, Sarah and Hagar will be used by Paul in this very way. In Romans, the two sons are used in the same way. Faith inherits the promises just as Isaac inherited the blessing.

These people of faith are no longer limited to Jews (or Gentile proselytes who become Jews through circumcision). These people of faith include the Galatian Christians, Gentiles who were not born into the promises, but only receive them through faith in Christ. These people include many here in this sanctuary today, Gentiles of many nationalities who have gathered to worship the same God who has given us all the same faith. Paul says, this entire arrangement that we now see fulfilled before our very eyes, was promised to Abraham! Those included are those who believe. Do you believe these things for yourself? Do not trust your parents hope. They must be your own hope.

As you can see then, Abraham was justified by faith, by believing the promise of God. This is how he was saved. His faith had an object. It had very real content. He couldn't see it, but not because it was irrational, not because it was a leap in the dark, not because it was blind, but because the time hadn't come yet for Isaac to be born. The content was about the future. It was about believing that God would make Sarah conceive even though it was impossible (see Rom 4:19-21). It was about trusting that God would deliver on his promise.

Today, of course, we look backward to the death and resurrection of Jesus. What we believe is even less preposterous (from a worldly point of view) because it actually happened ... in time ... in space ... in history ... in front of witnesses ... in an objective world ... exactly as God had promised and prophesied that it would. We do look forward, too, just as

Abraham did. But the content of our faith is the same: we look to Christ. Our perspective is different. Now we trust through faith that God will raise our bodies from the grave just as he did with Jesus. Anything that is future we trust because of what has now happened in the past.

It is tragic that people turn the gospel into "love, peace, happiness, hope, and meaning in life." That isn't the gospel. Those things may result from the gospel, but they are not the gospel. This completely obscures why Jesus came and what he did. He didn't die to give me meaning. He died to give me life, to save me from the wrath of God, from eternal punishment for my sin, to make it possible for God to acquit me of my crimes against him, to allow me to be raised from the dead in glory. The reason Jesus is the only answer is not because he gives meaning in life. Plenty of non-Christians have meaning in life. They are happy. They feel at peace. They experience love. But none of them have those things *in their relationship with God*. Their relationship with their Creator is only one of enmity, striving, belligerence, and hopelessness. And when they die, their fleeting feelings will leave them naked as they stand before the Judge and give an accounting of the deeds they have done in the body. And what are those deeds like?

OT Quotation #3 – The Content of Faith

Now we come to the third citation. "All who rely on works of the law are under a curse; for it is written, '*Cursed be everyone who does not abide by all things written in the Book of the Law, and do them.*'" This comes from Deuteronomy 27:26. This is the last word in a series of curses, which Israel was to call upon itself in a remarkable covenant ceremony. In Israel there is a valley that sits between two mountains.

Mt. Gerizim and Mt. Ebal

These mountains are Mt. Gerizim and Mt. Ebal. In the valley below there was a city called Shechem. Shechem is the place Abraham first went after God promised him the land (Gen 12:6). It is upon these two mountains that the entire nation of Israel was to ascend and yell back and forth to one another the curses of the law ending with this final curse. "Cursed are we if we do not do everything written in this law."

What kinds of things were they yelling? They were yelling moral laws. They were yelling laws that you can find in the law codes of the Hittites, the Babylonians, and the Egyptians. "Cursed is anyone who dishonors his father or mother." Hittites believed that was wrong. "Cursed is anyone who moves his neighbor's boundary mark." Babylonians believed that was wrong. "Cursed is anyone who misleads a blind person on the road." Egyptians believed that was wrong. In other words, the specific laws here were not applicable only for Israel. They were not invented by God here with Moses. They applied to all of God's children on planet earth. Thus, Paul's citation is not only applicable to Jews, but also to Gentiles. The law that Israel was given was but a reproduction in stone of the law he had written upon everyone's heart.

Why did God have Israel do this? It was to place them under the curse of the law to show them the absolute need for faith. It was to set them up for failure, because this was the only way that the promised Seed would eventually come. The point of this citation here is similar. It is to show that the opposite of faith is relying on works of the law. Works is the opposite of faith. If you rely upon works to save you, to justify you, to sanctify you, to glorify you ... you are under a curse. You heard that correctly. Has it sunk into your heart?

Why? Because to live by the law requires perfection—"ALL things" written in the Law. People will say that this isn't fair and that God would never require such a harsh thing. In this they fail to understand why God gave the law. God gave the law to show us our sin, our inability to equal God's own moral perfection. God gave us the law to show us what he is like and what we are like. And this is what the law does perfectly. Like a mirror it shows us what we are, only on the inside. Therefore, says the Apostle after quoting this verse, "It is evident that no one is justified before God by the law" (Gal 3:11). You can't get any clearer than this.

OT Quotation #4 – The Result of Faith

It is at this point that Paul cites his fourth quotation, and a remarkable one it is. He moves out of the Torah to the Prophets. He quotes Habakkuk 2:4, one of his favorite verses (cf., Rom 1:17). "The righteous shall live by faith." Before I explain this verse, it may be helpful here to see that Paul was not the only Jew who understood the important of this verse. It is recorded in the Babylonian Talmud that one Rabbi Simelai (3rd cent. A.D.) said, "Six hundred and thirteen commandments were given to Moses ... David came and reduced them to eleven (Ps 15)[12] ... Isaiah came and reduced them to six (Isa 33:15-16)[13] ... Micah came and reduced them to three (Micah 6:8)[14] ... Isaiah again came and reduced them to two (Isa 56:1)[15] ... Amos came and reduced them to a single one (Amos 5:4)[16] ... Habakkuk further came and based them on one, as it is said, 'But the righteous shall live by his faith' (Habakkuk 2:4)."[17] Prior to the NT being

---

[12] (i) He who walks uprightly and (ii) works righteousness and (iii) speaks truth in his heart and (iv) has no slander on his tongue and (v) does no evil to his fellow and (vi) does not take up a reproach against his neighbor, (vii) in whose eyes a vile person is despised but (viii) honors those who fear the Lord. (ix) He swears to his own hurt and changes not. (x) He does not lend on interest. (xi) He does not take a bribe against the innocent.

[13] (i) He who walks righteously and (ii) speaks uprightly, (iii) he who despises the gain of oppressions, (iv) shakes his hand from holding bribes, (v) stops his ear from hearing of blood (vi) and shuts his eyes from looking upon evil, he shall dwell on high.

[14] (i) To do justly and (ii) to love mercy, and (iii) to walk humbly before God.

[15] (i) Keep justice and (ii) do righteousness.

[16] (i) Seek me and live.

[17] b. Mak. 23b in Jacob Neusner, vol. 17a, The Babylonian Talmud: A Translation and Commentary (Peabody, MA: Hendrickson Publishers, 2011), 122.

written the Dead Sea Scrolls record this little gem, "This concerns all those who observe the law in the house of Judah, whom God will deliver from the House of Judgment because of their suffering and because of their faith in the Teacher of Righteousness" (1 QpHab 7.1 4-8.2)[18] (whom some have speculated is a Messiah figure 100 years before Jesus was born).[19] An ancient Jewish commentary on Exodus says this, "With all their professed faith, in Egypt, there was no real faith in the Israelites until they saw God's wonders on the Red Sea. Prompted by that faith they were enabled to compose and sing the exquisite song of praise. Through their faith the Israelites on the Red Sea became possessed of the Holy Spirit" (*Exod Rabbah* 23). The point is, even the Jews recognized that faith was necessary. Like Rome, they may have perverted the idea, combining law and faith. They may have placed their hopes in the wrong Messiah. But the idea was firmly rooted in their theology, because it came from their Scriptures! Those who say that Israel was saved only by works in the OT don't know what they're talking about.

Habakkuk's point is not that we are saved by a combination of faith and works, but by faith alone. Habakkuk has notable similarities to Genesis 15:6. First, both verses speak of righteousness (*tsedaqah*). Abraham's faith was credited to him as <u>righteousness</u>. The just (<u>righteous</u>) shall live by faith. Second, <u>faith</u> and <u>belief</u> are the same root word (אמן). Thus, commentators have suggested that Habakkuk may have Genesis 15:6 in mind when he writes.[20] But Habakkuk is hardly alone. The Psalm says, "I have taken the way of faith" (Ps 119:30 BBE). The Proverb says, "The one who speaks in steadfast trust (faith) will make known righteousness" (Prov 12:22). Another says, "A man of faith will abound with blessings" (Prov 28:20).

The promise here is what faith brings. The result of faith is life. That's what I said earlier. The righteous shall LIVE by faith. Faith raises us from the dead. Faith ensures that we will be raised from the dead.

---

[18] Cited in Richard N. Longenecker, vol. 41, *Word Biblical Commentary: Galatians*, Word Biblical Commentary (Dallas: Word, Incorporated, 2002), 119.

[19] For example, Michael O. Wise, *The First Messiah: Investigating the Savior Before Christ* (HarperCollins, 1999).

[20] Cf., O. Palmer Robertson, *The Books of Nahum, Habakkuk and Zephaniah*, The New International Commentary on the Old Testament (Grand Rapids, MI: Wm. B. Eerdmans Publishing Co., 1990), Hab 2:4.

Faith gives us new life. It gives us life in Christ. But this can only come through faith. It can never come through law.

OT Quotation #5 – The Reason for Faith

There is a good deal of debate about the translation of Habakkuk, because "faith" can also mean "faithfulness." The translation would thus be, "The just shall live by *faithfulness*." But faithfulness is a *work*. In English, faithful means "strict or thorough in the performance of duty." That we would be justified by a duty is an idea impossible to Paul who says in the very next breath, "The law is not of faith."[21] Imagine if that really meant, "But the law is not of faithfulness?" That would mean the law is not of duty. But the next thing Paul says is that "the one who *does* them shall *live* by them." In other words, the law IS of duty and that's the whole point of the law.[22]

This verse gives us the promise held out in the law: life. If you obey the law perfectly, you will have life. That's what the law itself teaches. In this way, the law and faith both hold out life. The problem is, the law can't give you life. The best it could do (as it did in Jesus' case) is to show that you are already *live*. But nobody keeps the law perfectly (except Christ), showing that they are in fact not alive, but dead. That's why, though life is held out in both the law and in faith, faith is so critical. The reason for faith is that the law can't give you life. But God through faith in Christ and the gospel promises life eternal and abundant.

---

[21] Some who maintain that "faithful" is the proper translation look to the LXX which reads, "The just shall live by <u>my</u> faith" (The Hebrew literally says "his" faith and "my" is a retranslation), in other words God's faith. But that makes no sense. Does God have faith? Thus they read it "the just shall live by God's *faithfulness*." This is true, of course. We do live by God's faithfulness. But this isn't what the passage says. Fortunately, we have Hebrews 10:38 which cites the LXX this way, "But <u>My</u> righteous one shall live by faith." This citation is from a variant in the LXX which transposes the "my" to a position before the righteous one rather than after it (Ronald Y. K. Fung, *The Epistle to the Galatians*, The New International Commentary on the New Testament [Grand Rapids, MI: Wm. B. Eerdmans Publishing Co., 1988], 143; O. Palmer Robertson, *The Books of Nahum, Habakkuk and Zephaniah*, The New International Commentary on the Old Testament [Grand Rapids, MI: Wm. B. Eerdmans Publishing Co., 1990], 182). This is the inspired, biblical rendering of the LXX and it also shows conclusively that faith is in view rather than faithfulness, since this is what the entire chapter of Hebrews 11 will prove.

[22] Contrary to John Piper and others who *badly* misunderstand the law at this point. See John Piper, "Did God Command Adam to Earn His Life," in *A Godward Life : Savoring the Supremacy of God in All Life* (Sisters, Or.: Multnomah Publishers, 1997), 171-73.

OT Quotation #6 – The Grounds of Faith

It is a serious error to turn faith into obedience, faith into faithfulness. When you do this you obliterate the law, the gospel, faith, faithfulness, religion, salvation, justification, and everything else. You attack Christ himself (however unintentionally), who is the only reason why we can be justified by faith in the first place. You attack his work and you attack, especially, his death. This is the function of the sixth and final OT quotation. One serious problem remains. How can God justly justify anyone by faith? If a person is wicked, God can't just let bygones be bygones. Someone has to pay!

In Galatians 3:13 Paul begins to get at the grounds of our justification, the grounds of faith, the reason why God can credit faith as righteousness. "Christ redeemed us from the curse of the law by becoming a curse for us." Friend, this is what you must believe. No other faith will save you, justify you, sanctify you, or glorify you. Only faith in the atoning work of Christ on your behalf will do this. Do you believe it?

This quotation is from Deuteronomy 21:23, "Cursed is everyone who is hanged on a tree." I've told you about how Israel would curse themselves. I've told you that anyone who wants to keep the law remains under a curse rather than a blessing. In Christ, the curse is turned into a blessing. For Christ became a curse, not through disobedience (as happened to Israel), but through vicarious obedience, through obedience in your place. He took the penalty of the curse, he suffered death and separation from God on your behalf while he was on that tree.

I've sometimes heard that if Jesus were alive today and God's plan was for him to die, that he would die in an electric chair. The cross was merely a convention of the time. That is not true. The cross was an extraordinary display of God's sovereignty over the Roman Empire. Crucifixion has not been practiced throughout most of world history. Only that narrow timeframe when Jesus was here was it really very common at all. God did this so that Jesus could die *on a tree* in order to fulfill the law.

I do not know all of the reasons why dying on a tree would bring a curse. I do know that the law has been tied up to a tree ever since the Garden of Eden. There is some kind of a relationship in the inscrutable mind of God that I have not figured out yet. The point is, that even in his death on a cross Jesus fulfilled the law. And he did it that the blessing might come to the Gentiles so that we might receive the promised Spirit through faith (Gal 3:14).

Christ's meritorious work all the way up to the cross is our only grounds of justification. Through faith, God imputes to us the meritorious works of Christ who loved his Father so much that he did everything he was required to do, everything that we are required to do as children of Adam. God imputed our sin to Jesus and he became a curse. God imputes his righteousness to us as a blessing. God does this for Jews and Gentiles alike, by faith.

Yes, faith is absolutely mandatory. Faith saves. But this faith must have an object. It must be full of content. That content is the gospel, the good news, the promise of God through Christ. The wise sages, pop singers, daytime talk show hosts, and Christian-turned-atheist friends have it all wrong. You have heard the gospel and so you are left without excuse. Only faith saves, because the law has no power to justify you. Faith gives life and the reason you need faith is because you cannot live by the law, because it demands perfection and you haven't done that. God can credit faith to you because Christ has died in your place, becoming a curse so that the blessing might be exchanged for that curse for those who trust in Christ's merits to save them. Do you believe this? It is the teaching of the whole of Scripture. It is the way God has always done things. Come to Christ and taste that he is good.

The Promise

[15] To give a human example, brothers: even with a man-made covenant, no one annuls it or adds to it once it has been ratified.[16] Now the promises were made to Abraham and to his offspring. It does not say, "And to offsprings," referring to many, but referring to one, "And to your offspring," who is Christ. [17] This is what I mean: the law, which came 430 years afterward, does not annul a covenant previously ratified by God, so as to make the promise void. [18] For if the inheritance comes by the law, it no longer comes by promise; but God gave it to Abraham by a promise.

Galatians 3:15-18

"I made *a promise, Mr Frodo*. A promise. 'Don't you leave him Samwise Gamgee.' And I don't mean to. I don't mean to."

Samwise Gamgee

Promises Made and Promises Broken

AMERICAN HISTORY IS A TALE OF PROMISES. Sadly, these are, as my favorite singer puts it, "promises made and promises broken, *measures of our demise.*"[1] These promises began in 1620, when my great (x12) grandfather, William Brewster drafted the first constitution in the Americas. Known as the *Mayflower Compact*, he and 40 other occupants of that maiden voyage attached their signatures to the following,

---

[1] Dan Fogelberg, "Promises Made."

Having undertaken, for the Glory of God, and advancements of the Christian faith and honor of our King and Country, a voyage to plant the first colony in the Northern parts of Virginia, [we whose names are written] do by these presents, solemnly and mutually, in the presence of God, and one another, covenant and combine ourselves together into a civil body politic; for our better ordering, and preservation and furtherance of the ends aforesaid; and by virtue hereof to enact, constitute, and frame, such just and equal laws, ordinances, acts, constitutions, and offices, from time to time, as shall be thought most meet and convenient for the general good of the colony; unto which we promise all due submission and obedience.

And thus, the greatest political wonder the world will ever see (at least until Christ returns in his kingdom) was born of a compact, a covenant ... of works.

Nearly 3,000 years earlier, the spiritual predecessors of my grandfather and his humble entourage were on the cusp of settling down in the land they had newly conquered. This new generation of Israelites, the children of those who lost their faith in the desert, came before their leader Joshua and said, "We will serve the LORD, for he is our God" (Josh 24:18). But Joshua, full of wisdom and understanding, knew that their words were full of ignorant arrogance. "You are not able to serve the LORD, for he is a holy God. He is a jealous God; he will not forgive your transgressions or your sins. If you forsake the LORD and serve foreign gods, then he will turn and do you harm and consume you, after having done you good" (vv. 19-20). But the people said, "No, but we will serve the LORD" (vs. 21). Then Joshua responded, "You are witnesses against yourselves that you have chosen the LORD to serve him." And they said, "We are witnesses" (vs. 22). Thus, Israel ratified a covenant of works brought by God to Moses on the top of Mt. Sinai.

Joshua understood that the covenant of works was good in many ways, for God had told Moses, "What great nation is there, that has statutes and rules so righteous as all this law that I set before you today?"

(Deut 4:8). Americans, too, realized that on the civil level, a covenant of works—laws and pledges—will actually set a people free. Laws will provide direction, stability, and righteousness while pledges to it will provide self-imposed safety and freedom.

But Joshua also knew that a covenant of works, especially between men and God, is only dangerously entered into. For when the pledges are broken and discarded, curses and disasters pour out upon a land like a tidal wave, devastating, destroying, and drowning everything in its path. Curses and disasters are becoming the norm in nearly every walk of life in western civilization. Evil is unbound. Immorality is promoted. Paganism is courted. Righteousness is censored. These *are* our curses which we embrace as lovers. Ironically, people live in greater fear today than ever before, they demand protection, and blame everything but the right thing because they openly embrace the very things that brought the disasters upon them in the first place.

This all started with broken promises. Our land is now filled with them. Politicians make promises and rarely keep them.[2] It wasn't always this intense, but massive promise breaking is certainly the norm today.[3] They keep making them and we are fools to believe them. As the song goes, "You made me promises, promises, knowing I'd believe | Promises, promises you knew you'd never keep."

The context of this song is relationships. Marriages are breaking up at record pace because those who promised unconditionally (not even in a covenant of works) "till death do us part" no longer care about their words. Go to a court of law today and you will still find that people who take the stand have to promise to tell the truth. Yet, our legal system is so filled with breaking constitutional boundaries that if these broken covenants were holes in Swiss cheese, there would be only holes and no cheese! Our culture is riddled with broken promises and broken covenants and we

---

[2] In 1916 Woodrow Wilson promised to keep the United States out of World War I. The next year, we went to war. In 1928 Herbert Hoover promised, "A chicken in every pot and two cars in every garage." The next year the market crashed as we entered the Great Depression. In 1988 George H. W. Bush famously promised, "Read my lips, no new taxes." In 1990 after making no headway with his opponents in Congress, he raised taxes.

[3] To date www.politifact.com lists over 40 broken promises of the current President. One could certainly track the same general trend for the last several Presidents.

wonder why every major moral category of crime and immorality are exponentially higher than they were only two generations ago. Our poets are so sceptical now that they sing, "Vows are spoken to be broken. Words are meaningless and forgettable."[4]

It is human nature to make promises, and it is human nature to break them.

Biblical Promises: Covenants

Now imagine if God were like us. It's not difficult to imagine if you confuse the biblical ways of salvation. You heard that correctly. I said "ways" (plural) of salvation. The Bible sets forward two ways of salvation. These two words of Scripture come to us through the promises of God. Yet, they are very different kinds of promises.

They are similar in that both hold out the promise of eternal life. They are also similar in that as promises, both come to us in the form of a covenant, which is why I mentioned covenants earlier. This is a covenant of works. Covenants of works are conditional agreements between two parties. They were very common in the ancient world, especially between great kings (called suzerains) and lesser kings (called vassals). Party A swears fealty and promises to perform X, and party B promises to reward with Y. But if party A breaks the promise, party B promises to punish with Z. In the Mayflower Compact, the covenant was between the members of the colony for the sake of the king and in the presence of God. In Israel's case, however, the covenant was between the people of Israel and God himself. They entered into this covenant legally because God had first entered into it with them through the law which he gave to them through Moses.

There is another kind of covenant in the Bible that also holds out the promise of eternal life. This is a covenant of grace, or as some have called it, of grant. This is an unconditional covenant where the promise and fulfillment is made unilaterally and not on the merit of the other party. God does attach a condition to this covenant, but it is not a condition in the same sense as meritorious obedience. The condition of this covenant is

---

[4] Depeche Mode, "Enjoy the Silence."

faith. Without faith, the promises are not inherited. We saw this last week in Galatians 3:6, "Abraham believed God, and it was counted to him as righteousness."

Faith is different from works. Work achieves the promise. Faith receives the promise. Works seize the promise. Faith believes that God has/will perform the promise. Work is the merit of man. Faith is the gift of God. Work says, "I will get this promise for myself." Faith says, "God has given this promise to me." The covenant of works says, "Thou shalt." The covenant of grace says, "I [God] will."

Galatian Problem: Confusion of Covenants

Here is where the problem potentially comes, and in the case of the Galatian churches, where it was centered at the moment the letter was written. God gave both kinds of covenant in the OT and some within Israel were under both kinds of covenant simultaneously. Not all Israelites were, but some were. But you ask, how could a person be under both covenants at the same time? The answer is the key to salvation. Get this wrong and you are hopelessly lost in your sin. Understand and believe and you are well into eternal life.

The churches of Galatia had been seduced by a demonic lie (Gal 3:1) which told them that they had to achieve some part of their eternal reward by merit. Some apparently believed that they were justified by works. Others believed that they were sanctified by their works. Paul sets them straight that the whole of salvation—from start to finish—is always and only by faith in Christ. What these false teachers couldn't (or wouldn't) understand is that the covenant which they were forcing the Christians back under was a covenant of works, eternal life by merit.

They had some reason to do this, because God in fact placed the nation of Israel under a covenant of works. But they greatly misunderstood the function and purpose of this OT covenant. This covenant (and this is where so many in the past and today go astray) was placed upon a nation for the legal possession of the physical promises that God had conditionally granted to them. Notice for example in the law God does not say the land is yours unconditionally for all time (per Dispensationalism and Zionism) but rather, "The land shall not be sold in perpetuity, for the land is mine. You are strangers and sojourners with me" (Lev 25:23).

In other words this covenant was corporate and thus binding upon all citizens. It was tangible and physical. It granted them a certain plot of land between Syria and Egypt, between the Mediterranean Sea and the Euphrates River on the condition of obedience. It was permanent *only as long as* the people obeyed the law and God didn't justly punish them for their sins. After breaking it, God reserved the right to preserve them in grace if he so chose or to kick them out of his land for as long as he desired. It was all up to the freedom of God.

The crucial thing here is that none of this is about *salvation*. Now, it is true that if someone wanted to merit their eternal life through obedience to this law, God would not stand in their way. But he never gave them the law *in order for them* to merit eternal life, because God knew that this was a stubborn and stiff-necked people long before he gave them the law on Mt. Sinai. Rather, as far as salvation is concerned, God set Israel under this covenant of works only to show them that they all fell infinitely short of fulfilling its terms and thus meriting the life that it held out for them. Its promises were corporate and temporal, not individual and eternal.

It is not a covenant of works that God gives to individuals to save them ... but a covenant of grace. Salvation comes by a unilateral promise of God to meet the demands of the covenant of works himself. Salvation comes by a unilateral promise of God to meet these demands as one of us, a servant and a seed of Adam the man. Salvation comes by a unilateral promise of God to meet those demands vicariously on behalf of those who cannot meet it for themselves, and if they will simply believe that God did this for them, they will be saved and sanctified.

Notice, this covenant of grace is not conditional in the sense of meriting anything yourself. Nor is this covenant of grace physical, at least not yet. There is no promise here of inheriting that plot of land across the pond simply because you trust in Christ by faith. No, this is a spiritual covenant granting eternal life in a kingdom which as of now is spiritual and cannot be seen with any human eye. Its Priest does not reside in a temple made by human hands. Its King does not rule in a castle made of stone.

The reason there has been so much confusion about salvation and about Israel over the centuries is because people ignorantly fuse these covenants together. They see that individuals did inherit real land (as in the case of Caleb; Josh 14:13). What they do not see is that someone like Caleb was under two covenants simultaneously: one covenant as an individual for salvation, the other as a member of a nation corporately. In Caleb's case it actually says that he "wholly followed the LORD" and that's why he was given Hebron. In other words, it was because of his obedience to Moses and Joshua that he was blessed (as opposed to the spies who were not).

Is God a Promise Breaker?

All of this is to say that it if you confuse these two covenants—which Reformed theology has understood to be the warp and woof of biblical theology, that you could very easily think of God as a being who breaks his promises. This is what our passage today is here to explain. Galatians 3:15-18 is a kind of parenthetical aside of the Apostle to show you that God is not a promise breaker and the reason why is because of his only begotten Son.

Where in Galatians might we get the idea that God has broken his promises? The idea comes from this confusion of the two very different covenants. Paul has been contrasting law and faith, works vs. trust in the preceding paragraphs. This contrast between law and faith is for him as great as the divide is between east and west. Yet, Paul has not argued that the law is evil, nor that it is invalid. He has argued that obedience to the law can never save a person because the law demands perfection (Gal 3:10, 12). What he has said is not that God will go back on his promise so that if you obey the law perfectly he will not give you eternal life. Rather, he has said that no one will keep the law perfectly (nor can he), and therefore eternal life will never be obtained by law-keeping. You cannot be justified by law-keeping, sanctified by it, or glorified by it.

But those who confuse the two words, the two covenants, law and faith, works and trust, fusing them into one, will quite naturally think that if God held out life to Israel by the law (which he did) that he did so because they are capable of attaining it. As John Wesley, Charles Finney, and Pelagius all thought, God would never command you do to something that was impossible. Add to this the idea that the Pharisees (and the Galatianizers) had that they actually were keeping the law! Now along comes this guy Paul who says that law-keeping Jews do not inherit the promises through obedience but through faith. Why isn't God holding up his end of the bargain? Paul's God must be a promise breaker, a capricious deity who changes the way of salvation from works to faith with no way to know which one you need today. This is all the more acute when you consider that Paul is now adding a new group of people into the salvation mix: Gentiles whom he says do not have to come under the laws of Israel to be saved. This is why he has spent the last few verses proving that none of this was ever true in the OT.

The Promise Fulfilled: The Seed

Let us go to our passage. "To give a human example, brothers: even with a man-made covenant, no one annuls it or adds to it once it has been ratified. Now the promises were made to Abraham and to his offspring (seed). It does not say, 'And to offsprings,' referring to many, but referring to one, 'And to your offspring,' who is Christ." This sounds completely out of place, until you realize that the Galatians were confusing the two covenants. This is what led them to confuse faith and works, to beginning with faith but finishing with law. Paul introduces this idea of a covenant here in order to clarify which came first in the history of Israel.

The covenant which came first was not the covenant of works codified on Mt. Sinai, but the covenant of grace given to Abraham. This means that for all Israelites, because Abraham is their father, faith precedes the law, indeed that faith creates obedience to the law. They were always saved by faith just like Abraham, and the law served some other purpose in their life than to save them. What Paul does here next is incredible.

The first thing he notices is that God gave a promise to more than just Abraham. This promise is repeated many times in the OT, but it begins in Genesis 12:7, "The LORD appeared to Abram and said, 'To your offspring I will give this land.'" Some translations read "descendants" (plural; NAS, NET, CEB, etc.). This is not entirely unjustified. They are taking the word as a corporate singular noun. All the Jews did this, which is partly what got them into trouble, as they confused the covenant of grace with works even here, as if God was granting salvation to them as individuals because he gave Abraham faith. Paul himself uses the term "offspring" to refer to many people later in this same chapter (Gal 3:29).

So it is not wrong to interpret the word as a plural *per se*. Obviously, there is some sense in which even unbelievers did inherit the Promised Land.

But this inheritance always pointed to a future and greater inheritance of which the Promised Land was itself only a shadow. This is the inheritance that Abraham himself awaited, a city with foundations whose architect and builder is God (Heb 11:10). More than this, the promises pointed forward to the one who would lead us into that greater Promised Land, and this person is our savior, the Lord Jesus. This is Paul's concern here. He wants to prove that in the ultimate sense, the promise of the inheritance of the land was not given to Isaac (though he was a man of faith) nor certainly to the whole nation of Israel (who were many of them faithless rebels), but to Christ and therefore God is wholly trustworthy.

His argument rests upon the noun as a singular rather than plural. In a remarkable feat of memory Jerome stated, "Passing my eyes and memory over all the Scriptures (which he personally translated into Latin), I nowhere find offsprings written in the plural but everywhere the singular."[5] I read this after having done my own computer search for this very thing. Jerome is, in fact, correct. The only place in OT or NT where you read of the plural "seeds" (*zeray, spermasin*) is here. What Paul is saying is that God came to Abraham (in fact, it was Christ himself who "appeared" to Abraham in the verse in question) and promised *to Christ* that He would inherit the land. This is incredible and proves the preexistence of Jesus Christ.

In my opinion, this promise is to be taken spiritually and physically. Christ becomes the king who reigns in a kingdom. While it is true that today his kingdom is spiritual, it is also true that it is literal. Christ reigns in heaven. One day, however, he will reign on earth as well. His throne will be set up in the new earth and he will rule the whole world. In fact, in Romans 4:13 Paul reminds us that the promise is not only of that little plot of land called Israel, but of the whole world. Gen 22:17 says, "Your offspring shall possess the gate of his enemies."[6] And this is, in fact, the way Jewish writings understood the promise as well.[7]

---

[5] Jerome, *Epistle to the Galatians* 2.3.15.
[6] Also verses like Ps 72:8, "May he have dominion from sea to sea, and from the River to the ends of the earth!"
[7] Sir 44:21, "Give them an inheritance from sea to sea and from the Euphrates to the ends of the earth"; Jub 22:14, "May you inherit all of the earth"; 32:19, "I shall give to your seed all of the land under heaven and they

Spiritually, those in the kingdom Christ inherits are also what (or rather who) he inherits. As the Psalm says, "Ask of me, and I will make the nations your heritage" (Ps 2:8). Or "You shall inherit the nations" (Ps 82:8). These things were spoken to Christ whom Paul identifies here as Abraham's "seed."

The word "seed" is the Greek *sperma*, and you can obviously see what English word comes from it. It refers to the physical descendant of a male. Christ-as-Seed theology has a long and rich history in the Bible which does not begin with Abraham. The first record of it is the promise given to Eve through the curse of the serpent, "I will put enmity between you and the woman, and between your seed and her <u>seed</u>; He shall bruise you on the head, and you shall bruise him on the heel" (Gen 3:15). Eve trusted this promise implicitly, and when she gave birth to her first son she apparently believed that he was the chosen seed (thus she named him Cain "the man"). Cain, of course, wasn't The Man. He murdered his faithful brother Abel. But God replaced Abel by giving Eve another son whom she named Seth saying, "God has appointed me another <u>seed</u> in place of Abel" (Gen 4:25).

Genesis traces the line of Seth down through Noah whom God shows grace and saves through the flood. After the Flood recedes and Noah leaves the Ark God says to him, "Behold, I establish my covenant with you and <u>your seed</u> after you" (Gen 9:9). As with Seth, this promise is narrowed through a specific child of Noah. His name is Shem. God promises, "Blessed be the LORD, the God of Shem; and let Canaan be his servant" (Gen 9:26). But then it adds this Gentile promise before there even were Gentiles, "May God enlarge Japheth, and let him dwell in the tents of Shem, and let Canaan be his servant" (vs. 27). All of this promising to Christ is done hundreds and thousands of years before Abraham is ever even born. Abraham is only one in a long line both before and after him to whom God gives this same promise of a coming Seed.

To Isaac God said, "In your <u>seed</u> all the nations of the earth shall be blessed" (Gen 26:4). To Jacob, "I will give the land to your <u>seed</u> after you"

---

will rule in all nations as they have desired. And after this all of the earth will be gathered together and they will inherit it forever;" 2 Apoc Bar 14:13, "The world which you have promised to them" (also 51:3).

(Gen 35:12). You see, though they receive the promises by faith, it is always a seed after them that will receive the final promise. Num 24:7 says, "Water shall flow from his buckets, and his seed shall be by many waters, and his king shall be higher than Agag, and his kingdom shall be exalted." The LXX reads, "A man shall issue from his seed and he shall have dominion over many nations; and he shall be higher than the kingdom of Gog and his kingdom shall be exalted." The Targum is even more interesting, "From them their King shall arise, and their Redeemer be of them and among them, and the seed of the children of the Jacob shall rule over many nations."

Though not in the line of Christ, Aaron and his sons also receive this promise. It is the promise of a coming priest in the order of Melchizedek (Ps 110:4). "This shall be a statue forever for him and for his <u>seed</u> after him" (Ex 28:34). "He and his <u>seed</u> after him shall have a perpetual covenant of priesthood" (Num 25:13). In each of these passages, the promised Seed is attached to a covenant.

With Eve, it is the covenant of grace ratified by the skins of the animal. With Noah it is the covenant of grace sealed by the rainbow. With Abraham it is the covenant of grace with the sign and seal of circumcision. With Aaron it is the covenant of grace signified by baptism in his ordination. The promise is also given to David in a covenant that God makes with him. "When your days are fulfilled and you lie down with your fathers, I will raise up your <u>seed</u> after you, who shall come from your body, and I will establish his kingdom" (2 Sam 7:12). "Great salvation he brings to his king, and shows steadfast love to his messiah, to David and his <u>seed</u> forever" (2 Sam 22:51). "I will establish your <u>seed</u> forever, and build your throne for all generations" (Ps 89:4). "The LORD swore to David a sure oath from which he will not turn back: 'One of <u>the sons of your body</u> I will set on your throne" (Ps 132:11).

Do you see that this is THE storyline of the Bible? From Genesis to Malachi, the seed is always just beyond the people's reach, unless they apprehend him by faith. But now, in the NT, the Seed has come down to earth, incarnate of the Virgin Mary. His lineage is traced out by both Matthew and Luke to prove that he is the Seed. The miracles he performs confirm that he is the seed. The prophecies he makes about himself testify that he is the seed. His resurrection from the grave proves beyond a shadow of a doubt that he is the seed. This is our God and Savior, the LORD Jesus Christ, who is, will be, and always has been God Almighty.

The Law after the Seed

I have shown you that the promise to Christ came before Abraham, during Abraham, and long after Abraham went to be with the Lord. I have done it through the Seed. Paul does it in another way. He focuses on the Law given at Sinai and Abraham to who the promise came 430 years earlier. People often get confused about this number 430 years (Gal 3:17) for a variety of reasons.

First, there are other numbers that seem to skeptics to create a contradiction. Some say Israel was in Egypt for 400 years (Gen 15:13; Acts 7:6), others for approx. 450 years (Acts 13:19-20). Thus, to a skeptic, the Bible is hopelessly contradictory.[8] Second, Rabbis and Christians cannot come to a consensus on when to begin the countdown. The most popular counts try to harmonize the "four generations" in Egypt (Gen 15:16) with the four generations listed between Moses and Levi in Ex 6:16-20 with the fact that Paul says that the law came 430 years after (where they assume that this refers to the giving of the initial promise to Abraham).[9] This gives you approximately 210 years in the land of Egypt. The biggest problem, of course, is that the text says they are *in Egypt* for 400-430 years, not merely 210 years.[10] Others have proposed that Paul's statement allows for a much later beginning of the count. Notice, Paul does not say that the count begins at Abraham, but merely "430 years afterward." After what? One could easily deduce that it was after the promises of the Seed came to an end in the days of the Patriarchs. As we have seen, the same promise was given to Abraham, *then to Isaac*, and *then to Jacob*. Thus, some have argued that the count begins with the last promise given to

---

[8] See for example Farrell Till, "The 210-Year 'Solution', http://theskepticalreview.com/JFTHowLongInEgypt2.html

[9] For example, John Gill discusses these views in his comments on each of these passages. He accepts the basic arguments here of the Rabbis.

[10] Some manuscripts like the LXX and Samaritan Pentateuch thus add, "Egypt *and the land of Canaan*" in order to reconcile the problem, but these additions seem to be more a matter of harmonization than actually translating the original text.

Jacob and to his seed. They take it very literally that Israel was in Egypt for at least 400 years after that.[11]

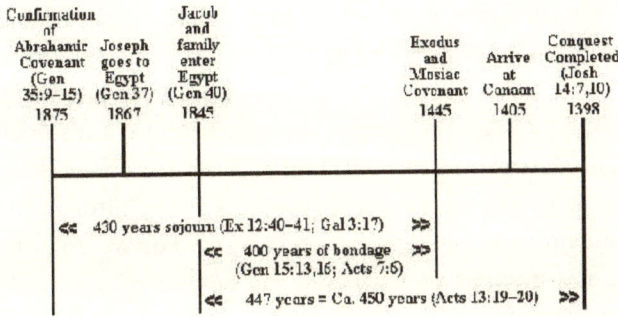

Confirmation of Abrahamic Covenant (Gen 35:9–15) 1875	Joseph goes to Egypt (Gen 37) 1867	Jacob and family enter Egypt (Gen 40) 1845		Exodus and Mosiac Covenant 1445	Arrive at Canaan 1405	Conquest Completed (Josh 14:7,10) 1398

<< 430 years sojourn (Ex 12:40–41; Gal 3:17) >>

<< 400 years of bondage >>
(Gen 15:13,16; Acts 7:6)

<< 447 years = Ca. 450 years (Acts 13:19–20) >>

The suggestions that we should begin the count sometime in the life of Jacob seem much more plausible to me (especially given the fact that 1 Chron 7:20-27 record as few as 10 and as many as 12 generations between Jacob and Joshua as opposed to the 4 or 5 assumed by a reading without gaps). But whatever view you take, please do not miss the point.

The point is that the national covenant of works given to a corporate people concerning land, temples, and other blessings and curses came centuries after the promises were received by faith. Thus, receiving the promises *never came* by law but only through faith, for the promise was continually given and regiven to the Patriarchs concerning the things Pharisees and false teachers believed were theirs by obedience to the law. Galatians 3:18 explains, "For if the inheritance comes by law, it no longer comes by promise; but God gave it to Abraham by a promise." Notice, it does not

---

[11] See H. W. Hoehner, "The Duration of the Egyptian Bondage," *Bibliotheca Sacra Volume* 126:504 (1969), 306-16 (http://faculty.gordon.edu/hu/bi/Ted_Hildebrandt/OTeSources/02-Exodus/Text/Articles/Hoehner-DurationEgypt-BSac.htm) who sees the count beginning in Genesis 35:9-15 and J. R. Riggs, "The Length of Israel's Sojourn in Egypt," *Grace Theological Journal* 12 (1971), 18-35 (http://faculty.gordon.edu/hu/ted_hildebrandt/otesources/02-exodus/Text/Articles/Riggs-EgyptSojourn-GTJ.htm) who sees it beginning in Genesis 46. Each article cites several proponents of his particular Jacobian starting point view. The chart (above) comes from Hoehner's article.

say, "For if the inheritance no longer comes by law," as if it once did. He says that it never comes by the law, because it has always come by promise.

To receive the promises of God you must have a promise. Is that obvious enough? The law is not that promise, but rather a curse which threatens to punish when it is not carried out perfectly. The law came after the promise to point the way to Christ. As Ambrosiaster said 1,500 years ago, "Once the promise had been established, the law was given subsequently, not so that it could undermine the promise but so that it might point to what was to be fulfilled and when it would come."[12] But Christ was the very promise promised to Abraham. He is, ultimately, what the land, the remnant, and the blessing is all about. For we do not even look forward to a new body or a new heaven and earth as much as to being with our Savior in friendship.

This is eternal life, "That they know the only true God, and Jesus Christ whom he has sent" (John 17:3). To know God's Fatherly pleasure rather than the displeasure of a judge, to know Christ's brotherly kindness rather than the sharp side of his unsheathed sword, to know the Spirit's internal calling, his inner groaning, his leading you to Christ rather than to see his fiery hand of judgment ... this is to have eternal life. Many people, including self-professed Christians, see none of these things good or bad. They ignore the displeasure of God because until they see him face to face God's common grace makes it possible to ignore it. On the other hand, they are not consumed with the kindness and peace that they have received from the King who have pardoned their sins. Often, the two go hand in hand. To not acknowledge your terminal condition is to not be able to see the delight in the remedy which has been provided. But many have known it only to forget it as they take the grace of God for granted and begin turning to worldly pleasures rather than continuing in their first love. Thus their hearts grow cold and dead over time.

The solution is to consider this day what Christ has done in his sacrifice on that tree those many years ago now. My job is to help you do that. I have no greater task as a preacher than this. Consider the cost to himself, how he was punished unjustly, how he was forsaken by his friends, treated

---

[12] Ambrosiaster, *Epistle to the Galatians* 3.17.

by his enemies, and deprived of the eternal fellowship he had with his Father from all the ages. Consider and internalize that he did this for your sake. Not for someone else, but for you. He did this so that you might know him, know life, and know peace. He did it all by a promise that he has kept, a promise that was made in the mysterious council of the Godhead in eternity past, a promise that was given to saints through whom Messiah was to be born, a promise that was made by God to God for the sake of those whom he has chosen. Consider and believe. Believe the promises and the trustworthiness of God. "For all the promises of God find their Yes in him. That is why it is through him that we utter our Amen to God for his glory. And it is God who establishes us with you in Christ, and has anointed us, and who has also put his seal on us and given us his Spirit in our hearts as a guarantee" (2 Cor 1:20-22). Oh, what glorious promises belong to those who believe in the Son of God.

Galatians

The Origin and Purpose

of the Law

¹⁹ Why then the law? It was added because of transgressions, until the offspring should come to whom the promise had been made, and it was put in place through angels by an intermediary. ²⁰ Now an intermediary implies more than one, but God is one.

Galatians 3:19-20

Origin of the Law According to the Nations

ONE HUNDRED YEARS BEFORE CHRIST DIED, a Greek historian named Diodorus Siculus wrote about the origin of the law as it had been passed down to him. He said, "They say that the first person who convinced the people to use written laws was Menes, a man both lofty in spirit and the most altruistic in his way of life of any lawgiver in memory." Menes is a prehistoric figure said to have been the first human ruler in Egypt after the gods. It is a curious and little known fact that Menes is carved into the south wall frieze on the United States Supreme Court building, along with 18 other world lawgivers including: Hammurabi (1700s BC), Moses (1400s BC), Solomon (900s BC), Lycurgus of Sparta (800 BC), Solon the grandfather of Plato (638-558 BC), Draco (600s BC), Confucius (551 – 478 BC), Caesar Augustus (63 BC - 14 AD), Muhammad (570 – 632 AD), Charlemagne (742 – 814 AD), Louis IX King of France (c. 1214 – 1270 AD), John Marshall (1755 – 1835 AD), and Napoleon (1769 – 1821 AD).[1]

---

[1] http://www.supremecourt.gov/about/north&southwalls.pdf

In accordance with Diodorus' Chronology, Menes is the first in the procession.

South Wall Frieze, U.S. Supreme Court

After telling us about Menes, Diodorus then goes on to give the following account of the origin of the law which he himself finds impossible to believe. "He claimed that <u>Hermes</u> had given these laws to him as a source of many substantial benefits; and this, they say, is just what Minos of Crete did among the Greeks and Lycurgos among the Lacedaemonians, the former asserting that he had received his revelations from <u>Zeus</u>, the latter from <u>Apollo</u>."[2] Of course, Zeus and Apollo are gods who ruled in the Greek version of the Divine Council on Olympus, the mountain headquarters of the gods and the place where they dispensed justice. Hermes is also a god. We've mentioned him in our study of Galatians already, and we will see him later in Galatians 4.

Diodorus finishes with these astounding but very accurate words to those unfamiliar with the history, "*And it is a tradition as well among <u>most other nations</u> that this kind of inspiration was the case,* being the cause of many blessings to those who believed. Among the Arians, they record, Zathraustes (Zoroaster) pretended that the Good Spirit (<u>Ormuzd</u>) gave him the laws; and among those called the Getae, who aspire to immortality, Zalmoxis in like manner credited the familiar <u>Hestia</u> with the revelation; and among the Judaeans, Moyses attributed them to the God called by the name of <u>Iao</u>" (*Jehovah* or *Yehu*).[3]

---

[2] Diodorus Siculus, *Bibliotheca Historica* (*Library of History*) I, in Edwin Murphy, *The Antiquities of Egypt: A Translation, with Notes, of Book I of the Library of History of Diodorus Siculus* (New Brunswick: Transaction Publishers, 1990), 119.

[3] Ibid, 119-20. Note: Since the preaching of this sermon scholarship has suggested that Paul does not have in mind the transgression of Adam in mind in this section of Galatians (as he does in Romans 5), but the transgressions of the Watchers in Genesis 6:1-4. This fascinating insight fits in nicely with the supernatural view of the ancients, but also of what follows in this sermon where God is still the ultimate source of all law. See Tyler A

The Origin and Purpose of the Law

It is tempting to give in, as Diodorus himself did, to the notion that these people were mad or that they made up a supernatural origin of law in order to better render the obedience of the masses to their own very human novel ideas.[4] But we know better. Law does not have a human origin, but a supernatural origin. At Eden, Ararat, and Sinai (all mountains), God gave the law to the man (Gen 2:16-17; 9:3-7; Ex 20:1ff). This is why law is transcultural and certain things are always wrong everywhere at all times. There simply is no good explanation for the universality of Law if human beings are its originators. Moral relativism is absurd.

Yet, given our own understanding that the LORD is the source of Law, it is still tempting to dismiss this idea that it's coming to man had anything whatsoever to do with what the Hebrew OT refers to as the gods (in accordance with Diodorus) or the Greek OT translates as angels. This morning our text is concerned with the law. It answers for us two basic and important questions: How did the Law get here and what is its purpose in our lives, especially as Christians. The first question is not asked as an end to itself. God doesn't just tell us how the law came to us so that we might be able to answer Bible Trivia on *Jeopardy*. The answer helps you to see the divine (heavenly) nature of the law and how rebellion against it is rebellion against the culture of heaven and especially, its King who sits upon its throne and oversees justice around the globe. But it also forces you to see the vital difference between the covenant of works and the covenant of grace. This difference is the difference between the direct oath of God and the indirect giving of law through mediators.

The second is the more practical question of what you are supposed to do when you come to a (the) law in the Bible. How are you supposed to think about it? What is your attitude about it supposed to be? Do you think properly about the law? Are you confused about its purpose? Do you understand why God gave it? Do you approach it the correct way?

Stewart, "Fallen Angels, Bastard Spirits, and the Birth of God's Son: An Enochic Etiology of Evil in Galatians 3:19–4:11," A Paper Given to the *Society of Biblical Literature*, 11-2015.

[4] His disbelief is seen in the next sentence, "For all of them believed either that their intent was wonderfully and thoroughly divine if the result would be of benefit to the mass of men, or else they knew that the common people would obey more readily if they were faced with the majesty and might of the beings said to have devised the laws."

Have you ever thought about its origin and how significant this is to your own obedience of the law?

The Origin of the Law

The first of our two main questions is "How did the law get here?" The answer is found at the end of vv. 19-20. This question actually comes after the question about the purpose of the law, but I want to treat it first because it serves or helps us understand the second question better. The law "… was put in place through angels by an intermediary. Now an intermediary implies more than one, but God is one." This explains the origin of the law.

On one hand, you already know the origin of law. It comes from God. As I said earlier, God is the one who gave the law to Adam, Noah, and Moses. Since the law comes from God, we mustn't think of the law as something evil or wicked or demonic. I heard an unbelievable exposition of Galatians 4:9-10 from a Calvinist new covenant theologian where he taught that Paul said that returning to Jewish old covenant observance of days (including the Sabbath), months, seasons, and years was returning to "paganism" and the "demonic."[5] This "shocking" statement made by Paul proves to him that we no longer keep the Sabbath. In a week or two I will deal with this much more thoroughly. For now, one of the things I found curious was that he never bothered to ask what this must mean about the God who gave those laws in the first place. If a return to OT lawkeeping is pagan and demonic, what does this say about the God who gave it?

Elsewhere, Paul does not call the law demonic, but rather "holy, righteous, and good" (Rom 7:12; 1 Tim 1:8). The law is not a reflection of evil beings, but of a perfect, morally pure being. The law is not some invention of men, much less Satan, but of El Tsaddik: The Righteous God (Isa 45:21). They are "His ways" (Deut 10:12); "perfect, sure, right, pure, clean, and true" (Ps 19:6-9). They tell you what God is like. They show you his character. They teach you what is good. They show you what is right and true. Is this what you think about when you think of the law?

---

[5] A. Blake White, "Sabbath: Galatians 4:8-10," http://www.youtube.com/watch?v=Ec1aTdFqVuk

Perhaps you don't. Perhaps you confuse God's laws for man's laws and thus have a disdain for God's law because of your confusion. So many Christians grew up with legalistic rules that are found no place in the Bible, yet were passed off as being the "very words of God." God doesn't say you aren't allowed to play cards, to go to a casino, to kiss before marriage, to have your lips ever touch the fruit of the vine, to smoke a cigarette? Some people would hear a pastor mention these things and conclude that he is telling you to run out and do them all. Frankly, some of these things are not wise or responsible. Several of them have potential to lead you into real trouble. But none of them are condemned explicitly in Scripture or even by good and necessary consequence. My point is that a lot of people grew up thinking that these things were just as evil in God's eyes as breaking the Ten Commandments. Incredibly, some Christians even elevate them above the level of the Ten Commandments! And thus, when they come out of legalism, they have a tendency to think of all law as silly or arbitrary or absurd.

But there may be others of you who may not think of God's laws as good (you may not think of God's laws at all!) because you are presently engaged in breaking them, have no conscience about it whatsoever, are in denial, are not repentant, and therefore cannot see the beauty of God's actual laws because your sin has blinded you to the truth. Those of you in this condition need to keep listening to this sermon as I come shortly to the purpose of the law. Before I come to this, we need to finish thinking about this law being put into effect by angels through a mediator.

The Apostle is driving us to something that is very important to consider. The glory of the law is of a lesser glory than that of the gospel *because of this angelic mediation.* And yet, there is something here in this verse that is critical to see. There are disagreements over the exact meaning of Gal 3:20 and the end of vs. 19. Exactly who is this intermediary? Many think that it must be Moses. After all, Moses does act as a mediator on Mt. Sinai in Deut 5:5 ("I stood between Jehovah and you at that time"). The main problem with this view is that the mediator here seems to stand between God and angels, not God and Israel.[6] A second problem is that the Moses-as-mediator view basically makes vs. 20 unintelligible.

Notice that vs. 20 affirms God's oneness or what we might call monotheism. "God is one." This is the equivalent of the *Shema* when it says, "Hear, O Israel! The LORD is our God, the LORD is one" (Deut 6:4; cf. 1 Tim 2:5; Heb 8:6). Why in the world would Paul interject monotheism into a statement about the mediation of Moses? Good luck coming up with an answer to that one. The best you will be able to do is come up with some clever theological answer that destroys the actual words of the text. This problem is so great that most commentaries will note that someone has reported that there are 430 different interpretations of this verse, one for each year that Israel was in Egypt! In other words, scholars are baffled.

But the statement of monotheism makes sense if the mediator here is not Moses, but someone who seems to violate the oneness of God. If he appears to violate God's oneness, then Paul must explain that God is in fact one being. This means that the mediator must be God himself. But you ask, how can God mediate between God and someone else (be they Israel or angels)? The answer is that there is more than one person in the Godhead, and one of these persons (the second to be precise) is the one who wrote the law with his own finger in the form of the Angel of the LORD. Notice what Moses said in Deut 9:10 about the mediation of another individual, "When I went up the mountain to receive the tablets of stone, the tablets of the covenant that the LORD made with you, I remained on the mountain forty days and forty nights. I neither ate bread nor drank water. And <u>the LORD gave me</u> the two tables of stone written with the finger of God, and on them were all the words that <u>the LORD had spoken with you</u> on the mountain out of the midst of the fire on the day of the assembly." This is not the Father he is talking about.

---

[6] F. F. Bruce reports how some think, "The question of the identity of the "mediator" is even more fraught with problems' than the function of the angels." He then summarizes, "In their view the 'mediator' here is so closely associated with the angels that one might think more readily of the angels' mediator than of the Israelites' mediator" (*The Epistle to the Galatians: A Commentary on the Greek Text* [Grand Rapids, Mich.: W.B. Eerdmans Pub. Co., 1982], 178). Bruce agrees with this assessment.

In other words, the Logos (preincarnate Christ) is the mediator in Paul's mind, not Moses. Mediation is the function of Christ in the OT as well as the NT, for he is the only mediator between God and man (1 Tim 2:5; Heb 8:6; 9:15; 12:24). Here is the problem: If God is mediating between God and someone else (be it a man or an angel), then this implies there is more than one God. But God is "one God" and therefore this mediator must also be God in his essence, even though he is a different person than the Father.[7] Thus, I think that when Paul says, "it was put into effect by angels through an intermediary" that this is a proof text of Christ being the Angel of the LORD. That's all quite mind-blowing, but it does not yet address the real point which is that angels delivered the law. This is also a big idea to grasp (and perhaps new to you), but it serves an important point. Let's talk about this idea.

First, I want you to see that the NT affirms that the law was put into effect through angels in several places. Stephen says in his death speech, "You who received the law as delivered by angels did not keep it" (Acts 7:53). Hebrews says, "Since the message declared by angels proved to be reliable, and every transgression or disobedience received a just retribution ..." (Heb 2:2). The idea seems to come from Deut 33:2 LXX, "The LORD came from Sinai ... with ten thousands of holy ones; on his right hand were angels with him ... all his holy ones are under your hands; and they are under you; and he received of his words, the law which Moses charged us." Ps 68:17 adds, "The chariots of God are twice ten thousand, thousands upon thousands; the LORD is among them; Sinai is now in the sanctuary."

This is all quite strange, but it affirms that the pagans were not far off in some sense in what they told us about the origin of the law. They said that the law was given to men by the gods. The LXX often translates the Hebrew "gods" as "angels" (Ps 8:5; 82:1; 97:7; 138:1, etc.). What the pagans do not affirm is that the angels themselves received the law from God Most High. Nor do they affirm that there is a non-created angel that

[7] This is the answer given by Heiser, *The Myth That Is True*, 152-153, but it piggybacks off of Bruce's (and others) view that the mediator is the Angel of the LORD, the latter simply does not say that the Angel is also Christ (see Bruce, 180). Calvin also seems to take the Christ as mediator view in this passage where in the OT he mediated for Jews and now also for Gentiles.

mediates between the gods/angels and God. Thus, while law retains its supernatural origin for them, it loses its morally good, objective, and transcendent quality, because different (not to mention fallen) gods/angels can deliver different laws. The Bible allows for none of this, though it obviously shows that in some ways that pagans of old knew more about this stuff than we do.

The point of bringing up angels here is to show that the origin of the law was mediated through several steps of decreasingly powerful representatives. First, the Word of God mediates between the Father and Angels. The Word of God is God. Then, angels put the law into effect, somehow delivering it to Moses. I don't know how it happened; I wasn't there. Then Moses delivers the Law of God to the people. All of this mediation takes away from the original glory of the law, not by diminishing God's glory or the Law's, but by proving that the covenant of works is not directly mediated to people by God himself.

All of this is to say that this is not the way the covenant of grace works. The covenant of grace came directly to Adam, Noah, Abraham, Moses, and the Apostles through only the mediation of God through the Angel named Yahweh and then through the incarnate Christ himself—God with us. There are no created angelic mediators here, thus the glory of the covenant of grace and the promise of the covenant is greater than that given in the Law of God, for in the promise God himself swears in the first person to perform all that is necessary to bring about salvation.

The Purpose of the Law

With this, we are able to look now at the purpose of the law which has a fading glory compared to the covenant of grace that comes through Christ. Most people have absolutely no idea why God gave the covenant of works to Adam or to Moses or to them. In fact, their ignorance of the truth of this matter has only served to increase the function of the giving of this covenant in the first place. Think for a moment about the common idea that God would never command us to do something that we were not able to do. Have you ever had anyone say that to you before? There is a presupposition about the law here that goes mostly unnoticed. It supposes that the law was given *for us to keep.* Here we wade into deep and treacherous water in a hurry.

What kind of an insane person would not believe that the law was given for us to keep? If you believe this, doesn't that somehow prove that the law is therefore wicked? Why wouldn't God want us to keep his good holy law? Oh, the subtlety of the shifting language used by the devil. Notice, I did not say that God does not want us to keep the law. I said that the law was not given for us to keep. These are very different things. The first questions <u>God's desire</u> *for us* regarding the law. The second questions <u>God's purpose</u> for giving the law to us. You can't equate God's desire and his purpose like this, because God might have more than one desire in any one thing he has purposed!

The improper view of the law presupposes that human beings are intrinsically morally good. The proper view (Paul's view here) admits that human beings are fallen into sin, hopelessly wicked, and in need of a miraculous cure. Of course God wants people to obey his law. He wants it in the same way that a Father wants his junkie son to stop shooting heroin and taking crack. He wants it in the same way that I want my government to get its national deficit under control. But God knows our condition, and his sending of the law was for a different purpose than fixing us or setting us straight. Don't think I'm saying here that God's desire for his sons to stop is always ineffectual, because it isn't. That's what election is for. That's what the covenant of grace is for. That's what effectual calling is for. But as it pertains to the law, the point I'm making is that God did not give the law to bring this desire to completion. It's actually just the opposite.

The Apostle says, "Why then the law? It was added because of transgressions, until the seed should come to whom the promise had been made." What does it mean "because of" transgressions? This can point to either a cause or a purpose. If it is a cause, then it means that God gave the law because transgressions were many and therefore the law came in to restrain them. This is possible and it gets to the classic Protestant division of the Three Uses of the Law. The two main branches of the Reformation (Reformed and Lutheran) both affirm that the law has three main uses. Calvin taught that the first use was that of a mirror. Like a mirror, it shows us our impotence, iniquity, and consequent condemnation. The second use is as a restrainer, perhaps like a chain restrains a dog. This use curbs man's outward depravity by offering rewards or threatening punishment. You use rewards with your children to get them to do the right thing. This is exactly what you are permitted to do when you are dealing with law. Courts, jail, capital punishment, etc., are things that are meant to deter dangerous or immoral behavior. These are also good, especially when people live together and have need of peace with one another. The third use is a guide.[8] You hire a guide to take you through territory you have never been before, to lead you, to keep you safe, etc. This use of the law is for Christians. If the verse is saying that the law was given because of our sin and in order to restrain it, then we are dealing with the second use of the law. But this is probably not what is in mind because in parallel passages, the idea is clearly that that law was given for the purpose of calling forth or increasing transgressions, to make them utterly plain to one and all so that your evil behavior could not be excusable to you (See Rom 4:15-5:20). Paul sums it up in Rom 5:20, "The law came in to increase the trespass."

Oh, how we need to recover this view of the law today, not just in our country, not just in our churches, but in our own individual hearts. What is the impetuous for removing the stigma and laws on homosexuality in our nation? Is it not mostly so that people can stop feeling guilty for what they are doing and begin to experiment like the modern evolved people that they are? What is behind the abandonment of biblical worship in the church? Is it not so we can finally feel free to worship however we feel like it? What is sometimes behind particular theologies that tell us we are no longer under law but under grace? Is it not so we can break all kinds of OT laws without theological concern that we are offending God? People hear about freedom in Christ and use it as an excuse to sin, to break God's law, and they justify it on theological grounds.

But this starts on the personal level, not on a national or institutional level. How many of you here gossip regularly about your husband to other women? How many of you drink so much alcohol that you pass out

---

[8] You can find these discussed in Calvin, *Institutes*, 2.7.6, 2.7.10, 2.7.12. They are also found in the *Formula of Concord* Art. 6.

on a regular basis? How many of you yell at your children in anger, are short with them, are would just rather not even be around them at all? How many of you work on the Sabbath and think nothing of it? How many of you take the Lord's name in vain at work or have speech filled with fecal matter to fit in with the boys? How many of you are willing to admit that you do these things? How many of you want the law to do its work on your heart by condemning you when you are called on it by a preacher or a friend or a spouse?

You wonder all the time why life seems so out of control, why church seems so boring or irrelevant, why you can't get excited for studying the Bible or gathering with saints to talk about Christ, why your marriage is filled with anger at one another on a daily, weekly, monthly basis, why work is a drudgery to be tolerated at best, why being around Christian friends is not very exciting, why you would rather spend all your time playing video games, why you dread going to school, why your own soul seems like some ugly vacant lot, and you refuse to look into your own heart for the reason. You will not look into the mirror of God's word to see what you are and what you have become. You live in a constant state of denial, you wallow in your sin like a pig wallows in mud, and meanwhile your spouse, your children, your friends, the people in your church have to put up with it without any ability to do anything about it.

Now, you see, this kind of preaching makes people very uncomfortable and they even turn against it, saying "don't judge me." But this isn't about a person judging you. It is about the law judging you, a standard that not only you but also I am held up to. Its whole purpose for being here is to show you what you are already like—you, me, everyone. The law shows us our sin, but it does even more than this. It actually stimulates our sin.

It's like adding water to a lawn full of weeds or lighting a match in a room full of gas. When we hear not to do a thing, our rebellious hearts actually desire to find clever ways to do the very thing we are told not to do. Sin springs up in our hearts and explodes in our minds because of the law. In fact, the only power the law actually seems to have over sinful people is the power to make them want to break it all the more. One of the most ironic things that it does is actually stimulate rebellion by tempting you to try and gain righteousness through it. Anytime we hear the law and come away thinking, "Well, that wasn't talking about me," we are well on the path to self-righteous self-deception. How easy it is to sit through a sermon where a few examples of sins are given and come away thinking, "Well, he didn't talk about anything that I have a problem with." But just here you have a problem, a very serious problem.

For how can you hear any example of a sin and think that isn't you? Doesn't James say if you break one law you have broken them all? Doesn't this mean that all sins are interconnected? So think of something that you know you do. Take gossip, one of the worst sins in the church because no one wants to talk about it even though it eats away the foundation and unity of the body like a termite. Now take something you think you don't do, like stealing. Did you know that when you gossip, you steal someone's reputation. How about murder. You say I've never murdered anyone. You murder someone in your heart by speaking badly about them. You say, "Well I never take the Lord's name in vain." Really? When you gossip about a Christian you take the Lord's name in vain by speaking ill about a fellow *Christ*ian, one who bears the name of Christ. We also commit a kind of adultery by sharing very personal information with someone who doesn't need to know about it when most likely you haven't shared that information with the person you are gossiping about. You are also putting your sin above God, thus breaking the first commandment. Do you see how this works? The law manifests our depravity. But when we think that we aren't really all that guilty, then we are tempted to think that the law is within our grasp to obey, and this temptation bring many to seek to justify themselves by their own righteousness. Beware, lest you hear God's word today and come away thinking like the rich young man, "All these things I have kept."

Lead You To Christ

So now you say, "This all seems so hopeless. You've convinced me of my sin through the law and shown me its purpose to condemn me. But why would God do this if he loves his people so much?" It's because the law was never seen as the final solution, but actually pointed to the final solution in Christ. This is why you must distinguish between the law and gospel and you must understand what the law was given to do. The Apostle says that the law was added for this function, "Until the offspring should come to whom the promise had been made." In other words, the law was given to point you to your need for salvation from outside of your own righteousness. As one person says, "it confines all in the prison-house of sin, from which there is no exit but the way of faith."[9] As another says, "Only in that way would the necessity of Christ's coming and work be properly understood."[10]

This part of the verse is so critical because it shows you that the law was never given to be an end to itself. Returning to the theme of the seed (Gal 3:16), the Apostle says that because God made promises to Christ, that the law was given to increase transgressions (that is to manifest to you how rotten you are and so bring you to the end of yourself) only until you should come to Christ who is the end of the law. He is the end of the law because he obeyed it. He is the end of the law because through faith in him you are saved.

I was thinking this week about Jesus in the wilderness for 40 days being tempted by the devil in relation to the law being put into effect through a mediator. Think about the troubles this mediation of angels caused almost from the beginning. God gives Adam and Eve one little law. The devil (who is an angel, not a demon), comes to Eve and makes her question what the law actually said. "Did God really say ...?" (Gen 3:1). He then makes her doubt God's goodness and trustworthiness in giving the law, "You will not surely die." "You will become like gods (that is like himself and the other angels) knowing good from evil" (therefore able to dispense justice in the way that only they can?). In other words, the fallen angel in a sense mediated the law to the woman who mediated it to the man and through this mediation, the world was plunged into sin, because fallen beings (be they heavenly or earthly) twist the law to their own vicious ends.

Now think about Satan and Jesus. Satan tempts Jesus with three forbidden things and again takes the Scripture and twists it to his own ne-

---

[9] F. F. Bruce, *The Epistle to the Galatians : A Commentary on the Greek Text* (Grand Rapids, Mich.: W.B. Eerdmans Pub. Co., 1982), 175.
[10] Herman N. Ridderbos, *The Epistle of Paul to the Churches of Galatia*, The New International Commentary on the Old and New Testament (Grand Rapids, MI: Wm. B. Eerdmans Publishing Co., 1953), 137-38.

farious purposes. But Jesus did not succumb. Jesus is the one who gave the law and who mediates even between Satan and God in heavenly places. Jesus is the one who obeyed the law and inherited the promises given to Abraham. And Jesus is the one who mediated the covenant of grace, giving the promise to all whom the Father had chosen, through the effectual calling of the Holy Spirit through the gospel.

So you see, the law has its purpose in your life to drive you continually to your knees in repentance of your sins and then to lift up your head and point you to the Messiah. First, you must confess your sins, acknowledge them, and repent of them. This goes for anyone here, be you a person who has never really believed upon Christ or a person who has and yet finds themselves trapped in sins you know you commit but will not admit to yourself or anyone else. Then you must trust in Christ. Friend, you must understand that your sin will be punished if you do not turn to the Lord by faith alone. There will come a day of reckoning.

But those who believe in Christ have had all of their punishment poured out on the son of God and God will never hold your sins against you. Rather, he promises you the same rewards promised to the Perfect One who died in your stead. Peace will be yours, not only peace between you and God (which is most important), but peace with yourself. This peace in turn will lead to greater kindness, gentleness, patience, self-control, and all the other fruits of the Spirit that are promised to those that love God, or rather have been loved by God. Use the law correctly and flee to Christ for refuge from the coming wrath of God.

Sons of God

Knowing Your Identity in Christ

3:21 Is the law then contrary to the promises of God? Certainly not! For if a law had been given that could give life, then righteousness would indeed be by the law. [22] But the Scripture imprisoned everything under sin, so that the promise by faith in Jesus Christ might be given to those who believe. [23] Now before faith came, we were held captive under the law, imprisoned until the coming faith would be revealed. [24] So then, the law was our guardian until Christ came, in order that we might be justified by faith. [25] But now that faith has come, we are no longer under a guardian, [26] for in Christ Jesus you are all sons of God, through faith. [27] For as many of you as were baptized into Christ have put on Christ. [28] There is neither Jew nor Greek, there is neither slave nor free, there is no male and female, for you are all one in Christ Jesus. [29] And if you are Christ's, then you are Abraham's offspring, heirs according to promise.

4:1 I mean that the heir, as long as he is a child, is no different from a slave, though he is the owner of everything, [2] but he is under guardians and managers until the date set by his father. [3] In the same way we also, when we were children, were enslaved to the elementary principles of the world. [4] But when the fullness of time had come, God sent forth his Son, born of woman, born under the law, [5] to redeem those who were under the law, so that we might receive adoption as sons. [6] And because you are sons, God has sent the Spirit of his Son into our hearts, crying, "Abba! Father!" [7] So you are no longer a slave, but a son, and if a son, then an heir through God. [8] Formerly, when you did not know God, you were enslaved to those that by nature are not gods. [9] But now that you have come to know God, or rather to be known by God, how can you turn back again to the weak and worthless elementary principles of the world, whose slaves you want to be once more? [10] You observe days and months and seasons and years! [11] I am afraid I may have labored over you in vain.

Galatians 3:21-4:11

A New Old Apologetic

I SUPPOSE IT IS APPROPRIATE THAT The Who sings, "Who are you? I really wanna know. Tell me, who are you? 'Cause I really wanna know." The problem is, most people are unable to answer that question because they are lost. They don't know who they are. In Australia you go on a walkabout (made famous in the Crocodile Dundee movies), a long trek into the middle of the desolate Outback to find yourself. In 1965, Elliott Jaques coined the term used in the western world, "midlife crisis." Before that time, there was no term that encapsulated this utter sense of self-doubt and inner turmoil felt in midlife for having squandered youth while rushing headfirst into old age. People are looking for meaning in all the wrong places.

This serious problem of having no identity began when the pillars of western civilization were being torn down: Truth, absolutes, objective morality, history, and God's work through Christ in it. These are the pillars that ground people. Many Christians have been pretending for many decades now that the problem is not really all that severe, that all we need to do is somehow reach people where they are at, contextualize our message, and the world will jump at the chance to become Christians. In the process, many of us have abandoned the very same things in order to reach those who are lost *because they have abandoned them*. This sounds like insanity. Rather than reach them, exactly the opposite has taken place. Our civilization has utterly rejected Christianity and all that it stands for and is returning at breakneck speed to the paganism, spirituality, sensuality, demon worship, slavery, and bondage unknown since pre-Christian times, before missionaries first took the light into the dark world of the Gentiles.

People are once more embracing the ways and religions of druids, witches, and shamans, barbarian hordes, Goths, and Amazons, and could not be more proud of it. They are like the people in Psalm 2 who raise their fist against God and his Messiah saying, "Let us burst their bonds apart and cast away their cords from us" (Ps 2:3). They view slavery to God as the worst of all possible things in part because they see the opposite of slavery as autonomy (freewill), not realizing that all men are slaves on this earth. We are slaves either to a benevolent, omnipotent, loving heavenly Father, or to tyrannical, powerful, hateful spiritual entities that have always used mankind to further their purposes against the God who created them. These people do not know who they are or what they are bringing upon themselves in their rush to re-embrace the gods of old. They are like the dodo bird which was hunted to extinction because it did not fear the predator that was hunting it.

Meanwhile, Christians are far too comfortable pretending that the erosion—no, the deluge—flooding our culture is not really taking place. We sit in Christian bubbles like kings holed up in a besieged castle, drinking wine, being merry, having parties while the armies of marauders and invaders fill in the moat, fire the trebuchets, and launch the fiery arrows to bring our fortress down. We surround ourselves with ear ticklers as we ignore the writing on the wall. Many of us, strangely, want to feel just as free as our unbelieving counterparts as we too forget that we are slaves of Christ Jesus.

In many respects, we have the same problem as the world. We no longer know who we are or what God has done for us in Christ. For some reason unknown to me, many Christians don't even care to know. We are much too preoccupied with trivial things in life to be worried about grandiose philosophical questions of ontology or being. And so, we've stopped telling the story that gives us our identity. The story of the Bible is the story of what we were and who we've become, in and because of Christ. Because we no longer tell the story, we no longer know the story, or love it. We seem unable to see and feel what the story has done. We've lost our past. Thus we are unable to mount a defense of our faith with any kind force that is able explain to others why they shouldn't go back to the older identities, to its baser roots. The most powerful defense of the faith is one that comes from a person that has been utterly moved and transformed. It is one that does not come out of obligation (I really should tell my unbelieving friend about Christ, but I don't know what to say), but out of abundance (I can't help but tell you what has happened to me)!

What you will hear from me today is something that has moved me to the core of my being. Much like becoming Reformed, it has given me new understanding into my own identity. I'm going to tell you about what it means to be a son of God. I'm going to tell you what that means against the backdrop of having been enslaved, in bondage, in servitude, in darkness, blinded by spiritual forces that to this day have authority over this world—until the kingdom of God intrudes upon them through the gospel, snatching a person's identity and citizenship out of this world and into the world to come. I believe this message has the potential to combat the forces of evil, because that's exactly what it did in the past, as the Apostle Paul took this message to the Gentiles who were living in such dark and sorry times. This involves returning to the context of the gospel that Paul understood very well as he went from Gentile city to Gentile city. Everywhere Paul went he told the people about the remarkable days when God's Son walked this earth and accomplished something so powerful that we today no longer see what he did because he has so effectively performed his work in western civilization that the old ways were almost completely forgotten.

Today's text has two different foci. One is the slavery and slave masters who held us in bondage. The other is our new identity in Christ. These two things are each of such importance that I will spend two weeks on the passage we are looking at today. The focus of this morning's sermon will be our identity in Christ as sons of God. I am going to compare this with the slave masters who held the world in captive everywhere until the gospel came to a land and transformed its people who then transformed its culture.

I have to try and overcome something with some of you. A main problem is that what I am going to talk about is only, at best, partially understood and taught. We've only been told half of the story. This, in turn, has caused us to forget some very specific things the omnipotent God did for our ancestors in the faith who lived in diverse Gentile lands.

Paul's announcement that Jesus is God's son is absolutely shocking. That he would say *we* have been adopted into God's family as "sons of God" is equally as shocking. Both ideas would have been revolutionary to those people that were held in bondage and fear to supernatural beings that ruled over them, created terror in their hearts, made them worship them and do things that pretty much only missionaries to such dark places can understand today. How revolutionary does any of this sound to you at this point? Maybe that's part of our collective problem? We've forgotten.

Earthly Sons of God

Gal 4:4 calls Jesus "God's son." Is this his human or divine title? Gal 3:25 adds, "You are all sons of God" in Christ. Is this looking at things from earth's or heaven's perspective? I very much want you to understand the full history behind this phrase "sons of God." If you know the history, you can understand the present. Those who do not know history are destined to repeat it, or in this case, to fall back into it. You are probably familiar with a partial history of it, and this is excellent in as far as it goes. Here is what you probably already know.

The idea of a son of God has its roots in the OT. Israel is often the focus of our teaching on this, but the idea goes all the way back to Adam who was made in the image of God and is called the son of God (Luke 3:38). Hosea looks back upon a period of slavery even more infamous than that which occurred in America. "When Israel was a child, I loved him, and out of Egypt I called <u>my son</u>" (Hos 11:1). Moses had told Pharaoh that God demanded "Let my people go!" (Ex 5:1), because "Israel is <u>my firstborn son</u>" (Ex 4:22). This was sonship of a miraculous birth of a nation by God. It is spoken of in one of Moses' songs, "You were unmindful of <u>the Rock that bore you</u>, and you forgot the God who <u>gave you birth</u>" (Deut 32:18).

Heavenly Sons of God

Earlier in this same song, Moses refers to other "sons of God." The curious thing is that they are not Israelites (see Deut 32:8 ESV). Israelites were not even around back in those days. In fact, they are not even human. This caused some Jewish scribes so much consternation that they actually changed the phrase "sons of God" to "sons of Israel" in order to more easily accommodate the anti-supernatural worldview (other than God himself) which many adopted after the fall of the temple in Jerusalem.[1] (The original wording "sons of God" has been argued persuasively by Evangelical scholars).[2]

The idea that the sons of God are heavenly beings is easily proven from the Bible. Job, the oldest book in the Bible in terms of when it was written, tells us that as God was laying the foundations of the earth, determining its measurements, laying is cornerstone ... in other words creating it *while someone else was there watching*. He says that "the morning stars" were singing together and the "sons of God" were shouting for joy (Job 38:7). It is impossible for this to refer to humans, since humans did not arrive until sometime after these first acts of creation. Therefore, the Bible tells us that in some sense God has heavenly sons (plural). Let that sink in a bit.

Because the things the text actually says are so difficult for people to believe, the history of the phrase "sons of God" that Paul utilizes and echoes a half dozen times in our passage today has been left out of our biblical education. To get at this better, return to Galatians 3:1. In this verse, Paul reintroduces a theme he brought up in 1:8. The theme is of supernatural created beings that are able to hold some kind of sway over our thinking, either through teaching or through insinuation, temptation, or some other form of mental manipulation. Paul asks, "Who has bewitched you?" The word "bewitched" implies some kind of Satanic spell that is being cast over the Galatian Christians. Later in this chapter, he speaks of angels putting the law into effect. The supernatural has never been far from Paul's mind in this letter.

Sons of God: Rulers and Princes

What are these sons like? The verse in Job calls them "stars," which shows their heavenly natures. Elsewhere the stars are paralleled with rulers (Gen 1:16; Num 24:17; Ps 136:9). They are sometimes compared with the hosts of heaven (Deut 4:19), angels (Ps 148:1-3), and gods (Deut 17:2-3; 32:43). The heavenly host is parallel with seraphim (Isa 6:2-3). They

---

[1] See Alan Segal, *Two Powers in Heaven: Early Rabbinic Reports about Christianity and Gnosticism* (Boston, Brill Academic Pub, 2002).

[2] See Michael Heiser, "Deuteronomy 32:8 and the Sons of God," *Bibliotheca Sacra* 158:629 (Jan-Mar, 2001), 52-74. http://www.thedivinecouncil.com/DT32BibSac.pdf.

are identified as "holy ones" (Job 4:18; 15:15; 25:5). They are called watchers (Dan 4:13; 23).

The NT uses several different words for them, some of which come from the LXX, each of which carries out in one way or another, the idea of them as <u>rulers</u>: princes (*archōns*), angels (*aggelos*), stars (*aster*), powers (*dunamis*), authorities-powers-principalities (*exousia*), lords (*kurios*), dominions (*kuriotes*), names (*onama*), spiritual forces (*pneumatikos*), elemental spirits (*stoicheia*), gods (*theos*), and thrones (*thronos*).[3] One of these words (*stoicheia*) is in our passage today (Gal 4:3, 9).

To see that these heavenly beings are in some way rulers over the earth (like vassals who run the kingdom for the suzerain, or princes for the king), look no further than Satan, the glorious, beautiful, and very evil, angel of light. Let me give just a couple of examples. In John, Satan is called the "*Prince* [or sometimes 'ruler'; *archon*] of this world" (John 16:11; cf. John 12:31). If you have ever wondered why Satan can offer Jesus "all the kingdoms of the world" (Matt 4:8-9) and not get laughed at by the God of the universe, it is because God had given him charge of the world at some point in the past. He was its lawful (though very lawless) ruler.

A more relevant passage to what we are looking at this morning is in Ephesians 2:2 where it says the "*prince* of the power of the air, the spirit that is now at work in the sons of disobedience." A couple of other passages tell us that Satan is the "power" who holds men in "darkness" (Acts 26:18).[4] He is the "god of this world" who has "blinded the minds of the unbelieving" (2 Cor 4:4).

<u>Captives in Slavery</u>

So how does this ruling of princes of the air relate to our passage today? The Apostle tells us that "when we were children, we were enslaved to the *stoicheia* of the world" (Gal 4:3). If you are enslaved to something, then it is your master and it <u>rules</u> over you. For the Israelites, it was the Pharaoh. For Christians, it is God himself (Paul often refers to himself as

---

[3] See Matt 9:34, 12:24; Mark 3:22, 13:25; Luke 11:15; John 6:11; Rom 8:38; 1 Cor 8:5, 15:24; 2 Cor 4:4; Gal 4:3, 9; Eph 1:21, 2:2; 3:10; 6:12; Php 2:9; Col 1:16, 2:8, 10, 15, 20; 1 Pet 3:22.
[4] The ESV's "power" is the Gk: *exousia*. It can be translated as "dominion."

God's "slave"; Rom 1:1; Gal 1:10; Tit 1:1 etc). The Bible teaches us that for Gentiles who lived in darkness their entire lives, never seeing the light of the gospel, they were in slavery to these *stoicheia* which I have just mentioned can be identified as heavenly sons of God. This is a terrifying idea because these beings have fallen into sin just like men.

Returning to Deut 32, the passsage which I referred to earlier which tells us about the heavenly sons of God prior to talking about Israel as God's son explains that there was a time long ago when God gave the nations their inheritance (*nachal*), dividing mankind according to the number of the sons of God (vs. 7-8). It then adds that the LORD's "portion" (*chalaq*) of the peoples of the earth is Israel (vs. 9). He inherits them. The number of the sons of God is recorded in Jewish literature around the time of Christ as being "70".[5] This corresponds to the number of nations dispersed after the Tower of Babel incident.[6] Interestingly, Israel is not one of them, because God's portion, his son, must be created directly by him through a miracle of grace.

Throughout Deuteronomy, Moses has been telling the people all about this. Deut 4:19 warns Israel, "Beware not to lift up your eyes to the heaven and see the sun and the moon and the <u>stars</u>, all the <u>host of heaven</u>, and be drawn away and worship them and serve them whom the LORD your God has <u>allotted</u> (*chalaq*) to all the nations under the whole heaven." "Allotment" here is the same word as "portion" a moment ago. Deut 17:2-3 refers to the sun, moon, and stars as "other <u>gods</u>." Deut 29:26 tells us that Israel turned and worshiped "other gods … whom [God] had not <u>allotted</u> (*chalaq*) to them." Deut 32:17 tells us that these were "new gods" and it calls them "<u>demons</u>" (*shedim*) who earlier peoples never dreaded. In other words, these new guys which we would all agree are real entities (demons) are a different group of beings from those allotted to the nations at an earlier time.

---

[5] Targ PsJon Deut 32:8; 1 Enoch 89:59; 90:22-27; 3 Enoch 17:8; Jasher 9:32 (This Jasher may be an 18th century forgery of the Book of Jasher mentioned in the Bible). For a brief discussion and introduction to "70" in the Bible and surrounding nations see John Day, *Yahweh and the gods and goddesses of Canaan* (New York: Continuum, 2002), 23-24.

[6] On there being seventy nations in Genesis 10 see Umberto Cassuto, *A Commentary on the Book of Genesis: From Noah to Abraham* (Jerusalem: Magnes Press, 1964), 177–180; Allen P. Ross, "Studies in the Book of Genesis - Part 2: The Table of Nations in Genesis 10 - its Structure," *BibSac* vol. 137: 548 (Oct-Dec 1980): 342

(See Chart Below)

Deuteronomy Allotment Compared					
4:19-20	17:2-3	29:26	32:7-9	32:17	32:43
"And beware not to lift up your eyes to heaven and see the sun and the moon and the stars, all the host of heaven, and be drawn away and worship them and serve them, those which the LORD your God has allotted (*chalaq*) to all the peoples under the whole heaven.	"If there is found among you. . . a man or woman who does what is evil in the sight of the LORD your God. . . and has gone and served other gods (*elohim*) and wor-shiped them, or the sun or the moon or any of the host of heaven, which I have forbidden. . .	"They turned to the service of other gods (*elohim*) and worshiped them, gods (*elohim*) whom they had not experienced and whom [God] had not allotted (*chalaq*) to them."	Remember the days of old; consider the years of many generations; ask your father, and he will show you, your elders, and they will tell you. 8 When the Most High (*Elyon*) gave to the nations their inher-itance, when he divided mankind, he fixed the borders of the peoples according to the number of the sons of God (*beney elohim*).9 But the LORD's portion (*parad*) is his people, Jacob his allotted (*chalaq*) heritage.	"They sacrificed to demons (*shedim*), not God (*Eloah*), to gods (*elohim*) they had never known, to new gods that had come re-cently, whom your fathers had never dreaded."	"Rejoice with him, O heavens; bow down to him, all gods (Gk: *uioi theou*). . . And let all angels (Gk: *aggelos*) of the divine Strengthen themselves in him. for he avenges the blood of his children and takes vengeance on his adversaries. He repays those who hate him and cleanses his people's land."

What's going on here? The idea is that as God took Israel to be his own portion, to rule over them as their God, their King, and their Sovereign, he earlier gave the nations rulers that would be over them as well. But whereas taking Israel was an act of grace, the nations' allotment of the sons of God was punitive and retributory. Remember, the Tower of Babel ends in *punishment*. The peoples are scattered and now we learn that they are given heavenly sons of God to rule over them, just as they themselves tell us in all their ancient stories no matter where you go on planet earth.

You can see this same worldview apparent in the passage today. Remember, Paul is speaking to Galatians which were mostly Gentiles. He reminds them, "Formerly, when you did not know God, you were en-slaved to beings that by nature are not gods" (NRS). In the next verse he calls them the *stoicheia*. Stoicheia can refer to one of three things in ancient literature. 1. Basic principles of religious teaching like the Law. Since Paul finds it necessary to compare the *stoicheia* here to gods, it makes little

Galatians

sense for him to mean "law." Who doesn't already know that the law is not by nature a god? That's ridiculous.

It can also refer to 2. The basic elements of nature such as earth, water, air, and fire. Peter uses the word this way (2 Peter 3:10-12), but Paul does not seem to. 3. They are personal spiritual beings like demons, angels, or star deities.[7] Stephen (Acts 7:42–43) gets at this idea when he says that Israel was worshiping the heavenly host and were involved in star worship.[8] The very strange book called The *Testament of Solomon* uses the word this way too. Seven spirits appear before Solomon and reveal to him their identity, "We are the *stoicheia*, rulers of this world of darkness" (TSol 8:2-4). In that book, Solomon is constantly binding demons and enlisting their service to build the temple.

Paul says that these *stoicheia* are by nature "not gods" (he uses the plural). It does not mean that they do not exist. In 1 Cor 8:5-6 Paul explains, "For although there may be so-called gods in heaven or on earth— as indeed there are many 'gods' and many 'lords'--yet for us there is one God, the Father, from whom are all things and for whom we exist, and one Lord, Jesus Christ, through whom are all things and through whom we exist." In other words, these are real entities but they are not the true God, they do not have any power over Christians because Yahweh, their God, is God. They have no power to keep people in darkness when God calls them to himself. Paul is saying that by their very nature these *stoicheia* are lesser beings created by the uncreated God who is alone God.[9]

The Son of God

This leads us then to the main idea of Galatians 3:21-4:7 which is that Christians are now called sons of God. This is tied directly to the slavery of our former lives when we were held under the captivity of the *stoicheia*, who had rightful authority over us as those who had been given

---

[7] For these three ideas See Daniel G. Reid, "Elements/Elemental Spirits of the World," in *Dictionary of Paul and His Letters* (Downers Grove, IL: InterVarsity Press, 1993), 229-33.

[8] He appeals to Amos 5:25–27 where star worship resulted in Israel's exile (*DPL*, 231).

[9] See Michael Heiser, "The *stoicheia/*'Elements' or 'Elemental Spirits,'" *Behind the Façade* vol. 3, no. 10 (March 2005): 36-43. Heiser seems to agree that stoicheia in Galatians are star deities. I rather think they are demonic entities (i.e. the children of the sons of God), because Paul says these beings are by nature less even than the gods (who are themselves less than God).

the nations as their inheritance.[10] The term "son" occurs seven times in our passage, so obviously it is a major theme. You can see this in Gal 4:6-7, "Because you are sons, God has sent the Spirit of his Son into our hearts, crying, 'Abba! Father!' So you are no longer a slave, but a son." As you can see here, "son" is used of two groups. The first is actually an individual: Jesus. "God sent forth his Son, born of a woman, born under law" (Gal 4:4; also 4:6).

Earlier in the letter, Paul referred to Jesus as "God's son" twice (Gal 1:16; 2:20). Curiously, Luke tells us only one thing about Paul's message in those early days, "For some days he was with the disciples at Damascus. And immediately he proclaimed Jesus in the synagogues, saying, '*He is the Son of God*'" (Acts 9:19-20). Keep in mind, Damascus, like Galatia, is Gentile country. Why does this matter? It is because the Gentiles understood this "sons of God" history in a way that Christians (Jew and Gentile alike) today have all but forgotten. They understood it because they lived in it. What Paul was going to tell them would change everything for them.

He began by explaining that God had a single Son that was unique among all the other sons. He calls him "God's son." John calls him the "only begotten (or unique) son" of the Father. The same idea is behind both phrases. Jesus is nothing like the other sons of God. Yet, he was to be counted among the heavenly sons and now he is counted among the earthly sons as well. Does that blow you away? Let's look at John 10:34 to understand this better.

In this passage Jesus is confronted by the Pharisees who charge him with blasphemy. Blasphemy means equating yourself with God. Jesus' reply is to go to the OT Scripture, specifically Psalm 82:6 where Jesus answered them, "Is it not written in your Law, 'I said, you are gods'?" Bear in mind that Jesus says this in order to prove to the Pharisees two things. 1. There is OT precedent for him calling himself a son of God because

---

[10] This does not necessarily contradict note 10. If the ancient view that demons are the disembodied spirits of the children of the sons of God (cf., Athenagoras, *A Plea to Christians* 24-25; Justin Martyr, *2 Apology* 5; Origen, *Against Celsus* 4.92; Lactantius, *Divine Institutes* 2.15) is true, then the sons of God could have given their authority vicariously to these sons who would therefore also be rulers over men in some lesser sense. This would be why pagans have long sacrificed to demons as well as gods.

there are other sons of God (which it also calls 'gods').[11] 2. Identifying himself as one of these sons of gods *sets himself apart from the Pharisees*. It is critical to remember that after he said this, the Pharisees *still tried to kill him* for blasphemy (vs. 39; John 10:33)!

There are two basic explanations for what Jesus is doing that fail miserably at explaining why the Pharisees were so enraged by Jesus' answer. The first solution is Evangelical. It says that Jesus uses the idea of a "god" to refer to some kind of human rulers,[12] even though nowhere in the Bible is the term "god" ever used this way.[13] The idea goes that the sons of God, i.e., Ps 82:1, are human rulers and that the gods (the same people; vs. 6) are therefore also human rulers. By saying "you" are gods, Jesus is therefore equating himself with the Pharisees (who are the "you", apparently, of Psalm 82:6) as another human ruler. But if that is true, why then are the Pharisees still so angry at Jesus? Why do they continue to seek his death for *blasphemy*? Jesus says this in order to distance himself from them, to prove that he and the Father can be one, not to make himself equal to a Pharisee.[14]

The other option is the Mormon option. It sees "gods" as referring to beings that once were like us and who we will one day become. They count God, the creator, among them no different from any other god. Not only is this solution heretical, it no more solves the problem of why Jesus is quoting this passage than the first solution. How does it help Jesus' cause if he is simply telling the Pharisees, "I'm a god and you're a god. We're all gods, so why do you get mad at me for calling myself the son of God?" The Pharisees obviously didn't take this like a Mormon does. They thought calling yourself a god was blasphemy! Imagine if that's what Jesus was calling them!

---

[11] It should be pointed out that Jesus does NOT go to Exodus 4 to prove that he is a son like Israel is a son. He goes to a passage supercharged with the supernatural.

[12] Cf., *ESV Study Bible*, John 10:34.

[13] See Cyrus Gordon, "אלהים in Its Reputed Meaning of *Rulers, Judges*," *Journal of Biblical Literature* 54 (1935): 139–144.

[14] Michael Heiser has an excellent treatment of the quotation of Jesus from Ps 82:6 as found in John 10:34. See Michael S. Heiser, "You've Seen One *Elohim*, You've Seen Them All? A Critique of Mormonism's Use of Psalm 82," *FARMS Review* 19/1 (2007): 221–266 (especially 258ff).
http://maxwellinstitute.byu.edu//publications/pdf/review/440310681-19-1.pdf

The only other solution is that these "gods" Jesus refers to are heavenly beings ... angels if you will, rulers whom God set over the nations (a la Dan 10:13; 20; Ezek 38:2; 39:1; 3 En 26:12, etc.). In fact, this is exactly what the Psalm is about. "God has taken his place in the divine council, in the midst of the sons of the gods he holds judgment" (Ps 82:1). In other words, Israel's God is the high God, the uncreated God, who judges these lesser beings. What had they done? "How long will you judge unjustly?" (vs. 2). Because of their unjust judging, "All the foundations of the earth are shaken" (vs. 5). Wow. These beings, which he then calls "gods" (vs. 6) and "sons of the Most High" (i.e., sons of God) will therefore "die like men" (vs. 7). What sense does it make for God to punish a man by dying like ... *a man*? Isn't that self-evident? The conclusion of this matter is that "God" will become the judge of the earth. He shall inherit (*nachal*) all the nations (vs. 8).[15]

This has become one of my favorite Psalms, especially in light of Psalm 2 where it says, "I have set my King on Zion, my holy hill" (Ps 2:6).[16] Who is this King? "The LORD said to me, 'You are my Son; today I have begotten (*gegennéka*, LXX) you'" (vs. 7). What does this son receive? "Ask of me, and I will make the nations your inheritance (*nachalah*)" (vs. 8), the same thing you see in Ps 82:8. Here is the source of the only begotten (*monogenes*) son, a word which means "unique" or "one of a kind" rather than only son of any kind whatsoever.[17]

So what Paul is telling these Gentiles in every city in which he preaches, is that God has a unique son, a son that actually took on human flesh, who became a human being (and did not merely appear to be human as angels sometimes do), who was born under law in order that he might earn for himself the right to rule the nations according to the rules given to angels and men, laws which were greatly transgressed by both parties, but which Jesus obeyed perfectly. Think for a moment about the creation mandate. Here God creates the man "in his image" and immediately

---

[15] The same word is used in Deut 32:8 for the nations receiving their "inheritance."

[16] There is an interesting relationship here between the "holy hill" and the "divine council" which sat in deliberation over the nations from the top of the holy mountain.

[17] For example, Isaac is Abraham's "only begotten" son (Heb 11:17) even though Abraham had another son named Ishmael.

(without any pause or verses in between) says, "Let them <u>rule</u> over ..."
(Gen 1:26 NAS). To be an image bearer is to be a son of God and a ruler,
which is why Adam is called God's "son."[18] Man's relation to the angelic
rulers is evident in Psalm 8:5, "You have made him a little lower than the
heavenly beings (*elohim* or 'gods'; 'angels' in LXX and Heb 2:7)".

It seems to have been the case that God created the angelic beings to
preside as lesser kings over the heavens, while man was given dominion to
preside over the earth. God is, of course, always the high King, sovereign
over everything. But in his wisdom and kindness, he chose to let other
beings govern over his creation as those under his authority, who report to
him. The rebellion of men (all in the foreordained and foreknown plan of
God) meant that they would now in some sense be slaves of these heavenly
beings who themselves transgressed their positions of authority. Jesus
came to reclaim God's righteous rule over his creation as well as to reclaim
mankind's rightful place as rulers of this earth. That's one reason among
many why Christ's full humanity is an absolutely cardinal doctrine of the
Christian faith. If he did not become a man, he could not rule as a man,
nor could he save men and women, and bring them into positions as sons
of God. But it is also a reason why Christ's full deity is just as much a cardinal doctrine, for he could not reclaim this for God unless he were God!
But because Christ did all that he did, he has now won a great victory over
these fallen heavenly beings and now sits enthroned as the god-man over
them. This allows him to destroy strongholds and the authoritative rule
that these beings hold over all mankind until the gospel comes and sets
people free.

Implications of Being a Son of God

The idea does not stop with Christ. Paul says that we too are sons of
God through faith in Christ Jesus. Faith and faith alone gains us this

---

[18] Cf., Luke 3:38. That angels are also God's sons explains how in some sense they are able to say along with
God, "Let <u>us</u> make man in our image." Many Ancient Near Eastern scholars believe this is a "deliberative plural" where God is speaking to the angels (or divine council), rather than a reference to the plurality of the majesty or the Trinity. The Sons of God will now have counterparts on earth. Cf., Michael Heiser, *The Myth That
Is True*, unpublished, 38; Meredith Kline, *Kingdom Prologue* (Eugene, OR: Wipf and Stock, 2006), 43-44; Gordon J. Wenham, vol. 1, *Word Biblical Commentary : Genesis 1-15*, Word Biblical Commentary (Dallas: Word,
Incorporated, 2002), 27-28.

status. And the creation "waits in eager expectation for the sons of God to be revealed" (Rom 8:19 NIV). But how are we sons? Through adoption (Gal 4:7), which is a miraculous creation through election and effectual calling. We are sons through the Spirit of God who is sent into our hearts (vs. 6) by which we call God "Abba, Father." When the Spirit of God comes into a person's heart, God claims that person as his own property, thus freeing them from the slavery of Satan, allowing the person to truly be free from angelic and demonic powers and forces for the first time.

One of the implications of this is that we become "heirs" along with Christ. This is a remarkable word which if you understand can change your life. Christ, who created the world has now been appointed "heir of all things" (Heb 1:2). We therefore have this same heirloom as Jesus. We are heirs of the kingdom. We become rulers of the nations, which will bow down to us in the life to come. And we will even "judge angels," a remarkable and enigmatic verse found in 1 Cor 6:3 which only makes sense in light of this worldview. In fact, I want you to think about the doctrine of election here for a moment.

Remember how Isaac was told, "the older shall serve the younger" (Gen 25:23; Rom 9:12)? This is often how election works. With regard to the two different sons of God, which came first? Who is the older? The heavenly sons of God came first. They are the older sons. I propose what is happening with Adam in the Garden (and later to the elect through faith in Christ) is that God is telling the heavenly sons of God, you shall serve them.[19] This is very plausibly the cause of Satan's fall, just as it was for Esau when Jacob "stole" his birthright (even though God had given it to him). For a time, Satan thought he won.[20] But in the promise of the seed (Gal 3:16; Gen 3:15), he did not. Christ won the victory and returned rightful and righteous rule of the world to a man. By adoption we

---

[19] An old idea of the fall of Adam is found in the Life of Adam and Eve (*Vita* 11:2-16:4). In this book the idea is presented that Satan fell because Adam had been given the dominion that Satan originally thought was going to be his.

[20] His temptation was, "you shall become as <u>gods</u> knowing good and evil." The plural "gods" is probably correct (see LXX, TNK, PsJon, NET, KJV, GNV, BBE, VUL). The idea is that Satan was tempting Adam with the very thing he already possessed *but didn't realize*: the power to discern and make judgments, as he (Satan the ruler of the world) himself did, over good and evil. Satan knew this would backfire on Adam and figured that God would be so angry with Adam that he would return (or give) all rule back to Satan and the heavenly host.

are allowed to partake of this divine right as sons of God. Election reversed the fortunes of the fallen heavenly beings. Now, we will judge angels.

Such an announcement as this is almost beyond the modern western Christian's ability to accept. I have come to believe that this is due in no small part to the fact that the gospel has so powerfully dispelled the kingdom of Satan in formerly pagan, superstitious, mystical, magical, paranormally charged civilizations that we no longer believe very much that these creatures really even exist. In doubting their existence, we play however unintentionally, straight into the hands of atheists, naturalists, secularists, rationalists, evolutionists, all of which deny that there is a supernatural world beyond our five senses. This is not a tolerable situation biblically. But it is also a position that has given us a self-imposed amnesia about what God has done through Christ and what he has given to his saved children as a gift of his grace.

I cannot even imagine, nor do I want to, what it must have been like for my ancestors in Scandinavia and northern Europe who lived in constant of fear of demons, who sacrificed all kinds of evil things to the pantheon, who practiced magic to have any hope of overcoming these territorial powers, and who had absolutely not a clue on earth about the truth of God because they had been blinded by uncounted generations of deception. But that is the way all of our ancestors were. That is the way the Galatians were only a few years prior to the writing of this letter. Paul is trying to call them into the freedom of Christ by showing them where they have come and who they are now as rightful, justified, forgiven children of the Heavenly Father through faith in Christ.

Has such a thought of your past even once crossed your mind? I guarantee that the faster our civilization rushes to re-embrace the gods of old (which we are doing at breakneck speed), the more you will be glad you can see the truth for what it is. I do not desire a return to the true dark ages, when Gentiles were in slavery to demons and evil spirits, but I see it fast approaching. We are embracing paganism with the full fervor of a culture spellbound by these creatures and the church seems to be ignoring it, pretending it isn't really happening, or promoting bizarre charismatic views of Satan and demons that no thinking person who knows the Bible could ever take it seriously, thus making my job here today even more difficult. But this darkness brings with it intense hatred for Christ, a love for evil, blindness to what is true, good, and beautiful. But in Christ, there is freedom. The gospel sets us free not only from sin, but from the dominion and bondage of Satan. And people are today in a better position to understand this than they have been for a thousand years, if we will embrace what the Scriptures teach us and study these things to show ourselves approved.

Jesus said, "The truth will set you free." He is the truth incarnate. He is the power of God, the one who has defeated Satan so that you may no longer fear, but live in peace and surety. For, "Who shall separate us from the love of Christ? Neither death nor life, nor angels nor rulers, nor things present, nor things to come, nor powers, nor height nor depth, nor anything else in all creation, will be able to separate us from the love of God in Christ Jesus our Lord" (Rom 8:35-39).

May God give you the ability to see, know, and love the truth about your past and about your present condition given to you as a free gift of grace through faith in Christ alone.

One In Christ

²⁴ So then, the law was our guardian until Christ came, in order that we might be justified by faith. ²⁵ But now that faith has come, we are no longer under a guardian, ²⁶ for in Christ Jesus you are all sons of God, through faith. ²⁷ For as many of you as were baptized into Christ have put on Christ. ²⁸ There is neither Jew nor Greek, there is neither slave nor free, there is no male and female, for you are all one in Christ Jesus. ²⁹ And if you are Christ's, then you are Abraham's offspring, heirs according to promise.

Galatians 3:24-29

Three Case Studies

THIS MORNING I WANT TO GIVE YOU three case studies that relate to Galatians 3:28, "There is neither Jew nor Greek, there is neither slave nor free, there is no male and female, for you are all one in Christ Jesus." See if you can find the similarities and differences. Case #1. A popular Christian feminist author writes, "For nearly two millennia, the approach of the Christian church toward the role of women usually has been to sanction the view current in mainstream secular society, decreeing it to be the 'biblical' role for women. If the role of women changed in society, it would change in the church as well. This typically has been the determining factor in the stance of the church toward women ... with the exception of Paul who writes [in a patriarchal culture], there is 'neither male nor female' [in Christ]."[1]

Case #2. In college I remember a session in which we talked about slavery. Slavery, I was told, used to be acceptable to God. But today, it is

---

[1] Rebecca Merrill Groothuis, *Women Caught in the Conflict* (Eugene, OR: Wifp & Stock, 1997), 1.

outlawed by the Bible. Under no circumstances is slavery every allowable because Paul says in Christ, "there is neither slave nor free."

Case #3. A couple of years ago, when visiting Israel's only Reformed Baptist Church, we entered into a worship service where three different languages could be heard (two through interpreters, one from the pulpit). Russian, English, and Hebrew were in a room full of American, Russian, and Jewish Christians. It was pretty chaotic, but Pastor Baruch felt very strongly that this is the way things needed to be because in God's kingdom, as Paul teaches, "There is neither Jew nor Greek."

These three cases have a similarity. All use the same text of Galatians 3:28 to make a point about unity in Christ. However, there are also differences. The first two cases apply their situations to the city of man, while the last applies it in the city of God. The first case is a little different still, because it also tries to apply Paul's language in the church, just like case three. However, in this case, the argument is rooted in what is culturally acceptable ought to be acceptable in the church as well, and so it is still firmly planted in the city of man.

Frankly, the history of the church has proven one thing. People are capable of making the Bible say whatever they want it to say and apply almost any passage to almost any situation they desire. It is true that almost every Christian feminist book anchors their argument in Galatians 3:28. I can remember the first time I heard this position taught in a class. The professor argued that all roles (or functions) between men and women are now blurred together because of Paul's remarkable new insight. Nothing should prohibit a woman from doing anything a man can do. I can also remember thinking, that's not what Paul is teaching in this verse. That might be proven elsewhere, but certainly not here. I also remember raising my hand in the class on slavery and responding, "I don't think that verse says that slavery is inherently evil and that verse can be used as justification for something like the Civil War." Before you get the same rabid look in your eyes that I received when I made that comment in the class, please know that I think it is a moral sin to treat other human beings as sub-human at every time and every place. But I also realize that this same passage teaches that everyone is a slave to something. You can't get away from slavery.

But I had a different reaction when I went into Baruch's church. Yes, I was definitely not used to the near chaos of so many people packed into a small room. Their worship style was different from what I prefer. It was difficult to focus on the worship because of all the things taking place in that room. But I also thought there is something right about this. I did not have the same kind of reaction to what he was doing as to the other two cases. Why might this be? Let's go to the text and see if we can figure out exactly what it means that in Christ these distinctions are obliterated.

Fundamental Misunderstanding of the Law

Part of the problem people have when they abuse this passage is a fundamental misunderstanding of Law. As we've seen before, it is common for people to take a verse like Romans 6:14, "You are not under law but under grace," to mean "law has no place in a person's life anymore. It is abolished, done away with, obliterated into a billion tiny atoms." This view of law is a failure to understand the purpose of law and how it was never intended (when given to fallen man) to be a means of eternal life. When people misuse it like this, and see that grace has come through Christ, they think that God is setting aside one thing for another. That's exactly what's going on in this interpretation of Gal 3:28.

Can you see the similarity between "law has no place in a person's life anymore" and "in Christ there is neither male nor female," etc.? Both view a "new" situation as replacing an older situation, but the older situation they think has passed away has been misunderstood in the first place. I'm not bringing together two unrelated things here. Rather, in the text itself they are woven together like a fine tapestry. In the passage, it is *because* the law is not contrary to the promises that Paul ends up concluding "there is neither Jew nor Greek." So, if you get Galatians 3:21 wrong, you will misunderstand Galatians 3:28. Likewise, if you get Galatians 3:28 wrong, it is because you have misunderstood the point about law and/or grace.

To explain this better, it will be helpful to look specifically at Galatians 3:26-29. "In Christ Jesus you are all sons of God, through faith. For as many of you as were baptized into Christ have put on Christ. There is

Galatians

neither Jew nor Greek, there is neither slave nor free, there is no male and female, for you are all one in Christ Jesus. And if you are Christ's, then you are Abraham's offspring, heirs according to promise." The first thing to notice is how vs. 28 is sandwiched between "all sons of God" and "Abraham's offspring, heirs according to promise." In other words, the removal of distinctions between slaves and free, male and female, etc., is directly related to becoming part of God's family. In other words, this is *primarily* about status, not function.

Now, one of the problems someone might claim against my view of Gal 3:28 is that in some sense, all six of these groups were allowed to have the same status *in the Old Testament*. This view, they will argue, presumes that is not true. And so to say this is primarily about status might imply that somehow Paul did not think that Gentiles, slaves, or women were ever included in the God's family in the Old Testament. Is Paul saying that in the OT only free, male Jews were saved? Is that the implication of saying that now in Christ women, slaves, and Gentiles are now included into the family of God?

Of course not. Paul knows full well that Gentiles were included in the family of God in the Old Testament. He knows about Rahab and Ruth (both Gentile grandmothers of Jesus). He knows about Manasseh and Ephraim (Joseph's two sons born to an Egyptian woman) who are two of the twelve tribes of Israel. But Paul also knows that for a Gentile to be saved, *they had to become Jews.* They had to undergo the religious ceremonies of Jews, particularly circumcision. That's the concern here. In other words, these Gentiles had to come under Israel's covenant law. They had to become proselytes. They had to convert to Judaism in order to be saved. He is saying that this is no longer the case. Similarly, there is nothing in the OT that says slaves or women were not saved. In fact, you are told the very opposite. If that is true, then how is Paul talking about status and not function (like feminists and liberation theologians like to claim)? If people all these people were saved back then, and all these people are saved in Christ today, what's the difference?

The key to this is found in vs. 27. "For as many of you as were baptized into Christ have put on Christ." This verse is a direct allusion to the ordination ceremony of the priests of Israel found in Exodus 29:1-9. In that ceremony, before he could begin his ministry, the priest had to undergo a baptism in water in the laver of the tabernacle or sea of the temple. Then, he was given his new priestly clothing. After his ordination was complete, he was able to perform his ministry. Now, again, you might say, ministry deals with function (and to a degree it does). But first and foremost, it deals with status. Prior to his baptism and clothing, he was just a Jew. After his baptism and clothing, he was a priest. His status changed.

Paul relates the status here, not to a priestly ministry (though we will talk about that in a moment), but to bring "in Christ." At baptism, a person has moved, ceremonially, from being outside of the kingdom to inside of it. To be "in Christ" is to be saved. Baptism points outwardly to something that has taken place in the heart—the new birth or the baptism of the Holy Spirit. Now, baptism also points to a new status within the community, from ordinary Jew to one able to serve before God as a priest. But first and foremost, Paul is talking about salvation here. And he is doing it through an *analogy* directly related to an OT law.

You see, it was a law that the priest had to be washed and clothed. If he did not undergo this law, he did not get to be a priest. This status of priest was only available to free Jewish men. Slaves could not become priests. Gentiles could not become priests. Women could not become priests. This is exactly the same way it was with Gentiles who wanted to come into the kingdom of Israel. They had to become Jews. The point then, of our verse, is that the legal requirements for coming into the kingdom have been erased by Christ. (Actually, they were never there to begin with, but perverted people think that was the case). To be baptized into Christ is to be clothed with Christ, is to be in Christ. No longer do Gentiles have to become proselytes. No longer do slaves have to seek their freedom, because they are free in Christ. No longer do women have to feel like second class citizens to men, because they are one in Christ.

But if you do not understand that Paul is making a specific point about becoming heirs of the promises given to Abraham, that is if you do not understand that Paul is breaking down the divisions in order to make a point about how the strict demands of the law have been erased in Christ by using a specific analogy from a law of the OT, then you will make Galatians 3:28 say more than it is trying to say. You will squeeze more juice out of this verse than it has to give you. You will pit it against other

Scriptures in such a way that you have to turn the entire NT ethic into cultural relativism, where this alone is a higher principle and all other commandments regarding marriage or women or children or slavery, etc. were accommodations by the Apostles because they knew it would take a long time for the government and culture to change their attitudes to the higher ethical ideal.

What am I talking about? Consider some examples. In Ephesians 6:5 Paul says, "Slaves, obey your earthly masters with fear and trembling." When we make Galatians 3:28 say more than Paul is trying to say, you end up pitting the "in Christ there is no more slave or free" against verses like this. So the question becomes, how could Paul, who said there is no more slave or free turn around and tell slaves to obey their earthly masters? That's a contradiction. Therefore, they will say, Paul accommodated himself to the sinful culture of the time. That law is culturally relative. Today, you could just as easily throw it out of the Bible for all the good it is worth. If he had it his way, he would have told that slave to do everything in his power to get his freedom or else run away, because really, in Christ, there is no slave or free and he needs to live like that in the real world.

This is nonsense, and it is a deep confusion of the kingdoms. Notice, in Galatians 3:28, Paul's concern here is with the kingdom *of God*— being "in Christ." He isn't talking about how Christ has somehow magically eradicated all slavery in the city of man. But people torture the text to make it say all kinds of things it doesn't say. Of course, in Philemon, Paul writes to Philemon to set his slave Onesimus free, but he doesn't force him to do it based on some universal principle that Christ has eradicated slavery. He *asks* him to do it *for Christ's sake* because his slave has been of great value to Paul and the furtherance of the gospel. But these people twist the Scriptures, force them to contradict, make utter nonsense out of many different laws, and turn the whole biblical ethic into cultural relativism.

Let's look at another example. One feminist writes, "In the new covenant, all members are equal members, with full privileges of membership in the spiritual body of Christ. Men and women are not just 'equally saved' (whatever that means). Rather, men and women have equal status in the community into which their salvation has secured their membership. All are not simply equal in the community of believers, but all enjoy equal opportunity to participate in the spiritual and religious life of the community. This is what Galatians 3:26-28 is all about."[2] In other words, women can be pastors. In other place she writes that this is the most important text in the Bible on biblical equality and concludes, "It is a broadly applicable statement of the inclusive nature of the New Covenant, whereby all groups of people, regardless of their previous religious status under the law, <u>have now become one in Christ</u>."[3] Have *now* become one?

This misses the point entirely, and it shows you exactly what I have been talking about. Paul is not saying here that somehow *now*, in Christ, everyone is "equally saved." That isn't his point. And who argues that way anyway? Nor, is he saying that *now* everyone has become one in Christ, as if previously, in the OT, Gentiles, slaves, and women were not one in Christ in any sense. Obviously, Christ had not come in the flesh, and so there is a difference. But according to the NT, faith was always "in Christ" (John 8:56; 1 Cor 10:9; Heb 11:26; Jude 5 etc.). Do you see how this pits OT against NT, law against grace?

This verse is about eliminating the obstacles for people to achieve that equal status that all OT saints enjoyed but had to jump through hoops to obtain. This is the difference. It isn't about pitting faith against law, as if I'm somehow saying that OT Gentiles were saved by law and not faith. It is about showing how in Christ, the laws that set one aside as God's people have been torn down in Christ. It isn't about the functions that God's people have in the church, much less is it about annihilating inborn distinctions between males and females. It's like verse after verse has been justification, justification, justification, suddenly one verse about women becoming pastors, then back to justification, justification, justification.

Couldn't a person argue, on the basis of this kind of thinking, that because in Christ there is no longer male or female, that somehow homosexual marriages are now acceptable "in Christ?" In fact, not only could people argue that way. They do. Couldn't you extend this to say that in Christ there is no longer child or parent, and that this would mean children should be allowed to reverse the roles with their parents where chil-

---

[2] Rebecca Merrill Groothuis, *Good News for Women* (Grand Rapids, MI: Baker Books, 1997), 35.
[3] Ibid., 25-26.

dren discipline them or sue them and parents are now allowed to abdicate their authority and not train them up? After all, there are no more distinctions in Christ. Do you see the absurdities? They are almost endless.

Feminists take specific commandments where Paul clearly forbids women from being elders, or where Jesus clearly chooses only 12 men to be Apostles, and they make those culturally relative. If Paul were living in our modern, enlightened American culture, he clearly would not have made such old-fashioned arguments. He would allow women to be elders and pastors today. If Jesus were living today, we are told, he probably would have chosen 6 men and 6 women, because our culture would allow it. As if Christ was all about cultural sensitivity and didn't want to rock the boat. You will even read people saying that Jesus did not even need to be a man, but God accommodated to the culture of the day and sent Jesus as a man because that was acceptable.

Now, you might hear my argument with the priestly law and say that this means there are no longer distinctions in the priesthood. After all, doesn't the NT teach that we are a priesthood of believers? Yes, it does. Doesn't the NT teach that we are all able to offer "living sacrifices?" Yes, it does. Aren't we all attending to God's NT temple? Yes we are. Wasn't attending the temple in the OT the exclusive right of the priest? Yes, it was. So doesn't that mean women can be pastors? No, it doesn't. There is a disconnect going on here that is subtle, but dangerous.

The disconnect is that even in the OT, there were different classes of priests. Even back then not every priest was able to serve in the holy place. Levites where considered in some sense "priests." But their duties were clearly restricted to diaconal duties. But even within the priesthood of Aaron, there were distinctions. Only the High Priest was allowed to go into the Most Holy Place. So you see functional distinctions in the OT even when there is some sense in which all of the priests had a special status not given even to other Israelites.

So I solve this tension by doing two things. First, I try as hard as I can not to pit one Scripture against another. I think in some ways, we are all trying to do that. But honestly, if Galatians 3:28 is saying what I'm telling you that it says, then we have no contradictions with other passages about women or slaves or parents. The other view can't say that. But secondly, I refuse to accept the premise that NT laws given to the church are somehow culturally driven. This is a confusion of the two kingdoms again. Yes, case laws in civil societies are culturally driven, because we are talking here about the cultures of mankind. (People don't have fences on their roofs today). But laws in the church belong to a transcendent culture, the culture of heaven, the unchanging culture of God's invisible temple. There is nothing cultural about offering up prayers of incense or offering your bodies as living sacrifices. If there are laws pertaining to functions that seem to contradict principles like Galatians 3:28, then perhaps we've misunderstood *the principles*. I'm arguing this morning that this is exactly what has been going on, and its results have been devastating to the transcultural kingdom of Christ. There is no question that these kinds of arguments have made the church look exactly like the world, rather than being different from it.

Let's look now and see at what the point of all this is. The point is not to somehow suppress slaves, women, or Gentiles. Heaven knows that God has always viewed all people as equal in his eyes. Anyone who ever uses the Bible to create a sub-class of human being, to justify racism, to justify treating other humans as cattle or slaves by their very nature, here only to serve me, is worse than an unbeliever. This kind of sin knows nothing of the image of God or of the love of Christ.

The point is to get you to learn to read your Bibles properly and to see how you can make proper applications. We don't want to be Christians who are forced by our own theology to continually have to figure out ways to justify contradictions that we have created or to turn the culture of heaven into something that continually changes with the whims and winds of fallen sinful human beings. Look again at the point of this passage, and this time view it in terms of Galatians 3:28.

The law could not impart life (vs. 21). But Scripture imprisoned everything under sin, so that the promise by faith in Jesus Christ might be given to those who believe. You see? The law here has nothing to do with cultures and accommodation, but to creating slaves who cannot save themselves. The point of vv. 21-22 is that God imprisoned and made people slaves of sin so that God might make the promise to Abraham real by displaying his grace, his power, his sovereignty, his election. Through faith you receive the promises, and through faith there is no distinction in these classes, nor has their ever been. But when you view the law improperly, you think in an entirely different way, and confuse the entire passage at the core.

Again, vs. 23, "before faith came we were held captive under law." But, the law was our guardian until Christ came, in order that we might be justified by faith (vs. 24). Again, it is justification that is in view here, not functional outworkings of slaves or women or whoever. "Until faith came" is not talking about there being no faith in the OT. It is talking about faith coming ... to YOU. Before faith came to you, the law was given as a guardian (not as a means of attaining your salvation, but as a means of teaching you your need for faith). But now Christ has come to you, and he has come in such a way that no longer do you look to the promise of Abraham for a coming Christ, you look at the promise fulfilled in Christ. And by looking back on his death and resurrection you are saved by faith in what he did. Do you see anything in these verses about functions within the body of Christ?

"Now that faith has come, we are no longer under a guardian" (vs. 25). This does not mean we no longer have any use whatsoever for the law. It means that now that you are saved, the law has performed the work God intended it to perform, which is to lead you to Christ and the need for faith in him to save you from what you could not save yourself from: slavery. Christ has set you free. You are justified by his grace. But, of course, law still serves a function in your life. And that is the key component missing in these misreadings of Galatians 3:28. They suppose that whatever laws were given were culturally relative, in effect eviscerating the laws and making them of no purpose. Paul isn't making that kind of argument here. Don't make the text say something it isn't trying to say.

Brothers and sisters, in Christ you are all sons and daughters of God through faith (vs. 26). If you are Christ's, then you are Abraham's offspring, heirs according to the promise (vs. 29). The whole section and continuing on into the next is about showing you how the promises given to Abraham have come true in Christ. God has torn down the walls that once divided our entrance into the blessing that came by law, and he has torn them down in the obedient work of the Son of God.

If you have been baptized into Christ, you have put on Christ. You have become priests of the living God. You are able to serve before him in his temple: Gentile, free, male, female, child, adult, eunuch, whole, slave, free. This isn't talking about the functions within the body, nor the roles that obtain in it. Think for a moment about marriage and creation. God created them male and female, but the two shall become one. Did marriage obliterate role distinctions in the OT because "the two become one"? That's the same argument feminists and others use in Galatians 3:28. Even feminists will argue that in the OT there were role distinctions. Their whole premise is that these role distinctions are erased by the new covenant. But right there in Genesis 2:24 you have the same basic kind of idea of merging two into one that you have in Galatians 3:28. But neither verse is talking about such things.

If you are in Christ, you belong to him and he has made the way easy for you to come to him. You don't have to become a proselyte. You don't have to try and search out freedom. You don't have to become a man. You don't have to wait until adulthood. You don't have to try and seek physical wholeness. All you "do" is trust in Christ by faith. Then the promises are yours. God is proven true. You are Abraham's child, sons and daughters of the living God.

Galatians

A Father's Love for his Wayward Child

Paul's Perplexity about the Galatians

[12] Brothers, I entreat you, become as I am, for I also have become as you are. You did me no wrong. [13] You know it was because of a bodily ailment that I preached the gospel to you at first, [14] and though my condition was a trial to you, you did not scorn or despise me, but received me as an angel of God, as Christ Jesus. [15] What then has become of the blessing you felt? For I testify to you that, if possible, you would have gouged out your eyes and given them to me. [16] Have I then become your enemy by telling you the truth? [17] They make much of you, but for no good purpose. They want to shut you out, that you may make much of them. [18] It is always good to be made much of for a good purpose, and not only when I am present with you, [19] my little children, for whom I am again in the anguish of childbirth until Christ is formed in you! [20] I wish I could be present with you now and change my tone, for I am perplexed about you.

Galatians 4:12-20

Paul the Arrogant Boastful Narcissist?

I'VE RUN INTO THIS IDEA IN REAL LIFE more than once. Someone comes to a verse where Paul says something like, "Brothers, I entreat you, become as I am," they throw up their hands, and in mocking ridicule say, "That Paul was the most ego-centered, narcissistic, self-important man who ever lived. Who does he think he is? How can anyone take his words as Scripture? It goes against everything Jesus told us about denying self, loving others, and seeking to be last." I've had roommates, family members, and

Christian friends all respond to the Apostle Paul this way. Some I know even lost their faith over it.

How tragic that people cannot learn how to read the Bible properly. How devastating that a misunderstanding would cause someone to lose their faith. How sad that the Bible gets twisted and distorted, especially, the words of the Apostle Paul, who in reality is one of the most *selfless* human beings that ever walked the planet, whose love for others caused him to tear his hair out when they turned against the truth, who was stoned and beaten for trying to give them the message of comfort, who became so ill at times—possibly over the stress he placed upon himself to seek the good of others—but still managed to shine the light of Christ upon those who dwelt in darkness.

What we have before us today is a gut-wrenching, tear-jerking, passionate plea of a minister to his flock, of a concerned mother to her wayward children, of an angry father towards those who are seeking to harm his sons and daughters. This is not the ramblings of a narcissist, but as one commentator writes, "… one of the finest practical applications of 1 Cor. 13, written by Paul himself. Though the Galatians have failed Paul, his love toward them never fails, for love is long-suffering and kind, and even now hopes all things."[1]

Let's begin by looking at how the bad interpretation stumbles out of the gate. Yes, Paul implores, "Brothers, I entreat you, become as I am." But he does not stop here. He is not putting the focus on himself for he continues, "… for I also have become as you are" (Gal 4:12). What is going on in this verse? We will quickly learn what it means to emulate Paul. But what does it mean that he became as they are?

What he means is that he would not let any lawful but potentially divisive thing stand in the way of showing these Gentile pagans the love of Christ and proclaiming to them the gospel. He explains exactly what he means here (in our verse) in the letter of 1 Corinthians, where he had the same approach. "To the Jews I became as a Jew, in order to win Jews. To those under the law I became as one under the law (though not being my-

---

[1] William Hendriksen and Simon J. Kistemaker, vol. 8, *New Testament Commentary : Exposition of Galatians*, New Testament Commentary (Grand Rapids: Baker Book House, 1953-2001), 176.

self under the law) that I might win those under the law. To those outside the law I became as one outside the law (not being outside the law of God but under the law of Christ) that I might win those outside the law. To the weak I became weak, that I might win the weak. I have become all things to all people, that by all means I might save some. I do it all for the sake of the gospel, that I may share with them in its blessings" (1 Cor 9:20-23). To the Philippians he writes something similar. "I count everything as loss because of the surpassing worth of knowing Christ Jesus my Lord. For his sake I have suffered the loss of all things and count them as rubbish, in order that I may gain Christ" (Php 3:8).

Just here, I have to sigh and take a deep breath. I remember the word of Peter who said about the words of Paul, "The ignorant and unstable twist to their own destruction" (2 Pet 3:16). It seems like I can't explain something Paul said by quoting something else Paul said without having to explain that for people, too. What I have just quoted, about Paul becoming all things to all men, has been run with by more than one person trying to justify all manner of unlawful things, especially in the realm of worship. And so I want to clarify my clarification.

I said a moment ago that Paul would not let any "lawful" but "potentially divisive thing" stand in the way. Never once do we find the Apostle perverting the moral law to win someone. He does not become a prostitute in order to win prostitutes. Never once do we see him tinkering with God's worship to make it "seeker friendly" in order to win "seekers." Rather he says, "I received what I also delivered to you…" (1 Cor 11:23). Paul isn't talking about that kind of thing. Instead, he has in mind living amongst people of differing customs and cultural habits in such a way as to not be a stumbling block to them in their daily lives. In other words, he is talking about "things indifferent": how you act at a meal, what you do with your time during the week, etc.

Not everything is an indifferent thing. Theft is not a thing indifferent. The worship that takes place in heaven with angels and saints is not a thing indifferent. But we have examples of things indifferent. If a Jew, for example, could not even stand to be in the presence of an uncircumcised fellow in order to even gain a hearing, then Paul (who was not obliged to this law) would have his companion circumcised in order to gain that hearing. And thus, when he took Timothy with him, he had him circumcised (Acts 16:3).

In Thessalonica, another Greek city, Paul took up a craft and worked with his hands to pay for his food (2 Thess 3:7-9). For those people, coming in with a message and expecting payment for that message was an offence and a burden, because apparently, those people were quite poor. It also appears that their lack of money was due in part to laziness, as many of them would not work for their own food (2 Thess 3:10). Paul did not do this because he "had" to under some kind of legalistic compulsion, but "to be an example to imitate" (see also 1 Thess 2:9-10; 1 Cor 9:14-15, etc.), which is exactly what he says to the Galatians in 4:12. In the verses which explain this, Paul says there what he says here, "imitate us." Obviously, this is not about "be like me," but "be holy, blameless, and learn to live godly quiet lives. Learn not to make other people unnecessarily angry. Learn to think of others before yourselves, etc." This is the chief end of living in community with one another.

Now, Paul brings this up here because it serves the purpose of a larger argument. What he is going to do is call back to their memory how he came to them, how they accepted him, how they so eagerly received his message. Then he is going to contrast this with what is presently happening to them because of the false teachers: how they now seem to scorn him, how they are being lured away, attacked, and reimprisoned, and how they are being flattered and are having their base desires catered to.

Everything has changed with them, so much so that Paul is perplexed about the entire situation. Thus, this passage is extremely relevant in a church (or day in the church) where God's people are being lured away, enticed, duped, and tricked by false teachers who not only introduce false gospels, but cause the Christians to mock traditional Christianity, to scorn orthodoxy, to ridicule traditional worship, to hate the old ways, and to leave the path trodden by the Apostles, church Fathers, and Reformers. That day is here, and it seems as if throughout church history, that day is always here. Therefore, you could not find a more relevant passage for the church than what we are studying today.

Let's continue with Paul's argument. The Apostle desires the people to become like him as he became like them, and even as—when he first came to them—they did him no wrong (Gal 4:12). What he means is, they had every reason, according to their cultural and religious beliefs, to harm him, to mock him, even to kill him, but they did not do that. Instead, they accepted him. Paul is talking here about something I'm betting you have never put together like this before. It is really most remarkable.

Received as an Angel

He says, "You know it was because of a bodily ailment that I preached the gospel to you at first, and though my condition was a trial to you, you did not scorn or despise me, but received me as <u>an angel</u> of God, as Christ Jesus" (Gal 4:13-14). You ask, what's so remarkable about that? Let's see if we can't reconstruct what he is talking about. You can thank God's using Luke to preserve some very important information about the visit of Paul to the heart of Galatia, the city of Lystra (Acts 14:8-19). When we read Galatians in light of Luke, it is very interesting.

The key to understanding what Paul is talking about is the phrase, "an angel of God." You remember that at the beginning of the letter, Paul condemned even angels, if they were to preach a gospel contrary to the gospel of Jesus Christ (1:8). In that instance, the angel acts as a herald, a messenger, which is what "angel" means. In this instance, being received as an angel is directly related to physical health.

It just so happens that in the Greek pantheon (and this would therefore be the religion of these Galatians prior to coming to faith in Christ), there is a god who functions as the chief messenger to the gods, but also as the chief healer of mortals. His name is Hermes. Hermes has had an impact upon our English language. The word hermeneutic, which means to interpret and is therefore related to *messages*, comes from Hermes. The word hermetic seal, which is a vacuum you place over things like foods to preserve them, comes from Hermes. Hermeticism is an esoteric, Gnostic magical religious system that adopted the caduceus as its symbol. You've seen the caduceus before. It is the intertwining serpents around a winged pole that is the symbol of most health agencies around the world. In other words, the caduceus is the symbol of *healing*.

(See Picture of Caduceus Next Page)

At any rate, you wonder how any of that is relevant? Acts 14:8ff tells us that when Paul and Barnabas came to Lystra, there was a crippled man who had never walked. He listened to Paul speaking. And Paul, looking intently at him and seeing that he has faith said, 'Stand up.' And the man began walking. Suddenly, the entire crowd lifted up their voices in unison and said, "The gods have come down to us in the likeness of men!" (remembering older times such as in Genesis 6:1-4 or angels coming to Sodom and Gomorrah). Luke then records, "Barnabas they called Zeus, and Paul, Hermes" (Acts 14:12). When Paul went to Galatia, because of his preaching and ability to heal, they thought he was Hermes, a god (or as the LXX translates 'god', an angel).

Zip back now to Galatians 4:13. Paul has come to these particular Galatian people because of an illness. In other words, he could heal others, but he could not heal himself. He acts like Hermes, but he doesn't act like Hermes.[2] Back in Acts, Paul and Barnabas were both indignant that the people were trying to worship them, and so they told them, "We also are men, of like nature with you, and we bring you good news, that you should turn from these vain things to a living God, who made the heaven and the earth and the sea and all that is in them. In past generations he allowed all the nations to walk in their own ways, though he did not leave himself without witness (in his common grace)." But it concludes, "Even with these words they scarcely restrained the people from offering sacrifice to them" (Acts 14:18).

---

[2] The Paul as Hermes connection in Galatians has been considered by many commentaries. R. Alan Cole, vol. 9, *Galatians: An Introduction and Commentary*, Tyndale New Testament Commentaries (Downers Grove, IL: InterVarsity Press, 1989), 25, 171; Max Anders, vol. 8, *Galatians-Colossians*, Holman New Testament Commentary; Holman Reference (Nashville, TN: Broadman & Holman Publishers, 1999), 51; Timothy George, vol. 30, *Galatians*, electronic ed., Logos Library System; The New American Commentary (Nashville: Broadman & Holman Publishers, 2001), 324; Clinton E. Arnold, *Zondervan Illustrated Bible Backgrounds Commentary Volume 3: Romans to Philemon*. (Grand Rapids, MI: Zondervan, 2002), 286.

With this as the background, understand what a remarkable thing Paul is saying to the Galatians. Let's assume that he is referring in Galatians to another city, since it is clear that in Lystra, Paul is not ill. Perhaps he is referring to the next city he went to (Derbe), since it says that Jews from Antioch and Iconium came to Lystra and persuaded the Galatians there to stone Paul and drag him out of the city, supposing that he was dead (Acts 14:19). Obviously, Paul would have been severely injured and may very well have gotten quite ill, since he was at the point of death. In light of this, it is very curious that Paul tells Timothy something almost identical to what we have going on here in Galatians and he refers to this very event, "You, however, have followed my teaching, my conduct, my aim in life, my faith, my patience, my love, my steadfastness, my persecutions and sufferings that happened to me at Antioch, at Iconium, and at Lystra—which persecutions I endured; yet from them all the Lord rescued me" (2 Tim 3:10-11). Timothy did what the Galatians are no longer doing.

So he comes to a city, where his reputation has preceded him. These people, too, accept him as an angel from heaven, a god among men (as Paul says, as the Lord Jesus himself). They have heard of his preaching and his healing. Yet, before them is an ill man who cannot heal himself. They could have despised and loathed Paul for not being able to heal himself, and they could have yielded to the temptation to do so.[3] But they did neither.

Paul says that his condition was a "trial to you" (Gal 4:14), but they did not scorn him. This is one of the most commendable things he says to these people in the entire letter. When you think about the whole idea of it all, it is a remarkable grace of God that they didn't stone him, too. But God used this event to allow Paul to proclaim the gospel to these people who were in bondage to Zeus and Hermes, and to set them free from the devastating religious darkness that they were under.[4] Can you see how all

---

[3] Hendriksen, 172.

[4] "Before Christ, the Galatians had been **slaves** to pagan gods such as Zeus and Hermes. When they believed in Christ, they had been delivered from this bondage. They could not claim any credit to say they had achieved a knowledge of God. God had taken all the initiative to form a love relationship with them so that he knew them. Now Paul asked them why they were turning back to the **weak and miserable** bondage of legalism which could not produce life or righteousness or freedom." Anders, 51.

of the spiritual-worldview stuff we have discussed in this letter has helped prepare you to understand the context here properly? You have truly entered into the way of thinking of these ancient pagans. Because of it, you are also able to understand why Paul is so upset. He knows that from which they have been set free, and for the life of him, he cannot understand why they would want to return to it. He himself was under bondage to the law as a Jew, and not in a million years would he want to return to that.

We are seeing the same thing occurring in our own day, as a once Christianized west becomes more and more pagan. Today is it cute and fun, running back to the gods with open arms. We act like frolicking little school children who don't realize they just met a child molester on the way home. If God is not gracious to us once more, I fear that in a generation or two, when there is no more light of the gospel allowed to penetrate a once glorious culture, people will be *begging for freedom* from these demonic creatures that now hold our culture in their clutches but make themselves seem so harmless. Only the gospel can set a person free from them, because only Jesus Christ has conquered them and won the victory.

What Has Become of You?

With that, Paul now wonders, "What has become of the blessing you felt?" (Gal 4:15). In other words, he is returning now to the place they find themselves today. They were once so quick to receive the weak things of this world which shame the wise things, in spite of the cognitive dissonance they had with their worldview and Paul's health. They were so receptive of Paul, when their entire worldview said they should not have been, that he says, "You would have gouged out your eyes and given them to me." Perhaps this is a reference to something that happened to Paul when he was stoned in Lystra?[5] It may just be hyperbole, to show how

---

[5] At the end of the letter Paul refers to the "big letters" with which he writes (Gal 6:11). Some commentaries will note that it is possible that the "bodily ailment" Paul speaks about could be something having to do with his eyes, but most dismiss it. However, if the ailment was brought on by stoning, it could account for weak eyes (they were damaged with a rock), for the big letters and why he used a scribe to write his letters (Rom 16:22) (the rocks damaged his hand), and it is possible that, being so close to death, he could have been easily overtaken with something like malaria or epilepsy (both have been suggested as the "ailment").

great their affection and tenderness was towards him when he arrived there.

Now, this is no longer clear. He writes, "Have I then become your enemy by telling you the truth?" (4:16). It is not clear what he is talking about here. Perhaps he is thinking of what he just wrote to them in this letter. Perhaps he is referring to the last time he visited them. Whatever the case, it has to do with the false teachers who are leading them astray, causing them to return to the very things (bondage to sin, the law, and the devil) that they were released from.

"They make much of you, but for no good purpose" (Gal 4:17). They are being flattered. Their ears are being tickled. They are being told the things they want to hear in the flesh. Their guard is no longer up, because they like what they are being spoon fed. Their cyanide tastes like sugar. They feel in charge. They feel powerful.

But "They want to shut you out." They are being told, "Do not listen to Paul. He does not have your best interests in mind. He does not want to give you power over your own life. He does not want you to obey God, but rather to break God's law. Stay away from him. Have nothing to do with him." The false teachers are attempting to isolate the Galatians so that they can pick them off like the lone animal that gets divided from the herd. It is easy prey.

They are doing it "so that you may make much of them." It is their own self-importance that is in mind here, not God's. This is an ironic thing to say in light of how I began the sermon. Paul says, "Become as I am." Now he says, "They want you to make much of them." The ideas are complete opposites. Paul wants them to emulate his selflessness, his weakness, his humility, and even their own original attitude towards him, so that they might return to Christ who is strong. But these men want to be flattered, to be propped up as great teachers, to be magnified and worshiped as those who have the "secret knowledge" to the "higher life." Paul wants the Galatians to emulate his actions. But these men want them to puff up their own persons.

Now, in vs. 18, he says, "It is always good to be made much of for a good purpose, and not only when I am present with you." In this verse, he is remembering that on that former occasion, when he came to them so distressed, he was the attention of their wholehearted devotion. This is the way they are acting now towards the false teachers. When he was there before, the attention they gave to him was "for a good purpose." That is, it allowed them to hear and to receive the gospel he had been preaching. It was because of their single-minded love and attention to him that they heard the gospel. But now, this same character trait is causing them great harm. It is a double-edged sword. This reminds me of how each of us has a strength and a spiritual gift, but how those gifts are often our greatest weaknesses.

The person gifted in speech is often heard, and if what is said is good or important, it is a good thing. Yet, this same kind of person very often never listens to others. And so the strength becomes a weakness. Those with gifts of serving are often a great help to the church or to a family, and this is a vital and important thing. Yet, such gifting can sometimes cause them to be too busy, like Martha, who didn't have time for Jesus. It can also cause the person to well up with anger, asking why others aren't so helpful as they are? The strength becomes a weakness. In the case of the Galatians, their ready desire to accept everyone allowed the gospel to come to them, and now it is, ironically, causing them to abandon it. You must beware. Know your gifts, the things you are good at, but know the weaknesses that accompany those gifts. Do not let yourselves be hindered by the trappings of sin that can result when you exercise your gifts.

The end of this section now sees the deep affection that Paul feels for these people bubble to the surface. "My little children" (vs. 19). Like each of the Apostles, Paul sees his job as a missionary as giving birth to new life-forms. Those who convert under his ministry are his children. He is their father. Or, in this case, he is their mother. "I am in the anguish of childbirth until Christ is formed in you!"

This is one of the few times that an analogy like this comes from an apostle (see 1 Thess 2:7). We see God, of course, giving this kind of imagery towards Israel. Jesus speaks this way about the end times. But here, *Paul* is speaking about giving birth. He is saying that he does not want their lack of faith to cause an abortion. The idea here is that a group is never fully secure, because they can always turn away.

Notice, I said "a group." Paul is not speaking about losing salvation. He is speaking to a group where some are saved and most are acting like they are not. He can't judge hearts, especially in a letter to everyone, but he can judge actions and confessions. As a group he is "perplexed about" them (Gal 4:20). Notice also the word "again": "I am again in the anguish of childbirth" or birth pangs. William Hendriksen writes, "Having been displaced in their affections by others, Paul's birth-pangs have returned." The birth pang may very well be literal, like the great suffering and stoning he endured in Lystra for the sake of Christ. Hendriksen continues, "He hopes with all the ardor of his soul that, for the sake of their own salvation, the Galatians will renew their former attachment to him. O that they might be his children once more, as children imitating him! O that they might become as he is (vs. 12), trusting solely in Christ for their salvation! O that they would cast aside all reliance on self, on law-works, as he, by the grace of God, had learned to do!"[6]

Is this not love showing itself in action? This is true love. Paul's tenderness for these people is as a mother to a child. His anger towards the false teachers is protective, like a father protecting his daughter from a pillaging enemy. People often think about love as a mere feeling, but here we see love as a verb. Love is patient. Love is kind. Love does all things.

Sometimes, love must be tough. Sometimes, love must be blunt. A child rushing into a busy street must be grabbed and spanked so that he will not do it again. It is for his own protection, not even necessarily because it was a sin, but simply because it was dangerous. Paul writes, "I wish I could be present with you now and change my tone" (vs. 20). He says this to let them know how much he loves them.

This then is how all pastors and elders ought to feel about each of their members and those who come to their churches. There needs to be great concern, but that concern also needs to be parental and focused on the long-term welfare of the children. Paul has displayed that in this passage, not in some narcissistic self-aggrandizing way, but in a most selfless compassionate way, by suffering for his child, by protecting his child, by training his child, by warning his child, by letting his child see how much he cares for him.

---

[6] William Hendriksen and Simon J. Kistemaker, vol. 8, *New Testament Commentary : Exposition of Galatians*, New Testament Commentary (Grand Rapids: Baker Book House, 1953-2001), 175.

I pray you would know that your pastor and elders feel this way about you. The things we do here, we do for your good, as imperfect as we are. We desire nothing more than for Christ to be formed in you. We want your delivery to be healthy and happy on the Day of Christ, so that you may know eternal love of a heavenly Father. Let us pray for God's church, here and abroad, that he would send pastors and elders who care about His children, that he would protect the sheep from the wolves, that the truth would be spoken, that the leaders might pattern their lives in such ways as to be emulated. And let us pray that God would bring many more people to himself through the selfless missionary activities undertaken for those who do not know Christ.

Two Women, Two Covenants

²¹ Tell me, you who desire to be under the law, do you not listen to the law? ²² For it is written that Abraham had two sons, one by a slave woman and one by a free woman. ²³ But the son of the slave was born according to the flesh, while the son of the free woman was born through promise.

²⁴ Now this may be interpreted allegorically: these women are two covenants. One is from Mount Sinai, bearing children for slavery; she is Hagar. ²⁵ Now Hagar is Mount Sinai in Arabia; she corresponds to the present Jerusalem, for she is in slavery with her children. ²⁶ But the Jerusalem above is free, and she is our mother. ²⁷ For it is written, "Rejoice, O barren one who does not bear; break forth and cry aloud, you who are not in labor! For the children of the desolate one will be more than those of the one who has a husband." ²⁸ Now you, brothers, like Isaac, are children of promise. ²⁹ But just as at that time he who was born according to the flesh persecuted him who was born according to the Spirit, so also it is now. ³⁰ But what does the Scripture say? "Cast out the slave woman and her son, for the son of the slave woman shall not inherit with the son of the free woman." ³¹ So, brothers, we are not children of the slave but of the free woman.

Galatians 4:21-31

The Birth of Two Covenants

THE FOLLOWING IS A MOSTLY TRUE STORY of real people who lived a long time ago. She was born and raised in the land of the Chaldeans, in a fertile valley along the Great River (Euphrates) in Ur, the home of an ancient wonder known today as the Ziggurat of Ur. She was civilized and educated in the law-codes of the great civilizations of the east: Lipit-Ishtar and Hammurabi. She was named Contentious[1] or Quarrelsome by her father, but she had noble blood, for her name also meant "my ruler," and she was among the most beautiful women in the world.

One day, an idol-worshipping Semite named "You May Breathe," but who was known in the native tongue of those people as "Wild Goat" or "Wandering Man," came across the contentious beauty arguing with some women in the city streets. He had been looking for a mate for his son "Exalted Father." When he came to his son he cried out, "Go and take for yourself the beauty named Sarai, then we will leave this God-forsaken place in search of riches and fame to the east. Abram eagerly complied, and together with his brother, sister-in-law, and nephew, they set out west and came to a place that they settled and named after their fallen brother, Haran.

Now, Sarai was barren and bore no children to the Exalted Father. But one day, The Mighty Angel came to Abram and said, "I will make you the father of many nations." Abram believed this promise and it was credited to him as righteousness, for the one in whom he trusted was none other than the Creator himself, the God of gods and LORD of hosts. He told his wife and she was grateful. Her disposition changed and she adorned her soul with a gentle and quiet spirit, which was precious in God's sight.

A year passed, then two, then ten. Still, Sarai bore no children. Then the day came when she was no longer able to bear at all. Her womb dried up. Her hope vanished. She believed the promise with her husband, but perhaps they had been going about this all wrong. Being the student she was, she remembered the provisions made in the laws of the lands to the east. Where she came from, the story was famous in both legend and law.

---

[1] All the names are taken from *Exhaustive Dictionary of Bible Names* by Cornwall.

"Laqipum had married Hatala," the daughter of an important governor. Hatala, like Sarai, was barren and Laqipum had in mind to give her a divorce. That day, the courts decreed "Laqipum may not marry another woman … but he may marry a hierodule," that is a temple slave, a shrine prostitute, even a very priestess of the goddess. This woman would not be an equal in the marriage, but she may bear him a son. But, if, after two years, there is still not child, "Hatala may purchase a slavewoman" to bear a lad. Then, after the child is born, "he may dispose of her by sale wheresoever he pleases, but he must pay her five minas of silver."[2]

The idea was ingenious and perfectly legal. Abram had grown powerful in Haran and Canaan and Egypt. Wherever he sojourned, God had prospered him. So Sarai took for herself an Egyptian slave woman named Hagar: "Flight" or "Fugitive." After the allotted time had passed, she approached her husband with her simple plan, "The LORD has prevented me from bearing children. Go in to my servant; it may be that I shall obtain children by her" (cf. Gen 16:1ff). But the best laid plans of men and women, if they are in conflict with the promises of God, will never pan out the way we plan. Like his father Adam before him, "Abram listened to the voice" of his wife (Gen 16:2; cf., Gen 3:17).

On cue, Hagar gave birth to a child. The slave woman gave birth to a slave son, for no son of a slave can be born free. A covenant was born that day. It was a covenant wherein a man tried to bring about the promises of God through his own strength in a way that seems right to him, faithful to God in his own eyes, but which despises the power of the Almighty.

When she saw her son, the slave looked with contempt on Sarai. The free woman began to panic. The law was unclear at this point. She had miscalculated. Not only could the slave woman be divorced, if Abram decided it, so could she! Her old nature reared its ugly head. The old quarrelsome disposition returned with a vengeance. Like her first mother, she blamed her husband, "May the wrong done to me be on you! I gave my servant to your embrace, and when she saw that she had conceived, she

---

[2] "Mesopotamian Marriage Contract," *Ancient Near Eastern Texts*, p. 543. See also Hammurabi #144 (*ANET*, p. 172 and Lipit-Ishtar Law code #24, *ANET*, p. 160).

looked on me with contempt. May the LORD judge between you and me!"

But Abram consoled his bride, his true love. "Behold, she is your servant in your power, do to her as you please." The anger of Quarrelsome boiled over at the maid and she dealt harshly with her, and Hagar fled. The Lord intervened on her behalf and she returned to Abram under an unsettling peace. But she and the child she bore would be the cause of trouble for him and Sarai the rest of their lives.

Then, one day several years later, God came to Quarrelsome and told her, "You will bear a son in your old age," and he repeated the same thing to Abram. He changed their names to Princess and Father of Many Nations. They laughed out of incredulous joy. A year later, the impossible came to pass. The dead womb revived, the Spirit of Power through the Word of Promise created a life through the union of two people almost 100 years old. And Isaac, a second covenant, a covenant of grace and promise was born.

Later, the slave woman's son began to laugh in mockery and disdain for Sarah's blessing and she made Abraham divorce the slave women. Abraham was not happy, but God told him to listen to Sarah, for there could no longer be any fellowship between slave and free, between works and faith, between hope and disdain, between flesh and promise. Only one could stay. The other had to leave.

Paul's Use of our Story

Galatians 4:21-31 centers upon this story as part of the climactic argument that these opposites can never be spouses in the same household. The household of faith cannot live with the slave of works and flesh and disdain and futility. The polygamous marriage is a destructive, corrosive abomination. But too many Christians, both yesterday and today, refuse to get this message. Like Abraham, they love two very different sons, because both come from their own bodies, though only one originates in the heavenly promise. Our pride does not want to let go of those earthly works we give birth to, because our stiff-necked pride refuses to let us bend our knees and heads to see the riches set before the one who humbles himself in God's sight.

Paul has completed his most emotionally charged appeal to the Galatians to turn back to Christ and away from those smooth-talking ear-ticklers who want to force them back into slavery to sin, the law, and the devil. Now, reason returns to the fore with a most ironic turn of the argument. "Tell me, you who desire to be under the law, do you not listen to the law?" (Gal 4:21). This will become a regular argument from the Apostle who elsewhere says to the Jews, "You who brag about the law, do you dishonor God by breaking the law?" (Rom 2:23 NIV). You must not let the power of the irony pass you by, for we all have those parts of the law that we hold rigorously to in legalistic self-righteousness and pride. Anyone who wants to keep the law so badly that they will be justified or sanctified by it must realize that they simultaneously refuse to read other parts of the very same law that tell them such a thing is impossible and absolutely contrary to the promises of God. This is picking and choosing religion as we want it to be, like the lawyer who asked Jesus, "What must I do to inherit eternal life?" (Luke 10:25), or the Ruler who asked him the same (Luke 18:18).

Jesus always answers, "Keep the commandments." Which ones, we ask? "Try the top ten," he replies. "Oh, I kept all those," we respond smugly. "How about, then, if you sell everything you have, rich man," or "How about if you let the dead bury their own dead, family man, and follow me," or "How about if you stop lusting and hating in your heart. Try those." Then, we go away sad, because Jesus searches our hearts and catches us in our idols of works that we worship. Tell me, you who desire to hold onto that one thing under the law in order to show God what a good faithful Christian you are, don't you listen to the same law and what it tells you about slavery? This is what Paul is saying.

I could think of dozens of places Paul could go in the Torah to make the same point. As a Reformed Christian, I usually think of passages of total depravity that are right there in the law (by which Paul means the first five books of the OT). Genesis 6:5, "Every intention of the thoughts of man's heart is only evil all the time." "The LORD has not given you a heart to understand or eyes to see or ears to hear" (Deut 29:4). "Fire came out from before the LORD and consumed (the sons of Aaron) … for 'Among those who are near me I will be sanctified'" (Lev 10:2-3). Each of these verses shows from the Law our inability to keep law as dutiful slaves.

But Paul chooses a more literary tact. He goes to the story of Ishmael and Isaac, of Sarah and Hagar and he uses this real life historical event to prove that in the law there are two competing covenants personified in the life-events of Abraham, the man of faith. Because this is a story and not a command, it works on a deeper level of the soul. Like a fable which tells a moral through story, Paul uses this to get across a point. But this story is no mere story. It is true history. And yet, God saw fit to typify the very struggle the Galatians are facing in the lives of Abraham and Sarah, because no one is immune from the struggle between the flesh and the spirit.

Two Sons of Abraham

He says, "Abraham had two sons." I've told you about them here. They are Ishmael and Isaac. They are born in that order, because God often lets us do things our way before finally showing us that it will be his way. It seems this is the only way we ever learn … through difficult trials of experience. Now, Ishmael, he notices, is born by a "slave woman." But Isaac, he notices, is born by a free woman (Gal 4:22). For nearly two chapters Paul has been talking about slavery under the law vs. freedom that comes in Christ. What better way to cap off his point than with two women who exemplify it in their very lives?

Next he notices that the son of the slave woman was born "according to the flesh," but Isaac was born "through promise." There is an antithesis: slave vs. free; flesh vs. promise. "Flesh" is anything we try to do on our terms, through our efforts, be they legal or not. "Flesh" is that which belongs to this evil age. It is that which is natural, that which is possible, that which is "common-sense." Sarah's entire plan was hatched because she knew the law-codes of the east and she wanted to help God bring about the promise. Sometimes the worst ideas are hatched with the best of intentions. And this is the way we so often justify our own continued grasping of our last few legalistic handholds. It isn't even that the laws of Hammurabi and others were *necessarily* bad. It isn't that refusing to drink alcohol or dance or (fill in the blank) are bad things. It is that we use them for the evil purposes of helping God's promise come to us. This is called synergism, our symbiotic desire to help God out, because what he says is just, well, too impossible, or his timing seems to be late, or the idea seems like it involves too much suffering or whatever. As we will see, God doesn't need our help to do anything, especially to fulfill his promises, thank you very much.

The "promise," you see, is God's monergistic sovereign work of power and grace to bring about the impossible all by himself. All we bring to this table is faith, belief that God has the power to do what he promised (Rom 4:21), just as we believe that God calls all things into existence by his word alone, that he gives life to the dead and calls things that are not as though they were (Rom 4:17). As he told Abraham and Sarah, "Is anything too hard for the LORD?" (Gen 18:14). Hope, life, salvation, sanctification, peace with God ... it all comes through Promise.

Allegory and Biblical Interpretation

This is a slightly different kind of a sermon, because it is a different kind of a passage. In Gal 4:24 Paul says this story of the slave woman and the free woman, the son of flesh and the son of promise "may be interpreted allegorically." I will not camp out on this for long, though I certainly could. Today, in conservative Christianity, allegory is demonized as the worst of all possible things an interpreter of Scripture could ever possibly think of doing to a text. And yet here we find the Apostle doing just that. Allegory is an ancient method of interpretation. It was used by the Jews (e.g., Philo) and by the Church fathers (e.g., Origen). There is no question that it has been used improperly, but then again, so has every other method of interpretation at our disposal, including literalism, redemptive-historical, historical-grammatical and the like.

Where allegory goes astray is when the interpretation of a text is used as a launching pad for the creativity of the interpreter, irrespective of the thing being interpreted. Think, for example, of my favorite whipping boy: Goliath. Allegory tells you "slay the Goliath's in your life." Here, Goliath becomes a mere symbol for "giant obstacles" in your life such as financial distress, debilitating health, or irreconcilable marital differences. In this use of allegory, it does not really matter at all if Goliath was a real giant slain by a real shepherd boy, much less does the historical-redemptive context of the story matter. Never mind that God will not allow his name to be mocked by his enemies. Forget that this battle continues the battle of the seed of Eve and the seed of the serpent. Don't worry that Goliath and David ultimately point to Christ vs. Satan. All that matters is that we get to the "deeper meaning" of the story, which, of course, always and only has to do with you and your immediate problems.

Paul does not use the story of Sarah and Hagar in this way at all. In fact, it is just the opposite. It is *because* the story is real history, it is *because* Abraham and Sarah really had to go through this, that their life can be used as an allegory for the same struggles that we go through. It is *because* Abraham and Sarah sinned that he is able to relate Ishmael to us figuratively as representing our own works righteousness and justification according to the flesh. It is *because* they believed the promise by faith that he is able to relate Isaac to us figuratively as a covenant of grace, a covenant that comes only through the miraculous work of a sovereign God. The history, therefore, grounds the allegory, and in the best possible sense, the story is interpreted allegorically in order to show you from the lives of the patriarchs, in the law itself, that we must never think of attaining righteousness through our imperfect obedience.

Two Women, Two Covenants

So how does the allegory work? The Apostle says, "these women are two covenants." Here you see in as clear a place as I know in the Bible, that there are two opposing covenants at work in the Scripture. Reformed Christians call these the "covenant of works/creation" and the "covenant of grace." They don't begin with Abraham, but he certainly finds himself right in the middle of both of them. Paul uses a little different terminology and perhaps it is why he chooses this particular story. For him, one is a covenant of slavery and the other a covenant of freedom. This terminology gets at a more practical implication of the covenants, the very idea he has been speaking about for several chapters.

The "covenant of works" is "from Mt. Sinai" and it bears "children for slavery." Paul says that Hagar represents this covenant, because in a very literal sense, she is Abraham's slave-woman. He then starts to get more focused, and against the false teachers, the attack is of much greater intensity. "Hagar is Mount Sinai" (Gal 4:25). When you think of Mt. Sinai, you think of the Law. Sinai was hinted at earlier, in chapter 3, when he said, "the law was introduced 430 years later" and when he said "it was put into effect by angels." So here, in Hagar, the irony is thick. Hagar, who is a woman at the beginning of the book of the law, ends up standing for the very law that these Galatians Christians are thinking they should return to. But Hagar is the slave woman!

Paul adds that Sinai is in Arabia. This is one of the chief reasons more recent treasure hunters have gone looking for Sinai, not in the Egyptian wilderness, but in today's Saudi Arabia. But the point is theological. Arabia stands outside the land of Promise, and as such it is a perfect representation of that which is opposed to the promise. But at just this point, Paul turns the table. A smug Jew would appreciate this imagery, but certainly not the next. "She corresponds to the present Jerusalem." Suddenly, Sinai and Hagar become Jerusalem, the heart and soul of the Promised Land, the capital of David, the home of the temple, the center of the Jewish world. What Jew in his right mind would make that kind of a comparison? None would. But a Christian, who has understood the truth of the matter, he would see it quite naturally.

What is "present Jerusalem?" It stands for all the Jewish people, those who had been given the law by God, given the promises, the Patriarchs, and the covenants yet refused to see the end of each as he presented himself to them ... the Messiah, the Lord Jesus. Present Jerusalem stands for the children of Abraham who are the children of the flesh. It stands for biological Jews. It stands for children born "in the natural way." It is those false teachers in the midst of the Galatians. There is one child of Abraham who better represents this than does their actual ancestor. So here is more irony. While they sprang forth from Isaac, it is Ishmael who represents these faithless people, for Ishmael is the son of slavery, the son born through quarrelling, scheming, jealously, and the return to the Garden of Eden. For Paul, "present Jerusalem" "is in slavery with her children."

Now, if I were to ask you the opposite of the "present," what would your answer be? Probably either "the past" or "the future." We would expect Paul would contrast "present Jerusalem" with something like "future Jerusalem," wouldn't we? He does not do this. Instead, he contrasts it with "Jerusalem above" (Gal 4:26). Above is contrasted with below, heaven vs. earth, spirit vs. flesh, God vs. man, but not "present vs. future."

This is because the Apostle understands a great mystery. Jerusalem above is just as "present" as "present Jerusalem." This is the glory of the covenant of grace and the kingdom of Jesus Christ.

But many Christians to this day do not understand this, and it is a great travesty. In Revelation 21, for instance, the Apostle John sees "the Holy City, Jerusalem, coming down out of heaven from God" (Rev 21:2, 10). Many Christians see this as some kind of post-millennial, futuristic city, not to mention a literal city resembling a Borg Cube, that will be visible with telescopes trained in the right place. The *National Enquirer* does stories on how it has been spotted from time to time. But what does John add? She is "prepared as a <u>bride</u> beautifully dressed for her husband." Who is the bride of Christ? It is the church. In other words, this heavenly Jerusalem of the Apocalypse is none other than the church of Jesus.

Now, there is a sense in which this city is not yet fully prepared. And yet, for both John and Paul, she is here now. As Paul puts it, "She <u>is</u> (present tense) our mother" (Gal 3:26). This is allegorically speaking, of course, but for the past 2,000 years there has been a sense in which the famous line by Cyprian ("He can no longer have God for his Father who has not the Church for his mother") is exactly right. It is exactly biblical to understand the church as "our mother."

The "mother" Paul has in mind has her roots in the law; that is in the story of Abraham. She is Sarah, the free woman, the first and best wife, the apple of Abraham's eye, the one who laughed in delight at the promise of God. She represents the church. She represents the covenant of grace. Notice, the two things are intertwined and cannot be separate, for God has chosen to use the means of grace (i.e., word and sacrament) in the church as the primary way of saving and sanctifying his people. And this takes place in corporate worship.

This is exactly why it is so tragic when people do not understand the present nature of the heavenly city. It makes church superfluous, tedious, monotonous, without purpose. They fail to have open eyes when they come together to worship God. They can't see that when they assemble, they come to heaven itself. They come to the heavenly Jerusalem (Heb 12:21). They come to thousands of angels in joyful assembly. They come to the place where names are written in heaven. They come to God who sits on his throne, teaches them from his holy mountain, and saves them.

How many children have been born spiritually in the past 2,000 years as they have heard the word preached just once or week after week, and one day, they suddenly come to the self-awareness that they believe! But how many today are keeping their children from the means of grace because other things are more important, somehow, than going to heaven itself! And how many things are Christians inventing that serve as cheap substitutes for the real thing, because it seems like it will "work." Such replacements are the schemes of Sarah and Abraham to make the promise come more quickly, more naturally. But the promise can never come naturally.

Think for a moment about what it taking place here in the heavenly city when a soul is saved. Salvation, though it seems to the natural mind to be perfectly ordinary, the product of a will bent towards God through excitements or emotions or reason, is actually the sole result of an extraordinary miracle of God which comes through his chosen means through the power of the Holy Spirit (as he says in vs. 29, "Born according to the Spirit"). I do not throw the word "miracle" out often or lightly. Ordinarily, miracles are rare. But in this one exception, God has chosen to make the miracle of the new birth a regular occurrence because of his grace. But how can I say that it is a miracle if it happens all the time? Because of the allegory.

Who is Isaac? Isaac is the son of the "barren woman." Notice that the Apostle now proves his allegory by quoting from Isaiah, who has also used the story in the same way. "Rejoice, O barren one who does not bear; break forth and cry aloud, you who are not in labor! For the children of the desolate one will be more than those of the one who has a husband" (See Isa 54:1 LXX). In Isaiah, this comes immediately after the most famous Messianic prophecy in the OT. It must therefore have more than one referent. It can refer to the Virgin Mary, for she is barren through virginity, and yet begets the Son of God through a miracle. In the broader context of the book, it can refer to the return of Israel from captivity, and the blessings that will ensue from the divine intervention in the days of Cyrus, when God ordained that he should, for no good reason, let the Jews return to their land and rebuild their temple. But it can also refer to the spiritual offspring of Abraham.

The verse has in mind Sarah (and possibly Hannah, who had a similar experience; 1 Sam 2:5). The birth of Isaac was truly miraculous, was it not? Abraham was 100 years old and said to God, "Shall a child be born to a man 100 years old?" Sarah was in even worse shape. Though she was younger, her womb was utterly old, shrivelled, and dead. She was well past any reasonable child bearing. Yet, because of the Promise and the Holy Spirit, Isaac was born to Sarah. Now, if the new birth is likened to the birth of Isaac, it stands to reason that the new birth is a miracle. If the new birth is the opposite of the birth of Ishmael, it stands to reason that the new birth is a miracle.

But too many people see the new birth the same way they see Christian obedience to the law (including going to church, worshiping with the saints, or living life during the week): the perfectly natural use of the human will applied to God's command to repent. Now, while it is true that Abraham and Sarah had relations (Isaac's was not the equivalent of a "virgin" birth, though Sarah would not have been a virgin), they could have been doing this 24/7 for the next million years and nothing would have happened. In the same way, people can respond "in the flesh" in a kind of temporary faith and human belief to the command, and for a moment they may bear fruit (Mark 4:5-6; Acts 8:13, etc.). But unless God does the work, bringing both the ability to conceive and the new life itself, nothing we do in the flesh will matter. All we do is give birth to slavery.

Now, of course, we do respond to God in the gospel call (just as Abraham went to be with Sarah before Isaac was born), and of course, we live obediently to God as Christians. But these are the *results* of new birth and the ongoing power of the Holy Spirit, and not the cause of it. Too many Christians get both things backwards, and it has caused no end of trouble in churches and lives because of it.

Cast Out the Slave Woman

And it is the confusion that must no longer be allowed to remain in your heart, whether it is confusion over salvation or sanctification or the place of the law or the legalism you still hold on to, for this confusion is a mixing together of oil and water. They cannot stay together, and if you try to keep them both, guess which one will always evaporate in the hot sun of works or doubt or suffering? Grace never wins that battle in a human heart so full of self-deception.

The confusion over the two covenants creates a battle that wages in your soul and for your soul. You want to have God be sovereign and you be sovereign. You can't have two kings. You want to be justified by grace and by your works. You want sanctification to be about you letting God work in your life, rather than the Word of God by the Spirit producing new life and fruit. But what happened in the story of the sons? "Just as at that time he who was born according to the flesh persecuted him who was born according to the Spirit, so also it is now" (Gal 4:29). I could apply this in all sorts of ways, as I'm sure you are doing even now in your head. But let me turn to the story instead.

Paul is referring to Genesis 21:9. The ESV does a better job preserving the word, "Sarah saw the son of Hagar the Egyptian, whom she had borne to Abraham, laughing." Other translations opt to explain what this laughing was about, so they say something like "mocking." What was Ishmael laughing about?

Remember, when God gave the promise to Abraham and Sarah, they both laughed (Gen 17:17; Gen 18:12). I tend to think it was a laugh of mixed feelings. Half was the laugh of faith and hope. Half was the laugh of incredulous wonder. The two of them ended up arguing over it with the Angel of the LORD later on (Gen 18:12-15) and Sarah was afraid. But when Isaac was born, Sarah laughed again saying, "God has made laughter for me; everyone who hears will laugh with me" (Gen 21:6). There is no longer any doubt, only joy. There was no more confusion over the promise and what it brought about. But Ishmael saw the happiness his non-mother had in the birth of Isaac. Later on, when Isaac was weaned, she caught Ishmael in a mocking laugh, making fun of Sarah (who earlier laughed) and Isaac and God, and Sarah became infuriated. The mocking of doubt, disbelief, and human achievement is embodied in Ishmael who was born out of all of it. Now, the child of the sin, the one of slavery, wars with the person of freedom.

Ishmael's laugh is what Paul refers to as "persecution," and it refers to the battle between flesh and spirit, a battle we all have and prove each time that we sin. It is a disbelieving incredulous mockery of God's promise, his power, his sovereignty, and his right to do things his way apart from us. We want to do it ourselves. We want to take the credit, or at least half of the credit. We want to hold on to our pride, our work, our accomplishments. It makes us feel good. It makes us feel needed. And so, rather than laugh at our good fortune and enjoy the blessings and the freedom, we laugh in disbelief at what God tells us. Like Abraham, we try to keep the family of slavery and freedom together, but in the end one must go.

Sarah realized this immediately. Now that the promise had come and she was happy in God's grace, she grew great disdain for her sin and the result that it produced, and Ishmael was that produce. She cried out to Abraham, "Cast out the slave woman and her son, for the son of the slave woman shall not inherit with the son of the free woman" (Gal 4:30; Gen 21:10). Do you see how the actual historical event serves as a figure of our own temptations to turn back again to sin, the law, and the devil? It is because it all really happened that Sarah was able to make the right judgment at that moment.

Basically, Sarah was telling Abraham, "Divorce this woman and send her away." Abraham loved his son Ishmael and did not want to be harsh to Hagar, but Christ came to him as the Angel and told him, "Do not be displeased because of the boy or Hagar. Whatever Sarah says to you, do as she tells you, for through Isaac shall your seed be named. And I will make a nation of the son of the slave woman also, because he is your offspring" (Gen 21:12-13).

God showed kindness to Abraham, Hagar, and Ishmael. But at the same time, he also shows us that the two covenants will continue to interact in our lives. This serves to test us, to see the quality of our faith. It serves to purge us, to purify our faith just like Abraham and Sarah. And it serves to always be a referent to you, so that you can see from where you came.

He concludes, "Brothers, we are not children of the slave but of the free woman." God has set you free. He has taken the covenant of works and sent it away. The fruit of that covenant no longer belongs in our homes. You have been set free from slavery to the sin and the law and the devil. The promise has come. The Seed of Abraham was born. He passed the temptation, obeyed the law, and bound the strongman to give you grace. Now you may enjoy your freedom and laugh at your good fortune. Do not be bound any longer to those things you continually hold on to, those areas of prideful legalistic obedience, empty powerless superstitions, or vain strongholds of sin. Be free! Turn to Christ. Love his church. Worship God. And give thanks for the covenant of freedom and grace.

Galatians

It is For Freedom

that Christ has Set Us Free

¹ For freedom Christ has set us free; stand firm therefore, and do not submit again to a yoke of slavery. ² Look: I, Paul, say to you that if you accept circumcision, Christ will be of no advantage to you. ³ I testify again to every man who accepts circumcision that he is obligated to keep the whole law. ⁴ You are severed from Christ, you who would be justified by the law; you have fallen away from grace. ⁵ For through the Spirit, by faith, we ourselves eagerly wait for the hope of righteousness. ⁶ For in Christ Jesus neither circumcision nor uncircumcision counts for anything, but only faith working through love.

⁷ You were running well. Who hindered you from obeying the truth? ⁸ This persuasion is not from him who calls you. ⁹ A little leaven leavens the whole lump. ¹⁰ I have confidence in the Lord that you will take no other view than mine, and the one who is troubling you will bear the penalty, whoever he is. ¹¹ But if I, brothers, still preach circumcision, why am I still being persecuted? In that case the offense of the cross has been removed. ¹² I wish those who unsettle you would emasculate themselves!

Galatians 5:1-12

Spurgeon and Pentecost

DWIGHT PENTECOST AND CHARLES SPURGEON had a public encounter. It goes that Pentecost told Spurgeon how much he had gained in holiness since heeding a "still, small voice" that told him to give up tobacco. Spurgeon replied, "Notwithstanding what brother Pentecost has said, I intend to smoke a good cigar to the glory of God before I go to bed tonight … If anybody can show me in the bible the command, 'Thou shalt not smoke,' I am ready to keep it; but I haven't found it yet. I find Ten Commandments, and it's as much as I can do to keep them; and I've no desire to make them into eleven or twelve." On another occasion, it is said that a brother reproached Spurgeon for his cigar smoking. He replied that he would give it up if he ever smoked to excess. "And what do you regard as excess?" asked the brother. "More than one at a time," Spurgeon said.

These quaint little stories make some people very angry. And there are other stories told about Reformed theologians who would intention-ally drink alcohol whenever perfectionists or Wesleyans came riding their high horses into town that positively cause steam to boil out the ears of the same people. When a person like Spurgeon responds like this to critics who say that you can't be a good, moral person if you smoke, he is attack-ing one of two forms of legalism as I see it in the Bible, one of which our passage has in mind today.

Two Kinds of Legalism

I would define legalism as any legally imposed threat to the free gos-pel of Jesus Christ, either in the form of biblical laws or man-made taboos. One kind of legalism imposes man-made rules upon people in such a way as to make them think that if they follow these rules, they will be victori-ous Christians living the higher life as opposed to carnal Christians who haven't put God on the throne yet. It is usually the case that man-made rules attack what we call sanctification (or growth in the Christian life), because few people have enough nerve to actually say that following non-biblical rules will somehow merit justification and God's favor. The idea is that sanctification is my work brought about my way which seems to me should be something God would approve.

Paul speaks about this kind of legalism in Colossians when he brings up the rules of the aesthetics, "'Do not handle, Do not taste, Do not touch' (referring to things that all perish as they are used)—according to human precepts and teachings." He says, "These have indeed an <u>appear-ance of wisdom</u> in promoting <u>self-made religion</u> (literally "will worship") and asceticism and severity to the body, but they are of <u>no value in stop-ping the indulgence of the flesh</u>" (Col 2:21-23). Jesus ran into this kind of legalism with the Pharisees who were obsessed with something we call "fencing the Torah (the law)." Jesus' entire Sermon on the Mount is directed at this. The teachers of the law say one thing ("You have heard that it was said ..."), but God (Jesus) says another ("But I say ..."). When Jesus says, "But I say ...", he is giving the actual teaching of the OT, the things that he originally told Moses on Mt. Sinai. But the Pharisees wanted to be clever. They thought that if they could put a wide enough fence around God's laws, through imposing human laws on top of God's laws, that while we might break some of those human laws, we would not be able to get close enough to God's laws in order to violate them. This is will-worship, and it is performed in ignorance of the truth.

It has always been strange to me that Calvinists who hate free will would sometimes give into it when it comes to self-made religion. But we are no more immune than any other Christian, because as Paul says, these things appear outwardly to us to be a good idea. If we can stop the outward sin, then the heart will take care of itself (never mind that the heart is desperately wicked and deceitful). They seem to be things that actually help us further our way down the road of religion and holiness. But we forget two things.

One, the religion that God loves is outward, not inward. It helps the poor and widow. It loves its neighbor and it's God. It is consumed with being kind and merciful rather than promoting itself in the eyes of others. Two, the law can create no power to help you keep it. If this is true of God's law, how much more those laws that we invent that God hasn't even spoken about? Thus, the law was actually given to increase our sin, not to snuff it out. This is the exact opposite purpose we have when we sincerely invent laws to help us contain our fleshly desires. In our ignorance or disbelief of what God tells us about the law, we end up cursing ourselves, like Adam and Eve before us.

The other kind of legalism is one that imposes God's laws upon God's people for the purpose of causing them to think that through obedience to them, they will be accepted or acceptable to God. This is very similar to the first kind of legalism. The purpose is the same. Like the first kind, this is sometimes used with regard to growth in the Christian life. As Paul says to the Galatians, "After beginning with the Spirit, are you now trying to be perfected by the flesh" (Gal 3:3). But this kind is also used even prior to sanctification, in the initial declaration of righteousness we call justification. People are made to think that if they perform God's laws that he will then look upon them with favor and declare them holy.

This, too, ignores something vital. Holiness in God's eyes is absolute purity. It is purer than 24 carat gold, cleaner than water from an artesian spring. Not a single sin can taint the waters of our holiness if we want to be justified by our works. Paul seems to be more concerned with this kind of legalism in Galatians 5 for he says, "You who would be justified by the law; you have fallen away from grace" (Gal 5:4). He uses circumcision, the ancient ceremony given to Abraham, as his law of choice. But beware, lest you think that Paul is picking on circumcision because it is a ceremonial law that has passed away. His concern is not with something that has passed away, but with using a law—any law—in the Bible to try and justify yourself.

Consider what he tells the Romans. "You who preach against stealing, do you steal? You who say that one must not commit adultery, do you commit adultery? You who hate idols, do you rob temples?" (Rom 2:21-22). Notice, these are the Ten Commandments. They have not passed away. Everywhere you turn in the NT, Christians are told to keep the Ten Commandments. What he is concerned with in both instances is keeping them to earn God's favor. So don't let circumcision trip you up as we move through the passage today. Keep in mind that Paul is using this law as an example, and it is one that he uses quite vividly as he saves some of his harshest condemnation anywhere in his letters for those who would impose this ritual upon the Gospel that trusts in Christ by faith alone.

Stand Firm

If we return to my Spurgeon stories for a moment, you will quickly see why he and so many other Reformed Christians have felt it vital not to give in to legalistic tendencies, but to resist them fervently. Paul begins Galatians 5, "For freedom Christ has set us free; stand firm therefore, and do not submit again to a yoke of slavery." Stand Firm! Against what? Against legalism and for freedom. This verse is the very heart and soul of the letter. It is worth taking a moment to consider.

For most of two chapters now, Paul has been telling us about the slavery we were under, whether we were Jews or Gentiles prior to coming to faith in Christ. Slavery is a terrible condition, but it is what the whole world is under in one form or the other, be it slavery to sin, the law, or the devil. But "Christ has set us free." If you skip over this too quickly, you will miss the powerful significance of this.

How did Christ set us free from sin and Satan? By becoming sin on the cross and giving up his own life by dying for us in our place. In other words, the freedom Christ won for us cost God everything. Father was separated from Son. The only begotten son of God tasted death that he did not deserve. God Almighty was punished with the fiercest wrath ever known, so that we might no longer be under slavery. If, therefore, we return again to fall under the whips of the masters who used to beat us mercilessly, we turn our back on Christ (he is of no advantage to us), we are cut off from Christ, and we have fallen away from grace.

This is what both kinds of legalism do. They cause us to stand between two opposites. They mix together incompatible compounds. What happens when you mix glycerol with nitric and sulphuric acid? It generates heat and results in a massive explosion. Trying to live with both freedom and legalism is like walking in the bright sun of a hot day with a leaky canister full of nitro-glycerine. (Have you ever seen the movie *Vertical Limit*)? At any moment it could explode. You do not want to die in that state, my friend. For if returning to law is really a cutting off from Christ because you have abandoned faith alone, then there is only one direction you will go in the explosion, and it isn't up.

How Serious Is It?

Therefore the Apostle commands us (it is an imperative, a command, not a choice), "Stand firm." "Do not submit again to a yoke of slavery." Legalism is not a room in the castle of heaven. It is the dungeon in the pit of hell. It is a different gospel altogether. What we are saying this morning is the working out of Paul's anathema at the beginning of the letter. "If anyone preaches another gospel ... let him be eternally condemned." It is serious business to stand up against a kind of religion that looks so good on the outside, but which is full of spiders and webs and all kinds of decaying corpses on the inside. That is why Reformed Christians have so often decided to die on this hill. The law and the gospel distinction is that important. We want you to hear that "good news" really is and must remain GOOD NEWS.

I want you to think for a moment about something. The gospel comes to a person with absolutely no cost and no obligation. It is utterly free. Just believe that Christ has done all of this for you, and God will look upon you with favor through the merit of Christ and you will be saved, because Christ did all things necessary to please the Father and he offers it to anyone without price. But what is so good about sometime later having to finally pay up? Who wants to return again to slavery? If I tell you, "Now brother and sisters, I know I told you that Christ was enough. And he is, in a way. But he really wants you now to be good little boys and girls. He demands now that you do what he says, if you want to stay in his good graces." This is not good news. But to those who do not understand the power of the Holy Spirit to change a person's desires, it sounds utterly abominable. Standing firm keeps the good news GOOD.

Consequences of Not Standing Firm

If we will not do this, the consequences are grave indeed. Verse 2: "Look: I Paul, say to you that if you accept circumcision, Christ will be of no advantage to you." Circumcision is the example he gives, only because this seems to have been the particular law the false teachers were using to begin their dastardly effacing of the gospel. What did circumcision do for Abraham? Well, Paul shows us in Romans that Abraham received circumcision as a sign of the faith that he had for many years prior to being circumcised (Rom 4:10-12). It was a symbol of the circumcision that God had given him in his heart (Rom 2:28-29).

But circumcision served another function in the inscrutable plan of God. Circumcision also set apart a physical people in their flesh. Last week I showed you through Hagar and Sarah that two covenants always remain side by side. This is seen in circumcision. Israelites were always supposed to have remembered that Abraham was given this as a sign of his faith. But under the terms of the law, if they chose not to believe that, then circumcision would stand as a sign of their conditional covenant of works, wherein God would bless them if they obeyed and punish them if they did not. You must remember, Galatians 5:1ff comes immediately after the "two covenants" which stand side-by-side in Ishmael and Isaac.

One covenant represents works and the other represents grace. But both are there as two potential means of salvation, as long as you meet the terms and conditions. The terms of grace are faith alone. The terms of works are perfect obedience.

It is the covenant of works that is clearly what the false teachers were forcing the Galatians to return to in their own particular teaching on circumcision. They were not pointing to faith that is shown in the sign, but to temporary physical standing in a covenant of works. Thus, verse 3: "I testify again to every man who accepts circumcision that he is obligated to keep the whole law."

Remember, Paul does not have a problem with circumcision *per se*. As it says in vs. 6, "In Christ neither circumcision nor uncircumcision counts for anything." He could have Timothy circumcised (Acts 16:3) without any feeling that he was forcing Timothy to come under the terms of the covenant of works. If you approach the law as he did, that it counted for nothing in terms of meriting God's favor, then it didn't matter if you got circumcised or not. As he finishes Gal 5:6, "But only faith working through love [counts for anything]." But if your attitude towards the law is that this obedience will make God like you or even somehow cause you to become more holy, then you have returned to slavery and must perfectly keep the law.

I did not make this idea up that you have to keep the whole law perfectly if you want to return to keeping any one part of it. Paul said it right here (Gal 5:3). James says it, "Whoever keeps the whole law but fails in one point has become accountable for all of it" (James 2:10). The Law says it too. "Be holy as I am holy" (Lev 11:45), which as Jesus said means "Be perfect" (Matt 5:48). What is the consequence of returning to the law? It is devastating.

Using circumcision as the launching point, Paul says, "You are severed from Christ, you who would be justified by the law; you have fallen away from grace." The verb *katargein* literally means "to cut off."[1] Do you see the word play with circumcision? It means that you have made

---

[1] Timothy George, vol. 30, *Galatians*, electronic ed., Logos Library System; The New American Commentary (Nashville: Broadman & Holman Publishers, 2001), 359.

Christ's death of no effect. This is not because Christ's death is ineffectual. It is effectual because of the power of the Holy Spirit to transfer you into the covenant of grace through election. But a return to the law is a return to the covenant of works and a desire to please God through your right-eousness rather than Christ's.

This is what it means, then, to fall away from grace. It is not a fal-ling out of salvation. Remember, Paul is talking to a group here. He is not singling out individuals. As a group, they are returning to works and abandoning grace. Anyone who does this within the group is in grave danger of proving their own profession of salvation through grace to be a lie. Their names were really not ever written in the Book of Life by God, but were forged there by us, as if we have the right to put ourselves in such a book as that! Paul is hopeful for true believers here, and for the group as a whole (Gal 3:10), that God's word will not return void in this instance, but will powerfully call the people back to their senses.

But there are subtle yet deadly forces that are surrounding the Gala-tians like bulls of Bashan, trying to get them to abandon Christ. So Paul wonders aloud, "You were running well. Who hindered you from obey-ing the truth?" (Gal 5:7). This is an interesting choice of words. To obey the truth is to obey the gospel. But to obey the gospel is to *believe* by faith and not by works of obedience.

Such deceivers are "Not from God who calls you [through the Holy Spirit and the Word]" (vs. 8). Someone else is calling to them, wooing them with a siren's song to the rocky islands far out at sea, where they will perish in the storms and obstacles of fleshly "obedience." This someone obviously sounds divine to them. Their message seems so pure, so good. It is definitely religious. It is from the Bible after all, that we learn about circumcision. God is the one who told the Jews not to murder or steal or take his name in vain. He is the one who said, "Do all these and you will live."

But he is also the one who said, "You can't do these things, because I am a holy God and I have not given you a heart to obey me or ears to hear me or eyes to see me." They don't want to remember those words, be-cause depravity is never a popular message. They only want to teach things that will puff up the pride of the listeners and, in return, make them appear before the whole world to be super-apostles, great teachers of wisdom and morals.

Paul uses the metaphor of leaven in bread (Gal 5:9). It is one of his favorite figures (see 1 Cor 5:6-8). He doesn't really explain it here. He just says, "A little leaven leavens the whole lump of dough." But in Corinthians he ties this language to the sacrifice of Christ. "Cleanse out the old leaven that you may be a new lump, as you really are unleavened. For Christ, our Passover lamb, has been sacrificed. Let us therefore celebrate the festival, not with the old leaven, the leaven of malice and evil, but with the unleavened bread of sincerity and truth." The context of Corinthians is the sinful actions of the church. The same will be true here very soon, as well, as he tells us that these Galatians, so high and mighty in their desire to return to the pure obedience of the law are at the same time, "biting and devouring one another" (Gal 5:15). In other words, as Sarah Palin might put it, "How'z that keepin' the law thing working out fer ya?" You can't even treat each other with a little love and respect! How do you think God will then be pleased with your circumcision?

Leaven is a substance you put in dough to make it ferment (like yeast) or produce gas and rise (like baking powder). It doesn't take a lot to work itself through the entire lump. This is the way the false gospel of legalism works, too. It doesn't take a big bite to see that suddenly, your entire way of thinking has been changed, and you have abandoned the gospel. It doesn't take very many people in a church to confuse the gospel to start kneading slavery to sin back into the bread of the church through gossip or bad Bible studies or corrupt influence. This is another reason why it is imperative to stand firm and not let yourselves give into your very natural desires to improve upon God's law or take his laws or your own and suddenly think that by them you are justified or sanctified.

We are an unleavened bunch, a group that does not find our satisfaction in the tasty bread that we bake with the yeast and baking powder of our own good works. We are the people who feed upon the Bread of Heaven, our Passover lamb, who was stricken by God because of our sin and so that we might be justified in his sight apart from our works, but only his.

Any other gospel than this is an abomination and a curse. Paul's confidence is that the Galatians will take no other view than the truth (Gal

5:10). But he adds his severe anger towards those who are leading his little children astray. "… and the one who is troubling you will bear the penalty whoever he is." He adds one of the most severe condemnations in the entire Bible for vs. 12, "I wish those who unsettle you would emasculate themselves." I will not be Victorian here and dance around what is going on, because you need to see how serious this all really is.

This word (*apokopto*) like the one earlier (*katargein*) means "to cut off." It translates the word "to crush" (*dakkah*)—as in testicles—in Deut 23:2. It means to castrate or emasculate. In other words, Paul is being very crude here, saying that if they are going to start with the tip, why don't they just (as the NIV says, "go the whole way") and cut the whole thing off! He is angry with a righteous indignation that is hardly, if ever, paralleled anywhere else in his letters, because this false teachings puts the Galatians in danger of hell fire.

Again, this is why we must stand up strongly and persistently against false teaching that tries to rob the good news of its power and us of our joy. One thing about legalists you will notice, they are NEVER happy people. And how can they be, when their whole life is consumed with outward perfection (and often oblivious to the inward heart), and all because of a false understanding of the purpose and work of the law? I want you to be happy people. I want you to be free people! I want your obedience to come from joy, not servitude and obligation. I want you to know the true power from the tyranny of sin, a power which can only come from being set free and living as it really were true … for *you*.

Friends, you are not justified or sanctified or glorified by keeping the law. The gospel sits right in the middle of the passage today. "Through the Spirit, by faith, we ourselves eagerly wait for the hope of righteousness" (Gal 5:5). "Who hopes for what he already has?" (Rom 8:24), Paul asks in another place. But through faith in Christ's righteousness, we believe that God looks upon us *as if we were righteous*, because this is the only way he may bring unrighteous people to heaven. He also does it because he loves his Son and is preparing us to be a spotless bride, *through the gospel*—word and sacrament—which alone cleanses us and washes us through the power of the Holy Spirit so that we may be presented holy and blameless on the great wedding day.

Like I said at the beginning, there are a lot of Christians who do not like the way Spurgeon responded to Pentecost. It makes them angry because they love their own self-righteousness. They love to be puffed up by their own works in holiness. It makes them feel good and worth something to God because of what they do for him. This is a reaction Paul knew far too well. He says in vs. 11, "If I, brothers, still preach circumcision, why am I still being persecuted? In that case the offense of the cross has been removed." What in the world is he talking about?

Let me get at this by going back to our opening story. I don't particularly like smoking. I think it is pretty disgusting and it clearly harms people's health. But like all gifts of God, it can also be enjoyable, especially when you are around a bunch of Reformed Baptist pastors after an ARBCA meeting. Moderation, common sense, and a little wisdom should be used here. Spiritually speaking, smoking is nothing and not smoking is nothing. It doesn't make you a lesser or better Christian. But what if it is something that could lead to sin, like drunkenness and alcohol (or fill in the blank). If you get drunk, it must obviously make you a lesser Christian, one that has lost God's favor, right? No!

Nothing we do in obedience or in disobedience makes us better or worse Christians. All that matters in this area is faith alone. This is where persecution comes in, because people hate this kind of a message. They think it is an excuse to sin. They think it shows disdain for the law of God. But this is because such people have not come to a knowledge of the truth.

The amazing and ironic thing that these people will never understand is this. Once a person is really saved by such a free message, God begins working in that person's heart to give them new desires and affections. Sometimes immediately, sometimes over a long period of time, the sins that once entangled begin to lose their excitement and appeal. We find ourselves wanting better things. We find ourselves wanting to obey and please God, because God is working out our new life by the Holy Spirit through the means of grace: word and sacrament. But the farthest thing on our mind now is that by doing or not doing we are somehow meriting God's favor, because we know that God is pleased with Christ and he looks upon us as he looks upon him for his sake.

The offense of the cross, that which is a stumbling block to Jews and foolishness to Gentiles, is our absolute freedom from the obligation to keep the law out of merit or pride. This is absolutely backwards from every other religion on the planet, including many falsely disguised so-called Christian teachings. The offense is that Christ has done it all and that you and I have nothing to add to his perfect work. It is natural to think that if we do something good, we will be rewarded by God with life, as long as the good outweighs the bad. It is natural to think that if the flesh can be subdued, the spirit and heart will follow (never mind that it is the heart that caused the flesh to act out the sin in the first place). Even when we know we grieve the Holy Spirit and bring about God's displeasure because of our sin (and we do), we also realize that it is always a loving Father's displeasure and that he never stops loving us or bringing about what is best for us as he promised.

People who hate grace persecute those who stand up for it. Get used to it and learn to recognize what is going on. If a person is being persecuted for their message because they tell people their only hope is outside of themselves to the Lord Jesus Christ, then they are being persecuted exactly as Jesus told them they would, because the world hates Christ, through Christ loved the world. Believe in his love and in his death, and God will save you from your sins. And do not give up faith alone at any point. For to do so is to put your soul in peril. Do not return to the yoke of the law. If you must to cling to something in the day of trouble, cling to Rock, for he shall never be moved or shaken. His burden is yoke is easy and his burden is light.

Freedom ... To Serve

¹³ For you were called to freedom, brothers. Only do not use your freedom as an opportunity for the flesh, but through love serve one another. ¹⁴ For the whole law is fulfilled in one word: "You shall love your neighbor as yourself." ¹⁵ But if you bite and devour one another, watch out that you are not consumed by one another. ¹⁶ But I say, walk by the Spirit, and you will not gratify the desires of the flesh. ¹⁷ For the desires of the flesh are against the Spirit, and the desires of the Spirit are against the flesh, for these are opposed to each other, to keep you from doing the things you want to do. ¹⁸ But if you are led by the Spirit, you are not under the law.

¹⁹ Now the works of the flesh are evident: sexual immorality, impurity, sensuality, ²⁰ idolatry, sorcery, enmity, strife, jealousy, fits of anger, rivalries, dissensions, divisions, ²¹ envy, drunkenness, orgies, and things like these. I warn you, as I warned you before, that those who do such things will not inherit the kingdom of God. ²² But the fruit of the Spirit is love, joy, peace, patience, kindness, goodness, faithfulness, ²³ gentleness, self-control; against such things there is no law. ²⁴ And those who belong to Christ Jesus have crucified the flesh with its passions and desires. ²⁵ If we live by the Spirit, let us also walk by the Spirit. ²⁶ Let us not become conceited, provoking one another, envying one another.

Galatians 5:13-26

Living Contradictions

OF OUR PASSAGE TODAY MARTIN LUTHER writes, A man is righteous and holy and does not sin insofar as he walks in the Spirit; but insofar as he is still prompted by lusts, he is a sinner and carnal. Therefore he has sin in his flesh, and his flesh sins; but he himself does not sin. This is a strange thought. The same man sins, and at the same time he does not sin. It is here that those two statements of the apostle John are brought into harmony. The first is found in 1 John 1:8: "If we say we have no sin, we deceive ourselves"; the second occurs in 1 John 3:9 and 5:18: "No one born of God commits sin." All the saints, therefore, have sin and are sinners; yet no one of them sins.[1]

When I read that this week I thought to myself, "Well, at least I'm not the only crazy person out there!" You see, I've thought for a very long time now that the Christian is a walking contradiction. I've never read anyone say my own thoughts to this so exactly.

This bizarre state we find ourselves in makes talking about the Christian life at the same time simple and difficult, obvious and confusing. What we have before us in Galatians 5:13-26 is perfectly simple to understand. God does not like sin. God does not tolerate sin. The law continues to show forth God's righteousness. The law never becomes obsolete. Who can't understand that? At the same time, it is difficult to understand this in light of the last three chapters where we are told repeatedly that to return to the law is to make Christ of no value? That is why so many Christians play games with the law on every conceivable level. Again, what we have before us is obvious. Paul talks about "the works of the flesh" (5:19-21) saying that they are "evident" or "obvious" (5:19). Everyone knows about the things mentioned in these verses. Even pagans like Aristotle (*Nicomachean Ethics* 2.5ff[2]) and Greek Stoics like Zeno (see Diogenes Laertius, *Zeno* 7.110-16[3]) made lists just like this.

On the other hand, it can be terribly confusing. At the end of this list Paul says, "I warn you, as I warned you before, that those who do such things will not inherit the kingdom of God." One scholar makes my point

---

[1] Martin Luther, vol. 27, *Luther's Works, Vol. 27 : Lectures on Galatians, 1535, Chapters 5-6; 1519, Chapters 1-6*, ed. Jaroslav Jan Pelikan, Hilton C. Oswald and Helmut T. Lehmann, Luther's Works (Saint Louis: Concordia Publishing House, 1999), Gal 5:21.

[2] He lists anger, fear, confidence, envy, joy, friendly feeling, hatred, longing, emulation, pity, and feelings from pleasure or pain.

[3] He lists: Covetousness, drunkenness, intemperance, pity, envy, emulation, jealousy, pain, perturbation, sorrow, anguish, confusion, fear, apprehension, hesitation, shame, perplexity, trepidation, anxiety. These move from outward to inward passions.

saying, "Although Paul is emphatic that we cannot by 'doing' the works of the law enter our promised inheritance (3:12, 18), but that entry is by faith alone (3:11), yet he strongly asserts here that by 'doing' these very different things we can bar ourselves from the kingdom."[4] How confusing. What are we to make of such a warning as this?

Flesh vs. Spirit

In light of these difficulties, perhaps the best place to start this morning is in Gal 5:17, for it shows the struggle between two opposites. "For the desires of the flesh are against the Spirit, and the desires of the Spirit are against the flesh, for these are *opposed* to each other, to keep you from doing the things you want to do." This verse is a summary of Romans 7 where it says things like "I do not understand my own actions. For I do not do what I want, but I do the very thing I hate" (Rom 7:15), or "I have the desire to do what is right, but not the ability to carry it out" (7:18), or "I do not do the good I want, but the evil I do not want is what I keep on doing" (7:19). It is amazing that anyone could argue that Paul— who talks the exact same way in both places—would have the Christian life in mind in Galatians, but the pre-Christian life in mind in Romans 7, but they do,[5] and that only further demonstrates the confusion that exists even in the strongest and best of Christian minds.

To appreciate our passage, it is critical to understand what is meant by "flesh" and "spirit." The word "flesh" occurs 6 times in our text, while the world "spirit" occurs 7 times, both are far and away more than any other words in the section. A lot of people have this idea that "flesh" is my

---

[4] R. Alan Cole, vol. 9, *Galatians: An Introduction and Commentary*, Tyndale New Testament Commentaries (Downers Grove, IL: InterVarsity Press, 1989), 217-18. In fairness to Cole, he goes on to explain how this "paradox" works, "Paul's whole point is that *those who do such things* thereby show themselves to be without the transforming gift of faith which leads to the gift of the promised Spirit, which, in turn, leads to the fruits of the Spirit, the seal of our inheritance. To all these things the Christian has died already, as Paul will show below; therefore he or she shows the reality of the 'faith that justifies', and the reality of the new 'life in Christ' that is within, by a clear break with all these 'works of darkness', familiar though they may have been in the past. It comes as a shock when Paul, in 1 Corinthians 6:11, after a similar list of loathsome vices, says, 'Some of you were once like that', although he does hasten to reassure the Corinthians of their new standing in Christ. Paul only gives this 'black list' to remind the Galatians of what their past slavery to sin had been before the gospel brought them freedom in Christ."

[5] For example, the excellent commentary by Douglas Moo, *Romans*, NICNT (Grand Rapids, MI: Eerdmans, 1996), 445.

body and "spirit" is my spirit, sort of the inner me and the outer me idea. The NIV renders a potentially disastrous translation of "flesh (*sarx*) as "sinful nature," especially if you somehow think that "spirit" (*pneuma*) here refers to your spirit (the NIV guards against this by capitalizing "Spirit").

That would mean that in any one Christian there are two natures. Does that sound heretical to you? It should. There is only one person ever born of a woman who had two natures. Jesus was fully God and fully man, two natures in one person. Christians are not like this. We do not have a good nature and an evil nature inside of us, battling it out in some Gnostic cosmic war.

What is a Christian, then? A Christian is a person with one regenerated nature (a "new creation") living between two worlds. We are new creations, united to Christ Jesus by faith, now in mystical union with him as a head is to a body, as a branch is to the vine, as a husband is to a wife. We have been resurrected now ("you have been raised up with Christ;" Col 2:12), but only as we are in union with Christ ("it is no longer I who live, but Christ who lives in me;" Gal 2:20). Our physical resurrection awaits the coming dawn of the age to come. So, mysteriously, we are both raised and not raised.

The Spirit we walk by is not our own spirit, but the Holy Spirit, God in us, the Spirit of Christ, giving us life, bringing new fruit, creating new desires.[6] Our problem is not, therefore, biological or ontological or metaphysical, but eschatological and ethical. We are in the already and not yet. We live in the present evil age, but we belong to the eternal age to come. Our feet are in this world, while our head—that is Christ—is in the world above. We are new creations in Christ, but the old creation, including the world, the flesh, and the devil which have been conquered, have not yet been judged. The kingdom of God has been inaugurated, but not consummated. Today it is invisible, tomorrow it will be visible. We see through a glass darkly, but then face-to-face. We taste now of things to come, but do not understand its power. We come to heaven in worship,

---

[6] On flesh vs. spirit see Richard Gaffin, *Resurrection and Redemption* (Phillipsburg, NJ: P&R, 1987), 106-109.

but we leave to go back into our daily routine. Do you see the difficulty? It is easy to understand, but impossible to comprehend.

If "Spirit" refers to the Holy Spirit, "flesh" refers only partly to my wicked body including my members, my mind, and my emotions. More broadly, it refers to the evil age in which I live. This includes the powers and principalities in heavenly places which align themselves against me for my undoing. It includes the temptations that come from without, from Satan who uses both good and evil things to get me to fall into sin. It includes the patterns of this world with all of its vices (like the things in the list in 5:19-21), but also its basic desire to run and flee from God. It includes my own wicked heart which continues to beat, longing for the day it will be resurrected on the Day of the LORD. It includes my body which is decaying and rushing towards death. All of this is encompassed in "the flesh."

Milk and Meat

Why, oh why, does Paul begin to contrast these two things here? It is because at this point, he has finished giving the milk of theology. Now it is time to move into the meat of ethical living. He has told us about how we are justified: by faith alone. He has told us that if we seek to merit God's favor through anything other than trust in the merit of Christ alone, that we will be damned for all eternity.

He has explained that the law was given to increase, not decrease sin. He has pleaded with us to not give into our base instinct, which is to try to please God on our own. He has denounced anyone who preaches another gospel than this. He has proclaimed that the gospel must remain at all times absolutely free for the Christian and that even once the Christian life has begun, it must stay free for them. All of that is behind him now. There is no more to be said about that. It is time to move into something both obvious and yet difficult to understand, to chew on the paradoxical implications of that which he puts before us now.

At no time is the Christian ever encouraged or commanded to break God's law or to even entertain breaking it in his mind. Yet, at no time is the Christian ever under an obligation to keep the law to merit God's approval. At no time does God ever approve of the works of the flesh. Yet, at no time does stopping the works of the flesh ever make God approve of us. At no time will a person who practices ungodliness be allowed to enter the kingdom of God. And yet, those who commit ungodly acts may always be forgiven in Christ and justified; indeed those who have been justified who commit ungodly acts always remain justified and will inherit the kingdom of God. Do you see why Paul waits until the end to speak of ethics?

People think, "Doctrine? Now that is the meat of Scripture. Doctrine is the hard food to chew on. It causes discomfort, smelly gas, sometimes loose bowls. Better to give people milk to swallow if their constitution can't handle real food. Better to just preach the law and get into all that divisive stuff." (I often wonder about the lactose intolerance from the milk, but that's beside the point). I am saddened when I hear such things. Knowing doctrine is our only way of being able to properly digest the meat of God's law. Doctrine is like a good tea or a probiotic or a digestive enzyme. It helps me swallow and digest the ethical part!

Knowing what the law does (doctrine), how God approves of us (doctrine), why God will look upon us with favor (doctrine), how Christ did everything necessary for our salvation (doctrine), how God applies salvation to us through election, effectual calling, faith and repentance, mortification of sin (doctrine), how God has already yet one day will resurrect us from the dead (doctrine) is the only way we can ever possibly hope to obey God's law in a way that pleases him, which is out of utter thankfulness, love, and no compulsion or duty of obligation. If people don't have that first, they will find infinite numbers of ways of perverting obedience into pride or discouragement, "look at what I did" or "look at what I can't do." They will turn the ethics into soteriology, a way to salvation. Humans have been doing this since the Garden of Eden. That's why ethics is the meat and always comes at the end of Paul's letters.

Freedom in Christ = Freedom to Serve

We talked last week about freedom in Christ and how under no circumstances are we to ever live as if we were not truly free in Christ. As Luther was once asked, "If you are right, we are free to do anything we want, including sin." Luther responded, "Yes. That's right." Before I finish the quote, listen to what he said and let it sink in. That is what freedom is. We have the freedom to sin, because whether we sin or do not sin, we are not saved by what we do or do not do. We are saved by faith alone.

But, of course, Luther was not finished. He concluded, "Now, what do you want?" His point is that Christians want to please God, because they have been given the desire to do so out of love and thankfulness. Martin Luther was hardly an antinomian (someone against keeping the law). Read his commentary on the works of the flesh (Gal 5:19-21) and you will see that quickly enough. He hates unbridled, unrepentant, flagrant hatred of God's law. Nothing is more repugnant to him, especially when self-professing Christians (like the Popes and bishops he regularly encountered) are the perpetrators.

Because he is finished with the doctrine, Paul is now able to set us straight about Christian freedom. What should we do with our freedom? Sin? By no means. "For you were called to freedom, brothers. Only do not use your freedom as an opportunity for the flesh, but through love serve one another" (Gal 5:13). What I love about Paul's ethic, and Jesus' ethic, and the whole Bible's ethic is that it is not the ethic of the mystic. There is no naval gazing here. It is not obsessed with the self. Paul does not focus on inward spiritual disciplines, but upon outward acts of love and kindness.

Notice, the same Paul who just a moment ago said, "If you accept circumcision, Christ will be of no value to you" and "every man who accepts circumcision is obligated to keep the whole law" (Gal 5:2-3) now says, "For the whole law is fulfilled in one word: 'You shall love your neighbor as yourself'" (vs. 14). He says "whole law" twice. In one instance, he stays away entirely from it. In the other, he rushes hands outstretched to embrace it. Is Paul crazy, schizophrenic, utterly mad? No. He has finished talking about the law as a means of meriting salvation, and is now talking about it as a means of acting righteously in the kingdom of God. You can only act righteously in the kingdom of God *if you are already in the kingdom of God*!

Paul's words here remind us of the words of our Lord, who was asked, "What is the great commandment in the Law?" (Matt 22:39; Mark 12:31). Jesus answered two-fold, "Love the Lord your God with all your heart, soul, mind, and strength, and love your neighbor as yourself." Jesus didn't make that up on the spot. Rather, he was quoting his own words which he gave to Moses on Mt. Sinai as recorded in Leviticus 19:18. It is so sad when people try to pit Paul against James and/or Jesus or Jesus against the OT, etc. All of them go back to this same verse as the summary of the law. None of them say, "Well, you know, now we are in the dispensation of grace, so don't worry about all that love business." It still pertains today, because love is a reflection of the unchanging heart of God.

Paul now adds, "But if you bite and devour one another, watch out that you are not consumed by one another" (Gal 5:15). This verse is completely ironic. These Galatians are being seduced into returning to the law of circumcision in order to become "good" little Christians. The temptation is to legalism. If you just do this one thing, God will be happy with you. But Paul told them, if you return to one law to make God happy, you have to realize that only perfect law keeping will do this. Your problem, dear Christians, is that you are not keeping the law perfectly, even amongst yourselves. You are biting and devouring one another. The list of vices we will come to in a moment probably summarizes at least some of what that means specifically. The imagery of the sinning is quite vivid. In the way they treat one another, they are acting like … cannibals! They are eating one another. If they are not careful, this ghoulish dinner will see them, not as the eater, but the eaten. Their little pecks and nibbles will turn into bites and swallows. Sin against other Christians is so horrible that it is like cutting them up, putting a skewer through them, cooking them over a hot fire, and eating them for dinner. Hannibal Lector might lick his lips, but the LORD God turns his face at our sinful banquet.

But we often think, well the sins God really cares about are in my heart. Yes, it is true that God cares about what is in your heart, for out of your heart comes all manner of sins. But acting upon your evil desires is even worse. Jonathan Edwards used to speak directly to the unconverted in his congregation, imploring them that if they will not trust Christ, at least do good and right things, so that it will not be as bad for you in hell. Each outward sin, he believed, added another coal to the fiery furnace below. When we sin against each other in the church, well, there is really nothing worse than that. The only body we are allowed to consume is Christ's body, because Christ's body is the only food that will sustain us, that will save us. If we eat one another, we will be consumed.

This whole idea of "walking by the Spirit" (Gal 5:16) is so misunderstood today, but it is really quite simple. It isn't mystical or magical. We are not talking about higher life, victorious Christian living, holiness perfectionism, or putting God on the throne of your life; but very simply, "serve one another." Paul actually defines what it means to walk by the Spirit. We are not left to guess about it.

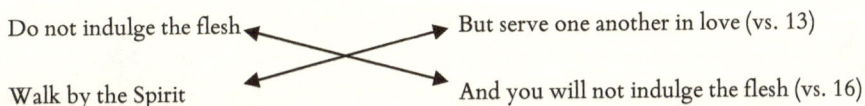

Do not indulge the flesh ——→ But serve one another in love (vs. 13)

Walk by the Spirit ——→ And you will not indulge the flesh (vs. 16)

Vs. 13 is an inverse parallel to vs. 16. He says, "Do not indulge the flesh" then he finishes, "you will not indulge the flesh." In between he says "serve one another in love" and "walk by the Spirit." Therefore, to walk by the Spirit is to serve one another in love. Simple to understand.

This is where the rubber meets the road. Paul does not say that walking by the Spirit is fasting and praying and reading your Bible every day. Those are not bad things, but it isn't what he says. He does not say learn all the theology and doctrine that you can as a church, then you will walk by the Spirit. Theology and doctrine are not bad things. He does not say, get involved in every activity in the church as possible, then you will walk by the Spirit. Getting involved in church is not a bad thing. He does not say stop doing evil things. Evil things are not good things. But what the Spirit of Christ loves most is the bride of Christ. He is the one washing her by the word. He is the one overseeing her until the Wedding Day. He is the one given to her as a deposit to come. The Holy Spirit loves the church, and therefore the church ought to love one another.

Notice that the law is given to prove all of this. The law expects that you will love yourself. Self-love is a good thing (self worship is a bad thing). What it adds is that you will love your neighbor as yourself. The law is broader than Paul's application here. "Neighbor" includes anyone you run into, especially your enemies, those who are hardest of all to love. Hopefully you won't think of any enemies in church here today, but I know people have had them in the past. Churches are full of that kind of thinking about one another. But in the church, especially, we are to love and serve one another, especially those we don't particularly like.

Serving does not mean "be and let be." It does not mean do good if they do good to you. It does not mean "harm none" (Wicca). It means going out of your way, in the church, to serve and help one another. It means looking for things to do and ways to help and then figuring out how to do them for people. Some of you here are so consumed with other things that you don't even think about how to serve those in the church. Work becomes all encompassing. Children take all your time. Health gets you completely down. Good things become idols. Bad things become excuses. And the church is harmed not even out of bad things, but out of not doing good things. Oh, how deep the applications of the law can go if we want them to!

We have seen vs. 17 and how there is a war within us. The Spirit of God wants one thing. The world wants another. We are caught in the middle, in a kind of no-man's land where we do what we don't want to do and we don't do what we want to do. Suddenly, we find ourselves returning to the law for help. Then, before you know it, we find ourselves either prideful again of how well we keep it or utterly depressed at how badly we pervert it. So Paul gives us good news in vs. 18, "If you are led by the Spirit, you are not under the law." This reminder simply encapsulates everything he has said for the last several chapters.

You are not under the law. You are free. We are not under the law. Use your freedom to serve one another. You are not under the law. Do not use your freedom to indulge the flesh. You are not under the law. What I have done here is move back and forth between law (imperative) and gospel (indicative). I call this the spiral of sanctification. The spiral starts with good news and through the Holy Spirit the good news changes you. It moves to law, which is holy, righteous, and good. But our flesh begins to take pride or lose faith because of the law. Then comes the good news to set us free again. Then we return to the law to see the things God loves. And the whole process starts over.

Together, this back and forth movement becomes up and down movement. The Spirit lifts us up through the gospel, and we knock ourselves down when we hear the law (or we puff ourselves up even higher than we ought). The good news is, we are already seated in heavenly places. We do not have to try to reach up into heaven any longer. And so our definitive sanctification becomes the grounds for progressive growth in godliness.

Definitive sanctification is that initial act of God setting you apart as holy and placing you in his temple as a vessel of worship. Progressive sanctification is the personal appropriation of the truth in the way you act, think, and live. It is all the work of God. Then it is all the work of you. You are not passive, but through the means of grace, God moves your will to desire change. Through word and sacrament, the Holy Spirit creates life and fruit in you. Then you go out and show forth the light and ripe food.

Works of the Flesh, Fruit of the Spirit

There are two contrasting ways you can act. One is the "works of the flesh." The other is the "fruit of the Spirit." Notice that one is a "work." The other is a "fruit." One is what you do to merit (or in this case, demerit). The other comes as a result of something completely outside of yourself. These works of the flesh are vices. Paul does not see the vices the way pagans do, with works of the flesh being things we don't ordinarily want to do, but only occasionally fall into because we are basically good. He sees them as the ordinary works of the flesh. It is our default mode, our sinful programming code. Also, pagans would view the virtues as things we can and should achieve on our own. Paul sees them, however, as the fruit of the Holy Spirit.

Christians commit works of the flesh. Unbelievers have a kind of fruit of virtue. Both kinds of people participate in certain kinds of ways in both categories. That is not the issue. The issue is that when Christians act virtuous, it is because of God's work in them, the fullness of his love overflowing through us. Conversely, when Christians sin, it is not what they want to do deep down, because they are in the Spirit. They have a war between pleasing God and carrying out evil desires.

Unbelievers have no war like this. Oh, they may war against the consequences of their sin, against being "found out," or against even some ethical principle they know is true. But they do not war against causing God displeasure. Also, when a non-Christian displays love or patience etc., they do not do it out of worship for Christ Jesus, but only out of self-exaltation or perhaps a higher ethic of pleasing another person. In no case does God's glory ever come into their mind, and this is the difference.

Also, many of the vices were viewed in the pagan world as either not so bad, or sometimes even perfectly acceptable. Those that were viewed as pretty bad were still viewed only this way because of how they affected us or those around us. They were never concerned with how God himself viewed them, and that is the root of the matter.

These lists are so extensive that we will look at both of them in more detail next week. Today, I can only just list some of them. The vices are perhaps just random things that came to the Apostle's mind, or some have tried to categorize them. Immorality, impurity, and sensuality seem to have sexual deviance in mind. Idolatry and sorcery seem to be more focused on religious practices. Enmity, strife, jealousy, fits of anger, rivalries, dissensions, divisions, and envy seem to be the way we treat one another. Drunkenness and orgies seem perhaps to return us to the first group or focus more on our own self-destructive behaviors.

The point I want to make here is the last phrase, "... and things like these." These kinds of lists are never meant to be exhaustive. Remember the man who came to Jesus and wanted a list, so Jesus gave him a list (the 10 Commandments)? But he viewed the list as exhaustive (not to mention only external). He thought that because he did all those that this was good enough. So Jesus added one more thing to his list, the thing he knew the man could not admit to keeping. If you are so smug as to look at this list and think, "I'm glad I don't do any of those," then I have another 650 laws in the OT for you to try.

What does it mean, though, that "those who do such things will not inherit the kingdom of God?" (Gal 5:21). Has Paul suddenly reverted to keeping the law for salvation? No. The best way to explain this is by going to another list, one that he gives to the Corinthians. In 1 Cor 6:9-10 Paul gives a similar list and says something similar about it, "The unrighteous will not inherit the kingdom of God." But he concludes this way, "And such were some of you." He then goes to definitive sanctification, "But you were washed, you were sanctified, you were justified in the name of the Lord Jesus Christ and by the Spirit of our God" (vs. 11). He is not so foolish as to spend 5 ½ chapters defending *sola fide* (salvation by faith alone) only to give it up here!

He does the same kind of thing in Gal 5:24. "Those who belong to Christ Jesus have crucified the flesh with its passions and desires." This is both definitive (we have died with Christ) and progressive (we mortify sin by putting it to death each time we are tempted). But the definitive grounds the progressive like an anchor grounds a boat in a storm. Paul is confident that the Galatians are believers, he has such a hope (see 5:10). So he concludes, "If we live by the Spirit, let us also walk by the Spirit. Let us not become conceited provoking one another, envying one another."

This "living by the Spirit" includes the following virtues: love, joy, peace, patience, kindness, goodness, faithfulness, gentleness, self-control. Paul says, "Against such things there is no law" (Gal 5:23). What he means is that you can't get into trouble being gentle with someone. No one has ever passed a law against being kind, and God certainly hasn't. The practical way to overcome vices is to engage in virtues just like the best way to kill weeds is to make your lawn healthy. Even Aristotle understood this. But in Christ, we understand that it is God who is working out our salvation through the Holy Spirit. These are the fruit that he gives to us because we live in the vine and draw our life from the resurrected life of Jesus Christ.

Therefore, in light of these things, I beseech you, come to the law with humility knowing that it is complicated. But come also to the law like a little child, knowing that it is obvious. You know what God desires. If you trust in Christ by faith alone, you know that he loves you. And if you are in Christ, you know what God is like. Therefore, do not leave here desirous to walk out and commit all manner of sins. But grow in the grace and knowledge of Christ (doctrine) and display such knowledge outwardly in the way you serve one another in love (ethics). May God give you grace to do so.

Galatians

Works from the Flesh

or

Fruit from the Vine?

[1] Now the works of the flesh are evident: sexual immorality, impurity, sensuality, [20] idolatry, sorcery, enmity, strife, jealousy, fits of anger, rivalries, dissensions, divisions, [21] envy, drunkenness, orgies, and things like these. I warn you, as I warned you before, that those who do such things will not inherit the kingdom of God.

[22] But the fruit of the Spirit is love, joy, peace, patience, kindness, goodness, faithfulness, [23] gentleness, self-control; against such things there is no law. [24] And those who belong to Christ Jesus have crucified the flesh with its passions and desires. [25] If we live by the Spirit, let us also walk by the Spirit. [26] Let us not become conceited, provoking one another, envying one another.

Galatians 5:19-26

Flesh vs. Fruit

THOUGH THEY ARE PROMINENT IN Galatians 5:19-26, the words "flesh" and "fruit" are actually significant ideas *throughout the NT*. The word "flesh" (*sarx*) occurs in 22 of the 27 NT books, a total of around 150 times. The word "fruit" (*karpos, akarpos*) occurs in 18 of the NT books, a total of a little over 75 times. In our passage, these two words show two sources from which a person may commit an action. We see, of course, that the flesh is the source of no good actions, but only flagrant acts of disobedience and sin. These are called "works" of the flesh. On the other hand, fruit that comes from the other source produces all kinds of good, God-honoring actions.

In the list, there is no hint that flesh ever produces a good action, or that the fruit of the other source ever produces a bad one. I think you would be hard pressed to find anything different anywhere else in the Bible. This leads to a difficulty since Christians do display the works of the flesh, and non-Christians display some form of the fruit of the Spirit. How do we rightly understand this? The answer to the Christian's dilemma is that we live between two ages, as I told you about last week. We have been raised with Christ, and yet our bodies have not yet been raised from the dead.

The answer to the non-Christian's dilemma is that they are image bearers. You must remember, it is the Holy Spirit of God who gives life, not just to Christians, but to all people (Genesis 2:7; 7:22; Psalm 104:30). The Spirit works in a general way to convict the world of sin (John 16:8). He came upon pagans like Balaam (Num 24:2) and Cyrus (Isa 45:1) so that they might prophesy and help God's people. Since the flesh cannot produce any good thing, and since the Holy Spirit comes in some way upon all people, we must therefore conclude that when unbelievers display fruit, it has to be the work of the Holy Spirit in some kind of common grace.

What then is the difference between the two people? This is the key question, because the Holy Spirit does not come upon all people in the same way. For Christians, the fruit they bear demonstrates their repentance and acknowledgment of utter dependence upon the Holy Spirit to regenerate them and give them life. For non-believers, as John Owen says, "Some indeed, receive him in a sort (or in a way), as to some ends and purposes, without any advantage finally unto their own souls. So do they who 'prophesy' and 'cast out devils' by his power in the name of Christ, and yet, continuing 'workers of iniquity,' are rejected at the last day."[1] It is the source and acknowledgment of Him that makes us differ, and those differences will continue on into eternity.

Work of the Flesh

---

[1] John Owen, *Works Vol. 2: Pneumatology* (London: Patenoster, 1826), 117.

This morning we will look at the two conflicting sets of actions and at the source of each. The first set of actions are vices familiar to both the NT, ancient Jews, the Greek world, and beyond. They are specific applications of the Ten Commandments, things forbidden by God that all people know because they are written on their hearts. There are fifteen things mentioned,[2] not an exhaustive list by any means. Some have tried to categorize the list. The most popular is 1) three sins of sensuality; 2) two sins of heathen worship; 3) eight sins with conflict; 4) two having to do with drunkenness. It may, however, just be a general list like a grocery list which may have some order to it, but is mostly jotted down as things come to mind.

Porneia. The first is a word used sometimes narrowly of prostitution (especially, temple prostitution), and sometimes broadly of immoral sexual relationships, hence the ESV's "sexual immorality." In the Greek world, as today, this vice was so common that it was generally not viewed as very bad at all, except when carried to excess. William Barclay writes, "It is significant that it is with this sin that Paul begins. The sexual life of the Graeco-Roman world in NT times was a lawless chaos … Paul lived in a world in which such sin was rampant, and in that world Christianity brought men an almost miraculous power to live in purity."[3]

Akatharsia. This word can mean dirtiness in the physical sense, pus or impurities in the medical sense, uncleanness in a ritual sense, or lack of purity or looseness in a moral sense. It is often used of ceremonial uncleanness in the OT. As with *porneia*, it seems to have sexual connotations here, though it can also refer to "error" (1 Thess 2:3). The ESV renders it as "impurity."

Aselgeia. The next word denotes licentiousness or debauchery or as Barclay puts it, "A love of sin so reckless and so audacious that a man has ceased to care what God or man thinks of his actions."[4] It can refer to exhibiting oneself, as in the idiot flasher caught this week in Boulder who said that as soon as they release him, he will do it again. But it can also

---

[2] Two more are in the textual traditions: "adultery" and "murder", but the evidence weighs out that these were later additions.

[3] Barclay, *Flesh and Spirit*, 24 and 28; cited in Longnecker, *Galatians*, Word Biblical Commentary, 254.

[4] Ibid., 31.

refer to any devising of lascivious behavior, and so the ESV translates it as "sensuality." These three words speak to our own sensually super-charged, sexually explicit western culture, which has uncanny parallels to the ancient Greek and Roman cultures. Paul says we are especially to watch out for this, because every other sin is committed outside the body, but these sins are committed against the body, which is the temple of the Holy Spirit. It is evident that these things are wrong, and we are not to do them.

Eidōlolatria. This word obviously means "idolatry," though it is never used in classical Greek or the LXX. Paul uses it with reference to an image of God (the second commandment) or the worship of another god (the first commandment), and also to eating food that had idolatrous associations but also more generally to being covetous or greedy. This last use of the word is interesting because it connects the first and last commandments together like a fastener links a chain. If you break any one commandment, you break them all.

Parmakeia. We get our word pharmacy from the next word. It can be neutral in meaning, but here it may refer to the use of drugs for poison or for use in sorcery (ESV) or witchcraft. This clearly has otherworldly implications, as the sixties proved to the world that had forgotten, certain drugs are doorways through to the realm forbidden for us to cross into. They do things to our souls that are unnatural. And they allow contact with creatures that are malevolent, powerful, and do not have our best interests in mind. We are to stick with the common, ordinary communication of God given to us in Word and sacrament.

Echthrai. The third list (if there is such a thing) begins with a word that means "enmity" or "hostility" or "hatred." The ESV renders it "enmity." This is not the word Jesus uses for hating your brother in your heart. It is an even harsher word that depicts the relationship to God when a person is a friend to the world (James 4:4).

Eris. This word means "strife" or "discord" or "quarreling" or "wrangling" or "contention." In the ESV it is "strife." Clearly, this word, the previous word, and several that follow have to do with how people treat one another and think about one another. In the context of Galatians, this would have to be focused especially on relationships in the church. Have you ever been in a church where people acted like this towards one another? Churches are not immune.

Zēlos. This word can refer positively to "noble passion" or negatively to "envy." It can mean intense devotion to God or to some other person or thing. It can refer to anger arising out of such devotion. It can refer to jealousy (ESV), an unfriendly feeling about someone else's well being or to envy and coveting, to have what is not yours, but which belongs to someone else. It is obviously closely related to the last few of the Ten Commandments.

Thumoi. This word also has a good and negative sense. It can refer to courage, or to rage or fits of anger (ESV). It is used of God's wrath (Rev 14:10) as well as Satan's rage (Rev 12:12) and human rage (Luke 4:28). It clearly refers to the last of these three here. Unbridled anger that shoots up like Mt. St. Helens erupting. Have you ever had this kind of uncontrolled anger?

Eritheiai. The next word is used in Aristotle for "canvassing for office" or "seeking office." More generally it is used for "working for wages." Over time, the word took on a negative meaning as something like "self-seeking" or "selfish devotion to one's own interests" or "selfish ambition." The ESV has "rivalries," which can certainly be caused by self-serving interests.

Dichostasiai. This word means "dissensions" (ESV) or "seditions." Its only other occurrence in the NT is Rom 16:17 where Paul warns the church to watch out for those who cause divisions. The word certainly applies to the circumcision party that is splitting the church of Galatia.

Aireseis. This word can mean a "choice" or "plan" or "purpose" or "preference." That doesn't seem to be the sense here. It can also mean "taking captive" or "capture." Hence, the ESV has "divisions." Different parties within Judaism arose (Pharisees, Sadducees, Essenes, Zealots) just as in the church we have many different denominations. These are not necessarily evil, but they certainly can be. So it could refer to "party spirit," or causing divisions within the church by grouping together into different factions or political parties that each seek to have their will imposed on the rest. Not only the Church, but individual churches have certainly seen much of this throughout the centuries. Most people seem think nothing of this, but it is listed in the same list as sorcery and sexual immorality. That leads to a point. Big sins and small sins are all listed here. There is no picking and choosing which sins you can enter into, which are really offensive, and which are acceptable. In God's eye, sin is sin. Notice, however, just how many of these sins are focused on how people act in the church. Fully half of them.

Phthonoi. The last of these words means "ill will," "malice," or "envy" (ESV). Envy seems to dominate the NT usage. It is closely related to jealousy. Clearly, God cannot stand abuse within the body of Christ. You must not treat one another in these ways.

Methai. The next word can mean "strong drink" or "drunkenness" (ESV). Strong drink, while not forbidden in the Scripture, certainly leads to drunkenness, which is. Why is drunkenness so bad? Because it makes a person lose control. Think about what happened to Noah (Gen 9:21). It opens the tongue to all manner of wicked speech. It causes people to make decisions they might not otherwise make. It makes them foolish and stupid. It causes chemical addiction that ruins people, families, children, and relationships, all while making the person think there is not really a problem. Basically, all of the other sins in the list are enhanced by drunkenness.

Kōmoi. The last word means "reveling" or "carousing" or "orgies" (ESV). These were often related to pagan worship (such as Dionysus). It does have a certain fit with drunkenness.

What do we notice about this list? First, it covers a broad range of sins. Second, it puts "big" sins in the same list as "little" sins, because in reality, there is no such thing. Third, some of these words have positive meaning, but each is being used to a destructive end. Fourth, half of them deal with violent, hateful, divisive actions in the church. Fifth, these are all works of the flesh. What each of these sins has at its absolute base is a love for self and disdain for others. Sexual sins treat the other sex as an object to be conquered rather than divine image bearers. Sins of worship seek guidance explicitly forbidden by God, often for the power and puffing up of the one participating in them. Sins of anger, jealousy, divisions and the like are all ways that we treat each other as sub-human. They are ways to usurp the power structure God has ordained and the fellowship God wants in the church. Sins of drunkenness are a sign that a person no longer cares about themself, but rather abandons self to other things. Ironically, they end up being just as selfish as the others, as the self-pity of the drunk is still selfish.

The Warning

After he completes the list Paul gives that ominous warning, "I warn you, as I warned you before, that those who do such things will not inherit the kingdom of God" (Galatians 5:21). What things? Things that originate in "the flesh." Do you remember when Paul says, "Flesh and blood shall not inherit the kingdom of God" (1 Cor 15:50). It is similar to this. Yet, in that same passage, he tells us that even heavenly beings have a kind of "flesh" (15:40), just as Jesus has a kind of flesh in his resurrected body. So what is going on?

In this passage, Paul tells us that the problem is that our flesh is "perishable" (42), "sown in dishonor" and "weakness" (43), "natural" (44). Adam was created a "living being" (*psuche*; *nephesh*; 45), but Jesus became a "life-giving spirit" (45), with a "spiritual body" (44), "raised in glory" and "power" (43), "raised imperishable" (42). Adam came from the dust and to the dust he shall return. Jesus has been raised forever and has ascended into heaven. This is, in a nutshell, what all things "in the flesh" do. They cannot inherit that which is eternal. They must be raised from the dead and sown as imperishable seed.

The warning is not talking about Christians who do deeds of the flesh, because as Paul acknowledges in other places and as I began with this morning, Christians do deeds of the flesh. But, something has changed with us. We "were washed", we "were sanctified", we "were justified" (1 Cor 6:11). Such "were" some of us. Past tense. How? Through faith and repentance. Calvin says, "Paul does not threaten that all who have sinned, but that all who remain impenitent, shall be excluded from the kingdom of God. The saints themselves often fall into grievous sins, but they return to the path of righteousness ... and therefore they are not included in this catalogue."[5]

---

[5] John Calvin and William Pringle, *Commentaries on the Epistles of Paul to the Galatians and Ephesians* (Bellingham, WA: Logos Research Systems, Inc., 2010), 166.

In another passage Paul says, "While we <u>were</u> living in the flesh, our sinful passions, aroused by the law, <u>were</u> at work in our members to bear fruit for death. But now we are released from the law, having died to that which held us captive, so that we serve in the new way of the Spirit and not in the old way of the written code" (Rom 7:5-6). This passage offers a nice transition to the next part of our passage in Galatians. First, it shows us what we were.

We were living in the flesh, but no more. Yet, there is that contradiction I spoke of all last week. We are still in the flesh, yet we are not living in the flesh. The explanation for this is a legal one and a mystical one. *Legally*, we died to the law. How? When we *mystically* died with Christ. We have been united with him through faith, in a *legal* declaration that we are not guilty and that Christ's righteousness is now our righteousness. *Mystically*, we have been raised with him in his resurrection. "It is no longer I who live, but Christ who lives in me," Paul said earlier in this letter (Gal 2:20), so that "the life I now live in the flesh I live by faith in the Son of God, who loved me and gave himself for me." So we both live in the flesh and yet do not live in it, because it is both I who live and yet Christ who lives in me; though I have not died, I have died, and though I have not yet been raised, I have been raised, because Christ went before me and did those things and God has united me to him in mystical union. Remarkable, isn't it? In Gal 5:26 of our passage here he said, "Those who belong to Christ Jesus <u>have</u> <u>crucified</u> the flesh with its passions and desires." In Corinthians he says, "Though we walk in the flesh, we are not waging war according to the flesh" (2 Cor 10:3), for we have divine power to destroy strongholds, arguments, lofty opinions, and everything that wages war against our flesh (vs. 4-5).

Second, in the Romans 7 passage, it says that the works of the flesh "bear <u>fruit for death</u>." "Fruit!" That is what Paul talks about next in Galatians, only this fruit is the <u>fruit of life</u>, the fruit of the Holy Spirit. He is the source of the fruit, not the flesh. If the source of the works of the flesh is the world, the flesh (that is our sinful minds and bodies), and the devil, then the source of the fruit of the spirit is the Holy Spirit.

Fruit of the Spirit

The second set of actions are virtues; also familiar to the NT, ancient Jews, the Greek world, and beyond. They are things against which there is no law. They are as follows:

Agapē. The first word on the list means "love." It is a word not found in classical Greek, which divided "love" into three categories: brotherly (*philia*); physical (*erōs*); and familial (*storgē*). The kind of love in mind with agape has had encyclopedias' worth of information written about it. You have heard much about it. It is a favorite topic of Evangelicals, and that is good. Agape is the kind of love that God himself has, which is expressed in verses like John 3:16. In Galatians 5 it is defined as "Faith expressing itself through love" (Gal 5:6) or "through love serve one another" (13) or "Love your neighbor as yourself" (14). It is a selfless, unconditional, serving love that always <u>does</u> (not just "wants" but "does") the best for other people. It is the highest moral end one can achieve (1 Cor 13:13), and all other virtues have it at their heart.

Chara. Next comes "joy," something esteemed highly in the Greek world, even used as a proper name, as it is in our own day. It is connected with happiness which resulted in finding your way between extremes and in the midst of pleasant circumstances. But Christians used the word in such a way that even in unpleasant circumstances, in the midst of the trials and sufferings of life, you could have joy. "Rejoice in the Lord <u>always</u>, again I saw rejoice" (Php 4:4). While Buddhism might say the same thing, it is because they deny that there is suffering! Christians embrace the suffering as real, but find its meaning in the suffering and death of Christ. Therefore, we may rejoice like none other.

Eirēnē. The third word means "peace." This is the universal quest of humanity, something they are always seeking, but never quite able to find. The Middle East cannot get peace. The U.N. will never bring peace. Treaties are worthless in a world full of treachery and distrust. But God gives peace. This is not merely the absence of war or pain or trouble of mind. It is a word that epitomizes the perfection of relationships. To have peace is to know that God not only does not hate you, but is positively reconciled to you as your friend and father.

Makrothumia. Next comes "patience." It means steadfastness, patience, or long-suffering in the face of persecution or provocation. When someone is out to get you, when trials come your way, when things are not going the way you would like, when the enemy is at the door, when the government is dissolving around your feet, when the teacher is being unreasonable in school, when you are being egged on to commit some sin with others on the playground or in the church, patience is a fruit of the Spirit. It is exhibited towards other people in the way you treat them, whether they are in front of you, or not ...

Xrēstotēs. ... for example, through "kindness." This word means "excellence" when referring to things and "goodness," "honesty," or "kindness," when referring to persons. It is found throughout classical Greek.

Agathōsunē. "Goodness" is a word, which like agape, is found only in the Bible. It is a synonym for "kindness." When you act kindly or goodly, you are acting for the benefit and betterment of someone else in a way that is not obligatory or begrudging, but free and willing.

Pistis. This word is usually translated as "faith" or "faithful." Like the other words, it has its roots in God who is "faithful" in all things. Because of its placement in a list like this, it does not refer to faith in God, but to faithfulness towards other people. It is the opposite of treacherous or untrue or apostate or cheating or adulterous or disloyal. Faithful are the wounds of a friend (Prov 27:6). Those who are faithful will have friendship wherever they go.

Prautēs. This word means "gentleness" which signifies "mildness" or "consideration" or "modesty" in dealing with people. It is teachable and submissive and humble. It is the opposite of harsh, ruthless, cruel, merciless. Yet, it is not the inability to get angry or have emotions. Aristotle defined it as somewhere in the middle. A gentle and quiet spirit is beautiful in the eyes of God.

Egkrateia. The last word means "self-control." It was talked about much by ancient Greeks. It is the opposite of overindulgence in both food or sex. It is the ability to keep yourself under control of your passions, be they lust or anger or covetousness or pride or any of the vices we talked about, and so it is a fitting way to complete the list.

One of the things I notice about this list is how it is singular (fruit) rather than plural (fruits). I don't know if I'm making too much of this or not, but what I think this may mean is that this fruit displays itself together, at the same time. What does it mean to love? It means all these other things. What does it mean to be patient? It means to act kindly and goodly and faithfully towards others. These are not gifts of the Spirit, but fruit. You are not to seek one of them, but not the rest. Each should be exhibited in your life on an increasing basis.

This is because this list of nine fruit of the Spirit are attributes of God, things that show his character to and through the world. In as much as he gives them even to pagans, he shows the world what kind of a God he is, and how true that is, since he gives them virtues even though they hate him. But there is more to all this than just "doing good things," as if these two lists were "don't do these things, do these things." In fact, that isn't at all what is going on.

Fruit from the Vine

To understand this, you need to understand the metaphor, because it is different from the previous one. That which comes from the flesh is a "work." That which comes from the Spirit is fruit. Though Paul can speak about "fruit for death," thus making the metaphor the same, here the idea is that in the flesh you are not in anything lasting and eternal, but in the Spirit, you have been transferred from one kingdom to another. There are several things to consider here.

First, how does a person get into the Spirit (or get the Spirit into them)? Not through the flesh, but through ... the Holy Spirit. That should sound obvious, but to so many people it isn't, because they glorify something that is impotent and they should know better. John says that we are born, "not of the will of the flesh" or "of the will of man," but of God (John 1:13). Paul says, "The natural person does not accept the things of the Spirit of God, for they are folly to him, and he is not able to understand them because they are spiritually discerned" (1 Cor 2:14). So, we don't get into the Spirit through the works or will of the flesh, but only through God's mercy. We have become spiritual by the Holy Spirit in order to be spiritual. This change does not begin with the flesh nor does it continue with the flesh. This leads to a second thought.

Second, becoming spiritual comes through the gift of faith and repentance. These are gifts of God (Acts 5:31, 11:18; Eph 2:8-9; Php 1:29; 2 Tim 2:25 etc.). A person receives these gifts through the word of God coming to them and changing their hearts through the conviction of their sin and a new desire to love and serve God. When they come, the person acts upon them. Have you exercised faith in Christ? Have you repented of your sin? You must, because without such things, you will not inherit the kingdom of God, even if you are 8 or 9 years old.

If you are still wondering about all of this, consider: It is incredible that John the Baptist could say to the Pharisees, "Bear fruit in keeping with repentance" (Matt 3:8). This shows that even Pharisees could bear fruit, but John's focus is on what really matters: repentance. Their fruit is not just outward, but must come from repentance. When Jesus said a little later in Matthew's gospel, "You will know them by their fruit" (7:16), at least part of this has to mean their repentance, for it is repentance that God uses as a means to generate the fruit. You know them by their repentance. Of course, the other side of repentance is faith.

I want to point out that both John (the Baptist) and Jesus say that every tree that does not bear good fruit is cut down and thrown into the fire (Matt 3:10; 7:19). This is similar to what I said a moment ago. This is similar, also, to the idea of Paul that those who commit vices will not inherit the kingdom of God. What is the problem? The tree is bad!

Imagine a scenario where your job was to take care of the peach orchard of a large land holder in Grand Junction. But you neglected your duty and all his trees died. You hear that he is coming back to check on the harvest, so you go to the store and purchase all the peaches they have at the store. You hire a bunch of needy, unemployed, unscrupulous people, and spend all day in the orchard stapling, gluing, nailing and screwing good fruit onto bad trees. You think that would be funny, because it wouldn't fool anyone. It is an absurd idea, and this is exactly what God sees in people who try to manufacture fruit apart from faith and repentance. Anyone who thinks they can fool God by doing good things, having a kind of fruit without repentance, is simply trying to glue good fruit to a bad tree. You aren't fooling God.

Jesus says, "Are grapes gathered from thornbushes, or figs from thistles? So, every healthy tree bears good fruit, but the diseased tree bears bad fruit. A healthy tree cannot bear bad fruit, nor can a diseased tree bear good fruit" (Matt 7:16-18). His solution is, "Either make the tree good and its fruit good, or make the tree bad and its fruit bad, for the tree is known by its fruit" (12:33).

How does this happen? By being found "in Christ." Jesus famously said, "I am the true vine, and my Father is the vinedresser (note, we are not the vinedresser). Every branch in me that does not bear fruit he takes away, and every branch that does bear fruit he prunes, that it may bear more fruit" (John 15:1-2). But he has hope for the disciples saying, "Already you are clean because of the word that I have spoken to you (the means of grace created their life). Abide in me, and I in you. As the branch cannot bear fruit by itself, unless it abides in the vine, neither can you, unless you abide in me. I am the vine; you are the branches ... apart from me you can do nothing ... By this my Father is glorified, that you bear much fruit and so prove to be my disciples" (3-5, 8). And a little later he adds the nail to the coffin of anyone still thinking all of this is done by the will of the flesh, "You did not choose me, but I chose you and appointed you that you should go and bear fruit and that your fruit should abide" (John 15:16).

Therefore, we come back to the heart of Galatians. All of this discussion about works of the flesh and fruit of the Spirit comes after saying in every conceivable way, you only have life through Christ, and you only have Christ through faith in him. This is why it is so important to keep going back to the gospel. But then, the gospel always has implications for the way we live. If we are in the vine, we are alive. And if we are alive, we produce that which comes naturally to living, healthy branches.

All of this has as its life-blood the sap of the Holy Spirit. He makes these things grow in us. He causes them to sprout. He infuses all of our works with fruit pleasing to God. The call here at the end of the chapter is a call of responsibility. These things come naturally, but they must also be cultivated. You cultivate them by being faithful to the means of grace, by diligently putting to death the misdeeds of the flesh, by praying to God repentance for your evil works, and by trusting his promises to justify, sanctify, and glorify you.

He says, "If we live by the Spirit, let us also walk by the Spirit" (Gal 5:25). To walk by the Spirit is to serve one another in love. In Romans he says, "Now that you have been set free from sin and have become slaves to God, the fruit you get leads to sanctification and its end, eternal life" (Rom 6:22). "The fruit of light is found in all that is good and right and true" (Eph 5:9). "Be filled with the fruit of righteousness that comes through Jesus Christ, to the glory and praise of God" (Php 1:11).

There is a great city that is coming down out of heaven. In the middle of the city there is a throne. Flowing from that throne there is a River of Life that makes its way through the central street. On either side of that street, beside the quiet still waters of the River, there is a tree of life. This tree has twelve kinds of fruit, yielding its fruit each month, never going dormant, always bringing healing for the nations (Rev 22:1-2). Make every effort, therefore, to be found in that city. For it is the city of the living God, the city of Christ Jesus and his church. The city which will last forever.

The Happy Sower

and

The Grim Reaper

[1] Brothers, if anyone is caught in any transgression, you who are spiritual should restore him in a spirit of gentleness. Keep watch on yourself, lest you too be tempted.

[2] Bear one another's burdens, and so fulfill the law of Christ. [3] For if anyone thinks he is something, when he is nothing, he deceives himself. [4] But let each one test his own work, and then his reason to boast will be in himself alone and not in his neighbor. [5] For each will have to bear his own load.

[6] One who is taught the word must share all good things with the one who teaches.

[7] Do not be deceived: God is not mocked, for whatever one sows, that will he also reap. [8] For the one who sows to his own flesh will from the flesh reap corruption, but the one who sows to the Spirit will from the Spirit reap eternal life.

[9] And let us not grow weary of doing good, for in due season we will reap, if we do not give up. [10] So then, as we have opportunity, let us do good to everyone, and especially to those who are of the household of faith.

Galatians 6:1-10

Structure of Proverbs

PROVERBS. CAN YOU TAKE A PROVERB OUT OF CONTEXT? It depends. If I say, "Well done is better than well said," or "A lie stands on one leg, the truth on two," both proverbs of Ben Franklin, it would be difficult. In these cases, the proverb *is* the context. To take it out of context would be to destroy the proverb completely. We often think of biblical proverbs the same way: as isolated little contexts unto themselves. A maxim here, an adage there. But is this true?

What if I read you this proverb: "Blessed is the one who finds wisdom, and the one who gets understanding" (Prov 3:13). How would you interpret it? If I told you that Greek philosophers loved sayings like this,[1] you might interpret it as an appeal to take a philosophy class at a school, certainly not the worst thing you could do. But what if I told you that the speaker *was* Wisdom, and that Wisdom is the Spirit of Christ? Now, suddenly, the meaning of the proverb changes. What you are to seek here is not bare knowledge, but knowledge gained through fearing the LORD. How about this one: "Be not wise in your own eyes" (Prov 3:7a).[2] What if I told you that Greek pagans spoke just like this? How would you interpret the meaning? Perhaps you might think that humility is an end to itself. But what if I finished the proverb as it reads in the Bible, "… fear the LORD, and turn away from evil." Now, again, we see that the proverb has a spiritual context. This is said to a believer as a means of persevering through the trials of life, not becoming conceited. Who knew proverbs could be so … complicated!

Why would I start a sermon on Galatians 6:1-10 by telling you about Proverbs? For two reasons. 1) Galatians 6 is filled with maxims or individual proverbs (technically called *sententia*),[3] similar to the book of Proverbs. 2) The sayings in Galatians 6 are set to a context, just like the

---

[1] For example, the famous proverb: "Curiosity is the beginning of wisdom."

[2] This one is similar to Galatians 6:3, "For if anyone thinks he is something, when he is nothing, he deceives himself," which as we will see below is similar to Greek proverbs like the one from Epictetus (55 – 135 AD), "If you think you are somebody for some, distrust yourself."

[3] All of the Greek maxims cited below come from Betz, *Galatians*.

book of Proverbs. At first glance, these might seem like a random series of ethical instructions:[4] "Keep watch on yourself, lest you be tempted," "Bear one another's burdens," "If anyone thinks he is something, when he is nothing, he deceives himself," "One who is taught the word must share all good things with the teacher," "Whatever one sows, that will he also reap." Read this way, they do sound pretty random.

It is popular to view this part of Galatians as Paul giving loose or diverse exhortations that defy grouping or structural order, but which deal with "personal and corporate responsibilities in the churches."[5] This provides some context at least. But, in my opinion, a very discernable structure is also here, one that is important to understand if you want to get the best possible understanding of what God is saying through Paul. We want to learn to read the Bible *properly*.

First, let me tell you what kind of structure it is and why it matters, then I'll show it to you. The structure forms a multi-layered set of chiasms. We've seen chiasms many times over the years in our study of the Bible. This is the first time I've noticed them in Galatians. A chiasm is a literary tool where you position your thoughts in a symmetrical order or pattern (such as A|B|C|B|A or AB|AB). By repeating ideas, it helps you remember what you have heard. But it does more. It can emphasize main points, and in the most common form of chiasm, a central idea comes to the forefront.

The main chiasm as I see it is this:

Vv 1-10			
vs. 1	**A.**	Restoration in the church	If anyone is caught in a transgression, restore him in <u>gentleness</u>
vv. 2-5	**B.**	Sowing	<u>Deceiving</u> oneself
vs. 6	**C.**	The Word	Those taught the word must <u>share</u> the word with the teacher
vv. 7-8	**B¹.**	Sowing	Do not be <u>deceived</u>
vv.9-10	**A¹.**	Reaping in the church	<u>Do good</u> to everyone, especially those of the household of faith

---

[4] So, commentators have said things like "There is no connection between one admonition and the next, except sometimes a similarity of subject or a catch-phrase; the collector is not pursuing a connected argument." (J. C. O'Neill, *Recovery*, 67; cited in Longnecker, *Galatians*, 270.

[5] Ibid., Longnecker, 270-71.

The center of this chiasm is vs. 6. This is a verse that every commentary says is the most enigmatic, random verse in the section: "Those taught the word must share the word with the teacher." Seen in the structure, this is not just one point among many. It is the central point of the entire passage. The main thought in the verse is *koinoneo*, the verbal form of *koinonia*: "sharing" or "fellowship." Fellowship is something that takes place in the body of Christ, which is the setting for all of these sayings. It has nothing to do with sitting around talking about sports. It has to do with sharing what you have with the body of Christ, be it talent or treasure or time or teaching.

The chiasm also helps you see the centrality of the church. In verse 6, the teacher is the *katechoun*. The student is the *catechoumenos*. The subject of their study is the *logos*. You are familiar with these words; they are the words of the gospel and of the church. Historically, catechumens are students *in church* who go through the basics of the faith and pass a test at the end. The gospel is what they are being taught to learn.

The edges of the chiasm point in the same direction. Vs. 1 - People caught in a transgression are to be gently restored by those who are spiritual. The language here is legal,[6] not in a court of law, but in a local assembly. On the other end in vs. 10, the instruction is to do good, "especially to the household of faith." This again refers to the local assembly. What you can see right away, then, is how understanding the structure gives you a better understanding of the meaning of the passage. I don't want you to be guilty of taking proverbs out of context. These are not just ethical shots coming out of Paul's theological six-shooter aimed at nothing in particular. They are very specific applications of walking in the Spirit, which in the previous chapter meant serving one another, in the body of Christ, in love.

Restoration in the Church - Galatians 6:1 (Chiasm A)

With that, let us go to the passage in its given order, working our way through the chiasm. Paul begins, "Brothers, if anyone is caught in any transgression, you who are spiritual should restore him in a spirit of gentleness. Keep watch on yourself, lest you be tempted" (Gal 6:1). He begins by thinking of a situation he can use to make concrete application

---

[6] See Betz, 295-96.

of the works of the flesh vs. the fruit of the Spirit he has just finished explaining. It is as if he is now saying, "You want to know what it means to walk by the Spirit, to display fruit, to serve one another in love in the real world? Here is what it looks like."

The situation in mind has three parts: 1) A description of the condition that would precipitate the procedure. 2) The procedure for handling the case. 3) A warning to those who administer the procedure. First, what is the condition? He writes about someone "caught in any transgression." Was there something specific in Paul's mind as he wrote this? Maybe. He has said these people are biting and devouring one another (Gal 5:15). But he also makes the application general: "any" transgression. He could be thinking about anything in the list of vices (Gal 5:19-21), which would include sexual vices, religious vices, communal vices (how you act towards each other), vices of alcohol, or "things like these." To make it more concrete, think specifically on the third category. It is easier to see how the situation could backfire when something like enmity, strife, jealousy, fits of anger, rivalries, dissensions, or divisions within the body are in play.

These things are easy to spot in a church, but it is not always easy to identify the source. The idea of the verse is that the person has been tempted (see 6:1c), they have given into the temptation and transgressed (6:1a), and they have been caught (6:1b). A word on how they got to this point. It says they are "caught" (*prolambanō*) in a transgression. This could refer to being caught, or to being "caught up in." Translations go either way.

This word can mean "to take or undertake" or "to be taken." Most commentaries say something like, "the person in question is ensnared by the tempter before he fully realizes what he is doing.[7]" They are "taken unaware" or "because of lack of caution."[8] This is true, but it neither excuses the sin, nor means that the sin in question is necessarily not that serious, as if this is just a little fault, error, or mistake.[9] All you need to do is think about Adam and Eve to see this. They were tempted. They were ensnared. They did not fully realize what they were doing. But their sin

---

[7] For example Hendriksen, 231 n. 170.
[8] Luther, Gal 6:1.
[9] Contra Hendriksen.

was inexcusable and utterly grave and serious, all at the same time. What is interesting to me is how Paul seems more interested in how the church handles the person, than in the person him or herself. How sins are handled are often a source of much worse works of the flesh than the original transgression. How is the church to deal with it? What is the procedure?

Let's start with Jesus, who gave us the procedure to follow in Matthew 18:15-17. It involves individuals, elders, and the entire church. It has increasing degrees of formal procedure to follow. First, a brother goes to the person and tries to help him. People almost always skip this step, because it's easier to make the pastor deal with it. I always ask people who want me to deal with other people if they have already talked to the person first? If the person does not listen, an elder is taken as a voice of reason and advice, and as a witness.[10] Finally, if the person is completely unrepentant, the entire church is involved and must cast a person out of its midst. In Galatians 6:1, you could be anywhere along this road. Therefore, anyone here could potentially be involved. Thus, what Paul says by way of warning must be heeded by every one of you, because you will all at some point see another brother in sin.

The first thing Paul says is that restoration should come at the hands of those who are "spiritual." This isn't talking about the super-spiritual Christian, but simply someone "more consistent [in this area?] in following the promptings of the Spirit."[11] This restoration must be in "a spirit of gentleness." Note, Paul takes the lead here in a gentle way himself, bringing this very topic up in an affectionate way: "Brothers." Gentleness, if you remember, was a fruit of the Spirit. In other words, this is an application of Galatians 5. A situation has arisen in which the works of the flesh are being sown in the church. Now, how is the church to deal with it? With more works of the flesh? No, but with the fruit of the Spirit: gentleness, meekness, self-control.

The problem is, it is far too easy to respond in the flesh rather than the Spirit. This is why I asked you to think about those things like anger or factions or divisions. These things naturally tend to arouse the very

---

[10] The "witness" in the OT context was an elder of Israel.
[11] Hendriksen, 232.

same problem in others. You get angry at me and my natural inclination is to get angry at you. You get a mob to take me out and I'll get my mob to take you out. This is the very thing that destroys churches.

When we give into the flesh, we do so because we give into the same temptations that overcame the original transgressor! Thus, Paul warns us "Keep watch on yourself, lest you too be tempted." Here's a very relevant proverb: "A soft answer turns away wrath, but a harsh word stirs up anger" (Prov 15:1). This naturally leads to the second part of the chiasm: self deception.

Sowing and the Law - Galatians 6:2-5 (Chiasm B)

It is so easy to be a hypocrite, especially when we look at the sins of other people. The next section is Galatians 6:2-5. As I said earlier, without context, it seems like a string of unrelated sayings. It isn't. This section has its own chiasm (a chiasm within a chiasm). It is larger, and even more pronounced than the first one:

> A.   Bear one another's burdens
>> B.   Fulfill the law of Christ
>>> C.   If you think you are something
>>>> D.   When you are nothing
>>>>> **E.   You deceive yourself**
>>>> D^1. Test your own work
>>> C^1. Your reason to boast will be in yourself
>> B^1. And not your neighbor ("Love your neighbor as yourself" = the law)
> A^1. Each will have to bear his own load

Let me walk you through it. It begins, "Bear one another's burdens" (vs. 2a). It ends, "Each will have to bear his own load" (vs. 5). Bearing burdens is the common theme. Next it says that if you bear one another's burdens, you will "fulfill the law of Christ" (vs. 2b). What is the law of Christ? Love your neighbor (Gal 5:14). Thus, at the other end he concludes "and not in his neighbor" (6:4c). Do not compare yourself to your fallen brother in Christ! That is perverse. Verse 3 begins, "If anyone thinks he is something." Just before he speaks about the neighbor in vs. 4 he says, "then his reason to boast will be in himself alone." Thinking yourself something and boasting in yourself are the same thing. We are almost to the center. In vs. 3, you shouldn't think you are something "when you are nothing." To discover this you must "test your own work." The man or woman who tests themselves will quickly discover that they are just as full of sin and the desires to give into them as the person they are trying to restore. The real source of boasting can then be discovered!

The center of the chiasm, and thus the central idea of these verses, is the only part we have left: "He deceives himself" (vs. 3c). Do you see how this is related to verse 1? Keep watch on yourself, lest you be tempted. If you do not keep watch you will easily fall into temptation and not even realize it. Therefore, you will deceive yourself. You will not realize that you are nothing, because you are not testing yourself and looking into your heart. You will think you are something and you will boast in yourself. You will not fulfill the law of Christ and will not boast in yourself because of your neighbor's shortcomings that you, apparently, don't have any of. You will not bear one another's burdens, but will have to bear your own.

What is so amazing about this entire pericope (a passage in a text) is that each of these sayings has counterparts in the Greek pagan world.[12] You could take any one of them alone, as many commentaries do, but they clearly serve Paul's larger context of how, when a person is caught in a sin, they are to be restored gently. It is remarkable that Paul could take pagan thought (which, as Van Til said is not really pagan at all, but their borrowing or stealing from the Christian worldview) and apply it in the church in such a remarkable, literary, effective way.

How do you restore them gently? These verses specify what that looks like. Outwardly, bear one another's burdens. If you are tempted and if need be, share your temptation. Pray for one another. Help one another. Love your neighbor. Fulfill the law of Christ. Isn't this what the

---

[12] For example, Socrates (vs. 2 "bear one another's burdens"), "One must share one's burden with one's friends, for possibly we may do something to ease you." Epictetus (55-135 AD) (vs. 3 "thinks he is something, when he is nothing") said, "And if you think you are somebody for some, distrust yourself." Menander (342-291 BC) (vs. 4 "test your work"), "For of all, examine the conduct of life, but not the speech, because a respectable conduct of life is different from elegant language." All quotes cited in Betz, *Galatians*, 299; 302; 303; 305.

Word says? Don't think yourself better than another with regard to sin, humble yourself. Humble yourself *in front of them*, so that they will recognize that they are not alone in sin because you have shared your own problems (generally or specifically) with them! How often people caught up in sin are made to feel subhuman by the smug, condescending, "help" of another person.

Inwardly, understand that you are dust, that the flesh is deceitful, and you have many shortcomings. Test your heart. Take inventory of your sins and confess them to God. Repent of them. For goodness sake, do not compare yourself with your neighbor, as if his or her failure is the source of your boasting about your own goodness! Compare yourself with God, with perfection. Look upon the real source of comparison. Then recognize that you are what you are because of him. Then your boasting will not even be in yourself, but in Christ. What does Paul say elsewhere? "By God's grace I am what I am" (1 Cor 15:10), or "If I must boast, I will boast in the LORD" (2 Cor 10:17; cf. Gal 6:14; 1 Cor 9:16; 10:31, etc.).

The Word - Galatians 6:6 (Chiasm C)

Certainly, all of this is sharing the word with each other. I come now to the center of the chiasm. "One who is taught the word must share all good things with the one who teaches" (Gal 6:6). Like the sayings in the previous section, this one has Greek counterparts.[13] The Hippocratic "Covenant" (Oath) says, "To hold him who has taught me this art as equal to my parents and to live my life in partnership with him, and if he is in need of money to give him a share of mine."

If I had more time I would tease out this idea that pagans have proverbial counterparts to what is said in our text this morning. I've at least mentioned this a couple of times for a specific reason. Too many people have this dangerous mistaken notion that what makes us Christians is our laws, our proverbs, and our works. Nonsense. This is Paul's whole point in our passage today. The whole world has God's law written on its heart.

---

[13] Pythagoras (vs. 6 "share all good things with the teacher"), "Friends share everything in common," or the Hippocratic "Covenant", "To hold him who has taught me this art as equal to my parents and to live my life in partnership with him, and if he is in need of money to give him a share of mine."

What makes us Christians is that we acknowledge the source of the law because something has come to us that makes us want to do so. God has saved us in spite of ourselves, by crediting to us something we do not have by nature: righteousness. He has done it through the gospel, the one John calls the Word, the *logos*, the same thing Paul talks about here.

Scholars are perplexed about why Paul would put this saying here. Is this just a random proverb? I don't think so. It gets at the heart of how the fruit of the Spirit is cultivated. For the Apostle, sharing all good things is at the heart of this. The sentence begins in Greek with *koinoneo*: Fellowship.[14] What is true fellowship? At the heart of sharing is the Word. He focuses in on the teacher and student. In catechesis, the student is supposed to say back to the teacher what he has learned. Specifically, Paul has in mind here the idea of all that is good. The law, of course, is good, if used lawfully. But the gospel is *really good*, because Jesus is Perfectly Good. Jesus is the Good Word.

If the Galatians would have sat down and discussed Paul's letter, really trying to grasp its meaning, they would be on the right track. This, of course, would focus on justification by faith alone and not by the law, but it would then include the place and use of the law in the Christian's life. It is by sharing *these* good things that the fruit of the Spirit is cultivated in a life, because through fellowship and the Spirit the head knowledge becomes planted in the heart. This is how, I believe, vs. 6 fits into our text. It is the heart and soul of the entire thing. The good news undergirds even the maxims here at the end of the letter. The gospel supports the law. The Greeks might have their altruistic principles, their love of wisdom and goodness and beauty. But we have Christ who personifies, embodies, and gives meaning to them all ... and, who saves us from our sins! That is what makes us different.

Sowing Flesh or Spirit - Galatians 6:7-8 (Chiasm B[1])

The way we act as believers can be out of the flesh (the fallen wicked patterns of the world) or the Spirit, that is the Holy Spirit. The fourth part of our passage parallels the second part. It is vv. 7-8, "Do not

---

[14] By putting the word first in the sentence, it emphasizes the importance of "sharing."

be deceived: God is not mocked, for whatever one sows, that will he also reap. For the one who sows to his own flesh will from the flesh reap corruption, but the one who sows to the Spirit will from the Spirit reap eternal life." The word "deception" gives us our closest link in the two sections: "He deceives himself" and "Do not be deceived." The idea of sowing is implicit in vv. 2-5. To bear one another's burdens and fulfill the law is to sow the fruit of the Spirit. Now the idea becomes explicit, "Whatever one sows, that will he also reap" (vs. 7).

The proverb is a general saying that again has contact with the pagan world. One need think no further than the concept of karma in Hinduism and Buddhism (where it is sometimes even called the "fruits of karma"). But we are not talking about mere fate here. We are not even talking about the whims of fallen, wicked gods like they may see, punishing or blessing us in a cosmic cycle of cause and effect. We are talking about the difference between the flesh and Spirit, between two worlds and ages, one ruled by sin and the other by God.

Works of the flesh (quarrelsomeness, 5:15, 26; conceit, 5:26; envy, 5:26; living aloof from the needs of others, 6:1–2; pride, 6:3–4;[15] and other things) are here contrasted again with fruit of the Spirit. He is talking about fulfilling the law of love vs. not. To put it in the metaphor Paul uses, in which field will you sow your works? Will it be the field of the flesh or will it be the field of the Spirit? Will it be the temporary field or the eternal field? Will it be the wicked field or the holy field? Will it be the field of merit or the field of gratitude? If you sow in the field of the flesh, you will reap corruption (vs. 8a).

Whatever the seed is, it is the field that makes the difference. If you place your hope for salvation upon circumcision (fill in the blank) or upon obeying Jewish Torah, you will reap corruption, because of the hypocrisy that will remain in your heart. As Dr. Ridderbos put it, "corruption" (*phthora*) here is "not the cessation of human existence, but the positive existence of grief and woe, temporal and eternal."[16] Ultimately, it is the idea of eternal annihilation. It is eschatological, just like the term "flesh"

---

[15] As pointed out by Longnecker, *Galatians*, 281.
[16] Herman Ridderbos, *Galatians*, NICONT, 218.

is. For example, "Flesh and blood cannot inherit the kingdom of God; nor does the corruptible (*phthora*) inherit the incorruptible" (1 Cor 15:50; cf. Rom 8:21; 2 Pet 2:12).

This is contrasted (in the form of the final chiasm, vs. 8) with reaping eternal life by sowing to the Spirit:

> A. The one who sows to his <u>flesh</u>
>> B. From his flesh will reap <u>corruption</u>
> A¹. The one who sows to the <u>Spirit</u>
>> B¹. From the Spirit will reap <u>eternal life</u>

The idea is that you are throwing seeds of fruit into the field of the Holy Spirit who makes them grow. You are not to cast them into the field of the world, the flesh, the devil, your heart, your will, your intellect, your neighbor, your enemy, your philosophy, your emotions, your parents, your spouse, your girlfriend or boyfriend, your politics; but to God. You are casting your seed upon him. Such fruit that grows up in this soil is eternal fruit, the fruit of the eternal city and the everlasting kingdom, the fruit that comes from Father, Son, and Holy Ghost, the fruit he gives to his children. The consequences here are heaven vs. hell. It could not be any more pronounced.

Reaping in the Church - Galatians 6:9-10 (Chiasm A¹)

With the motivation of eternal life and eternal punishment pushing us, Paul concludes, "Let us not grow weary of doing good, for in due season we will reap, if we do not give up. So then, as we have opportunity, let us do good to everyone, and especially to those who are of the household of faith." "Doing good" is contrasted with restoring a person in "gentleness" in vs. 2. Both are fruit of the Spirit. Both are loving neighbor as oneself. Both are walking in the Spirit. Both are severing one another in love.

The idea of reaping is implicit in Galatians 6:1. By restoring a fallen brother with gentleness, you will reap a bountiful harvest in the church and will not find yourself giving into temptations of the flesh. In vv. 9-10 it is explicit. If you will not grow weary of doing good, in due time you will reap. It may not happen immediately, but neither do trees planted yesterday produce fruit immediately. So you must not give up. Perhaps here is the most difficult lesson of all. It is one thing to give you a sermon on Galatians 6:1-10 and to tell you all about it. If you were to share with me and with each other what you have learned from the word, that would be a help. But what about a month or a year from now, when you have forgotten all about it (hopefully the forgetting won't come by this afternoon)? What happens when a brother falls into sin, or when you are tempted yourself to get angry or upset at a brother, but you don't have any reminders? What are you called to do?

Do not give up. Watering plants takes a long time for them to grow to maturity. Seeing results in other's lives and often your own is not always immediate. The Bible knows nothing of instant gratification. God did not destroy the inhabitants of Canaan all at once in order to test Israel and to see if they would obey the commandments (Jdg 2:22-3:2). So also, God does not get rid of the flesh, but it stays here to test us and to, Lord willing, cause us to grow in the Spirit.

We are commanded to do good to everyone, but especially those of the household of faith (which in the NT context, meant the local assembly). You need to put a face to the problem. That is what the local church does. Here you have to learn to be kind and gentle to those who are different than yourself, people who do not ordinarily make up your circle of friends, people who are outcasts, strange, perhaps even a little weird. You have to learn these things not only with likeable people, but with unlikeable people. You have to learn it not with perfect people, but with fallen people, real people. Look around in this room. There are people here you have been angry with in the past, perhaps even the present. It is with these people that you will reap what you sow.

Do good to them, because Christ has done good to you. Be gentle with them, because Christ has been gentle with you ... and them. If the only one who actually has a right to get angry won't do it, neither, beloved, should you. Look within and do not be deceived. Then look without and behold the face of your beautiful savior, who has loved you, died for you, died for them, and has made it possible through the Holy Spirit where people once living only in the flesh, can now display the very fruit of heaven itself.

Galatians

For the Israel of God

[11] See with what large letters I am writing to you with my own hand. [12] It is those who want to make a good showing in the flesh who would force you to be circumcised, and only in order that they may not be persecuted for the cross of Christ. [13] For even those who are circumcised do not themselves keep the law, but they desire to have you circumcised that they may boast in your flesh. [14] But far be it from me to boast except in the cross of our Lord Jesus Christ, by which the world has been crucified to me, and I to the world. [15] For neither circumcision counts for anything, nor uncircumcision, but a new creation.

[16] And as for all who walk by this rule, peace and mercy be upon them, and upon the Israel of God. [17] From now on let no one cause me trouble, for I bear on my body the marks of Jesus. [18] The grace of our Lord Jesus Christ be with your spirit, brothers. Amen.

Galatians 6:11-18

"Israel" and the "Church"

ONE OF THE GREAT THEOLOGICAL PUZZLES of our time has been correctly identifying and defining "Israel" and the "church." Traditionally, our fathers in the faith did not find this as much of a problem as we Protestants have for the last 200 years or so. What happened 200 years ago? It was the advent of a new way of reading the Bible called "Dispensationalism." Over the years, Dispensationalism has taken on different forms,[1] and

---

[1] These forms have come in three main stages of its history. The first stage is the original stage formulated by John Nelson Darby (1800-1882) and systematized by C. I. Scofield (1843-1921) and Lewis Sperry Chafer (1871-1952). Next comes Dispensationalism popularized for a new generation with Charles Ryrie's (1925-)

thankfully each form has moved closer to the traditional understanding of many biblical doctrines. But one thing all Dispensationalists have in common is their view that Israel and the church are two completely different entities.

Lewis Sperry Chafer wrote in 1936, "The Dispensationalist believes that throughout the ages God is pursuing two distinct purposes: one related to the earth with earthly people and earthly objectives involved which is Judaism; while the other is related to heaven with heavenly people and heavenly objectives involved, which is Christianity."[2] Twenty years later Charles Ryrie asked, "What marks off a person as a dispensationalist? What is the *sine qua non* (the absolutely indispensable part) of the system? ... A dispensationalist keeps Israel and the church distinct."[3] He favorably cites Daniel Fuller (not himself a dispensationalist) who writes, "The basic premise of Dispensationalism is two purposes God expressed in the formation of two peoples who maintain their distinction throughout eternity."[4] Even Progressive Dispensationalists maintain this distinction. As Craig Blaising writes, "Traditionally, dispensationalism has always viewed the church as a distinctively *new* dispensation in biblical history. The church finds its historical origin in the 'Christ event'—that is the death, resurrection, and ascension of Jesus Christ—and particularly in the 'baptism of the Spirit' which Christ has bestowed equally upon believing Jews and Gentiles since that feast Day of Pentecost following His ascension."[5]

Classic Protestants, be they Lutheran or Reformed (i.e., covenental) have always disagreed with such sharp distinctions.[6] While we do understand that there was and continues to be an ethnic group of people called Israelites (and we even have disagreements among ourselves over whether or not God will do anything special with this national group of people

---

Dispensationalism Today. Finally, a new breed of Dispensationalists began formulating "Progressive Dispensationalism" (which is quite close to new covenant theology) in the 1980-90s.

[2] Lewis Sperry Chafer, *Dispensationalism* (Dallas: Dallas Seminary Press, 1936), 107.

[3] Charles Ryrie, *Dispensationalism Today* (Chicago: Moody Press, 1966, 95), 32-33.

[4] Daniel Payton Fuller, "The Hermeneutics of Dispensationalism" (unpublished Th.D. diss., Northern Baptist Theological Seminary, Chicago, 1957), 25

[5] Craig A. Blaising and Darrell L. Bock, *Progressive Dispensationalism* (Grand Rapids, MI: Baker Books, 1993), 16.

[6] This view follows generally in line with the view of the Roman church out of which Protestantism arose.

before the end of time), we understand that these Israelites were called the "church" in the OT. When I first heard someone tell me this, it was a brand new and shocking idea. No one told me that growing up!

The word *ekklesia* ("church") is used over 75 times in the LXX and nearly 15 more in the Apocrypha. This is hardly a word that Jesus invented, but Dispensationalists rarely seem to want to talk about this.[7] An example of the use of the word is found in Deuteronomy 4:10 LXX where God asks Israel to remember the things that happened in "the day in which you stood before the Lord our God in Horeb in the day of the *ekklesia* (church)." And who was the "Lord our God" they stood before? According to what I argued from Galatians 3:19-21, it was Christ, the eternally existing mediator between God and angels (and Moses). So *the church* at the foot of Sinai was *Christ's* church, the same language he uses for his church when he talks to Peter (Matt 16:18).

Why do I go into all of this here, at the end of Galatians? It is because in the conclusion to his letter written to the "churches" of Galatia (Gal 1:2), he calls them the "Israel of God" (Gal 6:16). This expression is found only here in the NT, but it is theologically in line with what Paul calls the church in other places: "children of Abraham" (Gal 3:29) or "true circumcision" (Php 3:3) or "true Jews" (Rom 2:29). Getting the meaning of this phrase right is at the heart of the entire letter, its theology of how a person is saved, its warnings against divisions within the church, its insistence that those of faith are children of Abraham, and its conclusion which summarizes the main points of Galatians. But because people have this predisposed hang-up against such beautiful continuity, they make that which is clear seem blurry, that which is obvious seem puzzling, and they try to confuse people even here in Galatians 6:16 with grammatical questions that cause one to doubt the only meaning that takes the rest of the context of the letter seriously: That Christians are Abraham's offspring, heir of God according to the promises. They ironically create the very kinds of divisions Paul has been trying to squash between Jews and Gentiles, divisions which his opponents have been trying to re-create, and

---

[7] For example, both *Dispensationalism Today* and *Progressive Dispensationalism* fail to mention even a single OT reference to the *ekklesia*.

which have caused so much theological and ethnic divisions in these churches already. This is what I want to talk about this morning.

Conclusion to the Letter

Galatians 6:11-18 makes up the conclusion to the letter of Galatians. In some ways, it is like any concluding letter in the NT, especially the last verse which is a blessing. In other ways, it is not. Paul doesn't ask anyone to pray for him. He has nothing to say about any particular person. His greeting is terse. The differences outweigh the similarities, and have caused some to see it not so much as a pastoral conclusion, but as a piece of Greek rhetoric called *peroratio* or *conclusio*.[8] The *peroratio* had three main parts. The first (the *enumeratio* or *recapitulatio*) sums up the main points. The second (the *indignatio*) arouses anger and hostility against the opponent. The third (the *conquestio*) stimulates pity. Basically, this is exactly what Paul's conclusion in Galatians does! Paul sums up the letter in vv. 12-15. Vv. 12-13 are a sharp attack against his opponents. Vs. 17 arouses pity, though Paul does not ask for any.

For our sake and that of the Galatians, what this conclusion does is remind us one last time of the most important things we have discussed, while presenting us with a final mutually exclusive decision on which way we will go. Will we follow those who insist on confusing the law and the gospel, especially creating legalism or a return to a function of the law that has never been able to save anyone? Or will we follow Christ by faith, being content with his new creation as it stands prior to eschaton (the consummation of all things), trusting that all the Apostle has taught us is really true, despite what we sometimes see with our eyes? Will we return to divisions caused by the law after starting with faith and the Spirit, or maintain the unity always found by the elect through faith alone? This idea of the "Israel of God" helps us see all of these things properly.

---

[8] This fascinating short discussion is found in Betz, 313 who is rather Liberal. Betz actually sees the entire letter this way and organizes his commentary around it. See Longnecker, 286-87 for some disagreement, but also on the importance of the idea for interpreting the letter.

A Judgment of Motives

The conclusion begins with something quite unusual for Paul. He finishes the letter with his own handwriting (Gal 6:11). Typically, Paul employed a full time *amanuensis* or secretary. Whether he was always the same person or Paul employed different people we do not know; but at least one of them—a man named Tertius—is forever remembered for putting himself at the end of Romans (16:22). Here at the end of Galatians, Paul takes the secretary's pen and finishes the letter himself!

It says that he writes in "large letters." There has been a lot of speculation about why (i.e., Paul could barely see, his hand had been permanently injured and he couldn't help himself, etc.), but probably the best reason was given 100 years ago by J. B. Lightfoot that the boldness of the handwriting answers to the force of the Apostle's convictions.[9] It might be akin to ALL CAPS on Facebook or **boldface** in an email. It also would prove that this was Paul and not some forgery. Apparently, they would have known what his handwriting looked like, and they could compare it with what they had. Thus, if someone wanted to throw the letter away because they did not like what it said, they could not use the excuse of a forgery to do it! Today, this little verse is important for Christian apologetics, as it confirms that this really is a letter from Paul, a fact which even the most liberal scholars admit.

So what did Paul want them to take notice of? What was so important that he had to write it himself in large letters? It is one final return to the main issue of the letter and a final jab at those preachers of a false gospel whom he condemned at the beginning when he says, "It is those who want to make a good showing in the flesh who would force you to be circumcised, and only in order that they may not be persecuted for the cross of Christ" (Gal 6:12). Now THAT would make the false teacher furious if they read it, because Paul is judging their motives. Is this wrong? Can we emulate Paul here, or was this some kind of special, infallible, Apostolic insight he had that no one else is given? These are important questions.

I don't know how many times I've heard people say we are not to judge, lest we be judged, taking Jesus entirely out of context. He actually

---

[9] J. B. Lightfoot, *The Epistle of St. Paul to the Galatians* (Grand Rapids, MI: Zondervan, 1957), 221.

finishes this statement by saying, "Make a right judgment" (John 7:24). Jesus judged the Pharisees all the time, because he knew what they were doing. But it does not take omniscience to do this. Jesus tells the disciples to judge! Paul is following Christ's command, and is making an *ad hominum* attack on the persons themselves.

If you are going to make an argument, it is best to stay away from this sort of thing, because it is a logical fallacy. You do not base your argument upon what you perceive to be a person's motivations or character. But the conclusion here is a piece of rhetoric. It isn't an argument. Paul has already made his argument and he returns to it here, trying to help the Galatians take it seriously by showing what the motivations really are behind the false teachers. When used properly, wisely, and shrewdly, it can have a powerful effect.

He says, the only reason these men are trying to get these Galatians to get circumcised is because they are really only looking out for their own interests, because they don't want to be persecuted by the unbelieving Jews who are already going after the Christians. It makes a lot of sense, doesn't it? And who would have been able to understand this any more profoundly than Paul who, because he refused to preach another gospel, was nearly stoned to death in Lystra in Galatia (Acts 14:19)?

This whole politically correct nonsense that loves to take Jesus out of context as much as possible is utterly foreign to the Bible. Christians are, in fact, to make judgments. How else can we possibly hope to stand firm in the faith once for all entrusted to the saints, if we are not allowed to say that false teaching is heresy, or that false worship is reprehensible to God, or that unlawful living is immoral because God's character never changes? People don't like it, but this is because they are being caught and called on their own immoral activities. Who wants to be told that they are wrong?

It is one thing to say that what a person is doing is wrong. It is another to assert reasons for why we think they might be doing it. Now, I do think caution and wisdom and charity need to be exercised in dealing with this topic. We don't have omniscience nor Apostolic authority. At the same time, sometimes, when things get really out of control in a church or in The Church, judgments like this need to come up, so that immoral motivations will be considered by people who are being led astray to the peril of their own souls. Read 2 Peter or Jude and you will quickly discover how true this is! The present crisis in worship, in the very idea of orthodoxy, even in the idea of objective truth are serious enough that those attacking them need to be shown for what they are. I don't have anyone specific in mind, and therefore I have no specific motivation in mind. But if the church refuses to tell it like it is from Scripture, then pretty soon, there won't be a church. And yes, while God promises to always have his elect and a church, he does not promise that for any one culture or any minimum size. Plenty of places have absolutely no church. Today this is a very real and present danger that is taking hostage the minds of young people so powerfully, that historic Christianity now looks like the only intolerable cult around that must be stamped out. Make no mistake about it. We are in a battle for the very souls of a generation. Will we have the nerve to speak up, or will we, like these false teachers prefer not to be persecuted for the cross of Christ? This is one of the questions Galatians confronts us with.

Hypocrisy

What is the cross of Christ? Why does he mention this? It is because the cross is the ultimate form of persecution. Jesus underwent such persecution that he was put to death for raising the feathers of the religious elites, calling them on the carpet, daring to suggest that they were hypocrites. You see, the problem with these false teachers in Galatia, or the Pharisees, or people today who run around with different gospels is that they are hypocrites.

Paul says, "For even those who are circumcised do not themselves keep the law, but they desire to have you circumcised that they may boast in your flesh" (Gal 6:13). He continues with the attack and judging their motives. At the heart is this idea of hypocrisy. A hypocrite is someone who says one thing and does another.

The hypocrisy here is that they make the Galatian Christians adhere to outward laws in order to be acceptable in the eyes of Christ-hating Jews, but meanwhile they themselves refuse to follow other laws that are just as important. The whole idea of backbiting and causing divisions and going against Apostolic authority are just a few of the things we might guess. Again, Jesus confronted this kind of attitude regularly with the

Pharisees calling them white-washed tombs, clean on the outside but full of dead rotting flesh on the inside. He called them a brood of vipers who loved to strike at unsuspecting victims of their hypocrisy, who cared about the food that went into the body, but not the filth that came out of it.

This is the necessary problem with everyone who makes you adhere to rules and regulations, be they biblical or things they invented to make you appear to be more holy. No one keeps the whole law. Yet, the idea is that if you keep one part of it (or some new part that you make up), all will be well. You will be "true Israelites." See how this term becomes so important: The Israel of God? By calling them this, apart from law-keeping, Paul is saying that they already have everything they are being told that they will have if they give up faith and return to the law!

The end of vs. 13 and then vs. 14 are two sides of boasting. On the one hand, in their hypocrisy, these false teachings, in making the Galatians get circumcised, will then be able to boast in their flesh. Literally! By cutting off the flesh, everyone will know that they have won the battle of theology, that they have beaten the mighty Paul, if not with stones, then with words, arguments, and ideas. They will be able to boast in what they have done. And this is what they WANT to do! They want to boast about how effective their teaching was, about how they have made inroads with those unbelieving Jews, about how there really can be reconciliation between Christ and ... not-Christ. These snakes were the first to insist on an unbiblical form of ecumenicism.

The Cross – The Crossroads of Christianity

But the opposite of boasting in ourselves, in our neighbors, or in our victories is to boast in the cross, in persecution, in humiliation, in the death of Christ which is the only thing truly sufficient to save me from my sins. Vs. 14, "But far be it from me to boast except in the cross of our Lord Jesus Christ, by which the world has been crucified to me, and I to the world." The cross of Christ was not a trinket to be worn around a person's neck to show that they were a Christian. It was a scandal to Jews and foolishness to Gentiles. It was a form of torture and shame and death. It was repugnant. But Paul boasts in it! He boasts in weakness, in shame, in humiliation ... in Christ. The cross is the only bridge that allows us to cross from our sin to God's righteousness. It is the only sacrifice that avails the forgiveness of sins. The only remedy to our own eternal death, is the death of the eternal God-man on the cross.

Thus, this verse and the next (vs. 15) return us to the most basic Christian message. As one commentary puts it, "The gospel of Christ crucified so completely rules out any other supposed means of being righteous before God that Paul found it utterly incomprehensible for anyone who has once embraced such a gospel to ever think of supplementing it in any way. For to hold before one's eyes 'Jesus Christ having been crucified' is to put an end to all forms of legalism."[10]

Paul then takes Christ's death as a figure of speech to say that he has been crucified to the world and the world to him. By "world" he refers to the things in this world that used to seem like advantages to righteousness, but which are now understood for what they are, obstacles.[11] Paul isn't saying that he no longer engages the world or that he is trying to escape material existence through yoga or mantras or nirvana. He is saying that no worldly thing that you can imagine, no law, no spiritual discipline, no prayer, no meditation, no form of asceticism or hedonism, no act of the will or thought of the mind ... nothing can make me righteous except the cross of Christ.

A New Creation

This is what the next verse helps us see. "For neither circumcision counts for anything, nor uncircumcision, but a new creation" (vs. 15). No law, no rule, no code, no commandment can ever make a person new. They have to be created by God, through the gospel of Jesus Christ, by the power of the Holy Spirit, through the only instrument that receives it: faith. Faith is not the one work you do, the one thing you add to the mix of ingredients. It is simply the thing that receives and accepts what God has done.

"Creation" is a wonderful figure to represent this, because creation comes out of nothing. Nothing does not create itself. But God speaks the

---

[10] Richard N. Longenecker, vol. 41, *Word Biblical Commentary : Galatians*, Word Biblical Commentary (Dallas: Word, Incorporated, 2002), 294.

[11] Ernest DeWitt Burton, *A Critical and Exegetical Commentary on the Epistle to the Galatians* (New York: Charles Scribner's Sons, 1920), 354, 514.

word and the thing is created. God says "Let there be light," and there is light. God says, "Dry bones, come to life," and they come to life. Creation is the act of God. It is similar to the metaphor of being born again. Nicodemus was tied up in knots over how you enter your mother's womb a second time. Jesus said this new birth must come from the Holy Spirit alone. All this comes back to the cross, because the cross allows God to justly bring a person to life though they have died through sin. That is why Paul will only boast in it. The cross, like the new creation, is the work of God through Christ. To God alone be the glory and the boast! You must come to this realization today, before it is too late. Do you believe that Christ is your only way to be saved, sanctified, and brought to heaven, or are you looking for something, anything else? Trust in Christ and give God the glory.

The Israel of God

Vs. 16 now adds what appears to some to be an old rule of the early Christian church. As we saw last week, it is in a formal structure of a chiasm.

> A. Whoever follows this rule
>   B. Peace
>   B.' Mercy
> A.' Israel of God

Peace and mercy are paralleled, and so are "whoever follows this rule" with "the Israel of God." The structure alone should be enough to tell you who the Israel of God is, but if it is not enough, that which we have just talked about, especially circumcision should make it certain.

Earlier in the letter, when the whole issue of circumcision first came up, Paul's point was basically to ask, "Who are the children of Abraham?" Is it those who are circumcised, or those who are of faith? The answer was obvious and was supported by the OT where it was always the case that the true children of Abraham are those who share the faith of Abraham. Thus, when he calls them "the Israel of God," he is including everyone who is full of peace and mercy. He is not singling out Jewish Christians or any other nonsense like that. Peace comes from a right relationship with

God through faith, and so it is first. Mercy comes from being in that right relationship and so goes out as a blessing to all who are of the faith of Abraham.

Here, I want to talk for just another moment about this important phrase: The Israel of God. Often times we are told as Reformed Christians that we believe in "replacement" theology, that the church replaces Israel. I hate the word "replacement" here. If Israel was the church, then the NT church does not replace itself. I much prefer words like "fulfillment" or even better "fullness." The NT church is everything the OT church was supposed to be, but only rarely showed it, even though it was called the church. It is full of Jews and Gentiles, which was only slightly true in the OT because the Jews didn't go into the world and share their faith like they were supposed to. It is full of equality. It is full of forgiveness and faith. All of this was true in the OT, but was only seen by them like a rare clear spot on an otherwise cloudy day. For moments, the sun would peak through, only to return to the gray world of their sin and disobedience to the covenant of Moses.

When we refuse to acknowledge that all who walk in peace and mercy are the Israel of God, we inadvertently (or not) create divisions between Jews and Gentiles within the church, while maintaining those distinctions even outside of it. This is not a good thing! It can be a serious error that can create the very kinds of divisions that the false teachers were trying to create. Just look at how Zionism and this supposed right of Israel to exist no matter what they do or at Messianic movements that take Gentile Christians and cause them to follow kosher and other kinds of OT laws in order to be "true Christians" has done and continues to do to this very day.

But in Paul's argument, the false teachers were telling the Galatian Christians that if they got circumcised, then God would accept them fully as the Israel of God. Paul, in turn, tells them here that they already are the Israel of God without ever having to get circumcised. Justin Martyr early in the second century understood it perfectly. Speaking to the Jew, Trypho, he said, "For the true spiritual Israel, and descendants of Judah, Jacob, Isaac, and Abraham (who in uncircumcision was approved of and blessed by God on account of his faith, and called the father of many nations), are we who have been led to God through this crucified Christ"

(Justin, *Dialogue* 11.5). Thus, understanding the continuity of the argument Paul makes in Galatians from the OT helps you to take these last few verses the way they were intended. Don't give in to the false teachers, because you already have all of the blessings of Israel in their best and fullest meaning in Christ.

Conclusion of Galatians

Paul concludes his letter with two short points. First, he says, "From now on let no one cause me trouble, for I bear on my body the marks of Jesus" (vs. 17). This is one final authoritative jab at the false teachers and a not-so-subtle warning to the Christians in Galatia. Paul has suffered at great personal cost to himself in order to bring them this good news. He has borne a heavy burden in this letter for his friends who are on the brink of giving up that gospel altogether. He will not continue to be patient or long-suffering. If they persist in such beliefs, if they continue to attack his authority, he is confident that he has done what was required of him: to tell them the truth. He has suffered for it. He has been counted worthy of being like Christ. That is enough for Paul. Likewise, the church should not be overly patient with heretics who seek to destroy the gospel of Jesus Christ. We must return to a biblical orthodoxy and relearn to call a spade a spade on the essential points of the faith as set forth in the ecumenical creeds of the church!

His final words are short, but they are still important. "The grace of our Lord Jesus Christ be with your spirit, brothers. Amen." This is a prayer for the people. In his conclusion to Galatians, Martin Luther shows the deep personal agony he felt for the millions who were perishing eternally because the established church in Rome had spiritually moved its headquarters to Galatia and was leading so many people down the road to hell because of legalistic teaching of righteousness. I too grieve for the many who are withering in churches because the law and gospel are not preached in our day, even in the most conservative political and ethical of our congregations. The prophet said, "My people perish for lack of knowledge." Please, hold the truth more dear to you than gold or diamonds. Love God for who he is and what he has really done. Accept nothing less.

Calvin gives a little more hope and sees things a bit more objectively. I leave you with his words. "[Paul's] prayer is not only that God may bestow upon them his grace in large measure, but that they may have a proper feeling of it in their hearts. Then only is it truly enjoyed by us, when it comes to our *spirit*. We ought therefore to entreat that God would prepare in our souls a habitation for his grace. Amen."[12]

---

[12] John Calvin and William Pringle, *Commentaries on the Epistles of Paul to the Galatians and Ephesians* (Bellingham, WA: Logos Research Systems, Inc., 2010), 188.

Galatians

Appendix: Galatians and the Gods

A Study of the Supernatural Worldview in Galatians

Note: This article was written prior to my sermons on Galatians. As such, I borrowed from it in relevant sermons. I thought it would be helpful to print it as an appendix in this commentary because of the supernatural ideas that are new to many people.

IN THIS ARTICLE I WANT TO LOOK AT THE supernatural side of Paul's letter to the Galatians, particularly angels and other spiritual beings called the *stoicheia*. This is a mostly unnoticed undercurrent in this letter, partly because Paul's strong emphasis on the Law and circumcision quite naturally sweeps us away, and for good reason. If you are anything like me, I think you will find this both stimulating and fascinating.

The letter of Galatians was written by the Apostle Paul to a group of mixed Christians (i.e. Jews and Gentiles) in the province of Galatia probably around 50 A.D. It was not written to a single church, but to churches (Gal 1:2). The term "galatia" can be used ethnically or territorially. If it is being used ethnically, then it refers to the original inhabitants known as the Celts,[1] and its probable audience is central and northern Galatia.[2] If it is being used territorially, then it is probably being written to the churches

---

[1] David Noel Freedman, Allen C. Myers and Astrid B. Beck, "Galatia," in *Eerdmans Dictionary of the Bible* (Grand Rapids, Mich.: W.B. Eerdmans, 2000), 476.

[2] See Hans Dieter Betz, *Galatians : A Commentary on Paul's Letter to the Churches in Galatia*, Hermeneia--a critical and historical commentary on the Bible (Philadelphia: Fortress Press, 1979), 5, 9-13.

Galatians

Paul planted on his first missionary journey which includes cities like Iconium, Derbe, and Lystra (Acts 14).[3] Both of these have intriguing historical correspondences to the curious other-worldly references in the letter. Let me explain that before introducing you to these ideas.

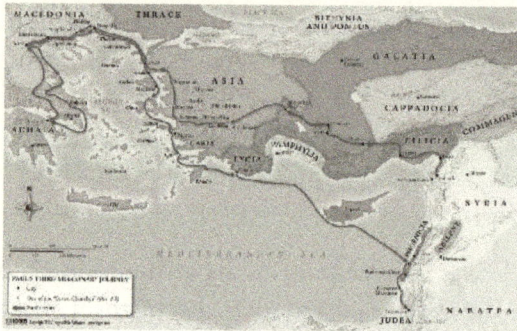

Most people think of the Celts as an ancient tribe that in inhabited Britain and Ireland, but the main territory they occupied was on the continent, primarily in Gaul and Germani. Gaul is an ancient term that describes the region that today takes up France, Luxembourg, Belgium, most of Switzerland, the western part of Northern Italy, and parts of the Netherlands and Germany on the west bank of the Rhine.[4] The people who lived here were called Scythians (also Sacae and later Saxons) by the Greeks. Josephus (37 – 100 A.D.), the Jewish historian, relates that Magog the brother of Gomer and grandson of Noah, was the ancestor of these people.[5] To the east of the Rhine in modern Germany and Scandinavia were the Cimbri and Teuton peoples. The Greek historian Strabo (63

---

[3] See F. F. Bruce, *The Epistle to the Galatians : A Commentary on the Greek Text* (Grand Rapids, Mich.: W.B. Eerdmans Pub. Co., 1982), 3-18.

[4] More technically, it is "a region of northern Europe bounded by the Rhone River on the east, the Alps on the south-east, the Mediterranean on the south, they Pyrenees on the south-west, the Atlantic on the west, and the English Channel on the north-west." John T. Koch, "Gaul," in *Celtic Culture: A Historical Encyclopedia* Vol. 1 (Santa Barbara, CA, 2006), 793.

[5] Josephus, *Antiquities* 1.123.
  http://www.perseus.tufts.edu/hopper/text?doc=Perseus:text:1999.01.0146:book%3D1:whiston+chapter%3D6:whiston+section%3D1

B.C. – 24 A.D.) wrote that the Romans who lived in Gaul called them "Germani" in order to indicate that they were the "authentic" Celts, for *germani* means "genuine."[6]

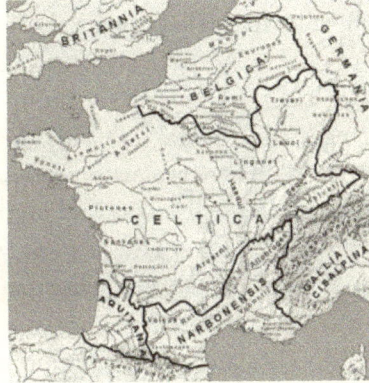

"Gaul" is thought by some to derive from a word meaning "power-ful."[7] Others suggest that "Celt" and "Gaul" have the same meaning, something like "potent" and "valiant men."[8] Why might they have been so powerful? Many ancient historians tell us that these Gauls, and especially their princes, were giants. (It is difficult to know if the Celts were all giants; if a remnant of giants had come into their midst and set themselves up as kings and gods, sort of like Goliath a descendant of Anak who was enlisted into the Philistine army; or if marriages between an ancient giant clan[s] and smaller Celtic clans had introduced genetic possibilities of very large Celtic children). The early 18th Century historian Paul Pezron says these Gauls "exceeded all others in bulk and strength of body; and hence it is that they have been looked upon to be terrible people, and as it

---

[6] *Geography of Strabo* 7.1.2. http://www.perseus.tufts.edu/hopper/text?doc=Perseus:text:1999.01.0239:book%3D7:chapter%3D1:section%3D2
[7] See Helmut Birkhan, *The Celts* (Vienna, 1997), 48.
[8] Paul Pezron, *The Antiquities of Nations; More Particularly of the Celtæ or Gauls*, Mr. D. Jones, translator (London: R. Janeway, publisher, 1706), 276.

were Giants."[9] For example, the Roman historian Julias Florus (2nd Century A.D.) describes one Teutobocchus (a blue eyed, yellow haired Gaul king) as "a man of extraordinary stature" who used to "vault over four or six horses at once" but "could scarcely mount one when he fled." When captured he "was seen above all the trophies or spoils of the enemies, which were carried upon the tops of spears."[10] The Greek historian Polybius (200 – 188 B.C.) laments that thanks to the Celts the Roman legionaries had become super fighting machines. "Once they had got used to being struck down by Gauls they were incapable of imagining anything worse."[11] There are many stories and legends of these giant Gauls/Celts to be found in the histories and mythologies of those peoples.

The Germani were even worse for they were the "true Celts" as Strabo explained. The Christians historian Hegesippus (110 – 180 A.D.) wrote that the Germans "are superior to other nations by the largeness of their bodies and their contempt of death."[12] The Roman Vegetius (4th – 5th Cent. A.D.) wrote, "What could our undersized men have done against the tall Germans." Columella (4 – 70 A.D.) says, "Nature has made Germany remarkable for armies of very tall men."[13] Sidonius Apollinaris (430 – 489 A.D.) reports that so many of the people were seven feet tall and up that he could not address them properly.[14] Augustine reports of a German (Goth) woman being paraded around the streets of Rome who "by her gigantic size over-topped all others."[15] As late as the 1500s, a German by the name of Aymon grew to 11 feet tall. The famed Baron Benten-

---

[9] Pezron, 48.

[10] Florus, *The Epitome of Roman History*, 1.38.3. http://en.wikisource.org/wiki/Epitome_of_Roman_History/Book_1

[11] Cited in Gerhard Herm, *The Celts* (New York: St. Martin's Press, 1975), 19. A particularly vivid and short history of the Roman wars with the giants of Gaul and neighboring Germany can be found in Charles DeLoach, *Giants: A Reference Guide from History, the bible, and Recorded Legend* (Metuchen, N.J.: Scarecrow Press, 1995), see especially the sections "Celtic Giants," "German Giant's Annihilation," and "Giants Who Became Gods." This includes history from the likes of Julius Caesar, Plutarch, and Diodorus among others. http://www.stevequayle.com/Giants/index2.html

[12] Hegesippus, *Histories* 2.9. http://www.ccel.org/ccel/pearse/morefathers/files/hegesippus_02_book2.htm. This book is a compilation of Josephus' Wars, and is usually thought to be pseudepigraphal (that is, attributed to Hegesippus, but probably not actually written by him).

[13] These sources are cited in Johann Georg Keyssler, *Travels through Germany, Hobemia, Hungary, Switzerland, Italy, and Lorrain* Vol. 1 (London, G. Keith, 1760), 51-52.

[14] Cited in Cornelius Tacitus (56 – 117 A.D.), "Treatise on the Situations, Manners, and People of Germany," in *Works* 4 (Philadelphia: Thomas Wardle, 1838), note 9.

[15] Augustine, *City of God* 15.23.2.

rieder—who was himself eight feet eight inches—"hardly reached up to Arymon's armpits."[16] Still another named Hans Braw was estimated at 12 feet 8 inches tall![17] So fierce were these Germans that, "The Gauls," reports Julius Caesar (100 – 15 B.C.), "had not been able to endure even the expression on their faces or the glare of their eyes."[18] The Romans called them "Berserkers," and for decades the greatest army on earth was continually slaughtered by these giants in war (and people wonder where Hitler got the idea of a "super-race" from)!

How does this relate to Galatians? In two ways. First, the Celts/Gauls seem to have inhabited the region of Galatia in very early times. Josephus stated that Gomer the son of Japheth the son of Noah settled in Galatia. "Gomer founded those whom the Greeks now call Galatians [Galls], but were then called Gomerites."[19] The name Gomer in Akkadian is Gimirru (they called them Gimmerai). Europeans called them Cimmerians or Cimbri. Many of these Cimbri migrated north and west into Gaul and became the Celts. Second, during the centuries long wars with the up and coming Romans (3rd – 1st centuries B.C.), these Celts began to leave Gaul *en masse* (many had undoubtedly continued past Gaul in earlier times). Some went north into Britannia, and there is evidence to suggest they migrated further west into North America where they became the tall blonde Adena people known to the Indians.[20] Others returned towards the place of their origin, migrating back towards Galatia. In fact, Galatia takes its name from the Gauls (Celts). It comes from a Greek word (*gala*) meaning "milk." Galatea means "she who is milk-white," as the Celts were the white skinned blonde giants of ancient times.

The migration of these ancient peoples seems to have begun in the region of today's Uzbekistan and Kazakhstan around the Jaxartes River which flows into the Aral Sea.[21] This matches the migration of the ancient Kurgan peoples, made famous in pop-culture by the Kurgan Immortal in

---

[16] Keyssler, 39.

[17] Ibid., 52.

[18] Caesar, *Commentary* 1.39.

[19] Josephus, *Antiquities* 1:123.

[20] See Frank Joseph, *Advanced Civilizations of Prehistoric America* (Rochester, VT: Bear & Company, 2010), 10-84,

[21] Pezron, 41-42.

the first *Highlander* movie.[22] These ancient Kurgans were depicted as extremely tall and of Caucasian descent in golden figures discovered near the Black Sea.

Left: 4th century B.C. Scythian horseman. Found at the Kul' Oba kurgan near Kerch (northern Black Sea). **Right**: Comb with battle scene, Scythian 430-390 B.C., Ukraine, Solokha kurgan. Located now in The State Hermitage Museum. Saint Petersburg, Russia. **Note** how the legs of the riders go *all the way to the ground*! These were either very small horses, or very tall men, much like Teutobocchus as discussed above.

Some moved northwest, north of the Black Sea, into Serbia and finally to Germany. Others went southwest, first into Margiana, Hircania, and Bactriana, and then south of the Caspian Sea into Armenia where they continued to migrate south (into Syria and Arabia) and west (into Galatia, Phrygia and beyond). It is curious the southern migrations go right past the ancient region of Babel, where Nimrod the "mighty hunter" (who in the Greek translation of the OT is called a giant; Gen 10:8-10) seems to have built the famous Tower of Babel. It also takes you near the regions of the giants kings mentioned in Genesis 14 (including Shinar, Elasar and Elam, and Goiim which may have been near Galatia).[23]

---

[22] Marija Gimbutas, "The Kurgan Culture and the Indo-Europeanization of Europe: Selected Articles from 1952 to 1993," ed. Miriam Robbins Dexter and Karlene Jones-Bley. *Journal of Indo-European Studies Monograph No. 18* [Washington, D.C.: Institute for the Study of Man, 1997]: xix + 404 pages

[23] These lands are filled with gigantic megalithic ruins (places like Göbekli Tepe, Baalbek, Gilgal Refaim etc.) which traditions say were built by giants.

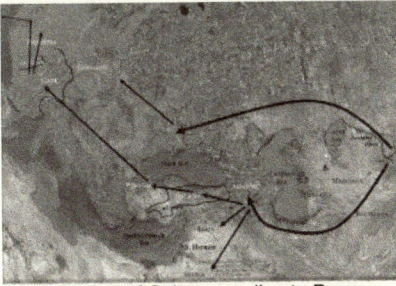

Migration of Celts according to Pezron

T. R. Holme, "The Kurgan Invasions"
http://www.trholme.com/garden-e-danu/GG6.htm

All of this is background necessary for enriching your understanding of the demonic worldview Paul presents in his letter to the Galatians. "How could that be," you ask? It is a good question. The answer is that for the demons were thought by many in ancient times to be the restless souls of the giants who perished in the flood.[24] These demons become the "evil spirits" of the NT, but in older times they were viewed as neither good nor bad, but as intermediaries between the gods and humanity.[25] The Galatians would have been intimately acquainted with such ideas for obvious reasons.

If "Galatians" refers to a geographical region of the Roman Empire, then it is likely that Paul is writing to the churches he planted on his first missionary journey. In one of these very cities, the Galatian city called Lystra, we read of a man crippled from birth whom Paul healed because he saw the man had faith in Christ (Acts 14:8-10). When this occurred, the people lifted up their voices as one and said in their native tongue, "The gods have come down to us in the likeness of men!" (vs. 11). So they called Barnabas Zeus and Paul they called Hermes because he was the chief speaker (vs. 12). How strange! Why did these Galatians think such a thing?

---

[24] Cf., 1 Enoch 15:8-16:1; Athenagoras, *A Plea to Christians* 24-25; Eusebius, *Preparation for the Gospel* 5.4; Justin Martyr, *2 Apology* 5.
[25] Cf. Augustine, *City of God* 8.23.1; 9.8.1. Augustine does not deny that the demons are intermediaries; he denies that they may be trusted because he sees them as fallen, evil beings.

Galatians

Hermes was worshiped as the god of magic and healing by the Greeks,[26] but he was also a great teacher of wisdom and understanding,[27] the ultimate messenger god of the pantheon. He has exact counterparts in Jewish (Pênêmûe), Egyptian (Thoth), and Roman (Mercury) traditions. A "messenger" in both Greek and Hebrew is also an angel. Hence, it is very curious that Paul tells us in the middle of his letter, "You received me as an angel of God" (Gal 4:14).[28] Why? Because they thought he was Hermes! Yet, Paul says, "It was because of a *bodily ailment* that I preached the gospel to you at first ... yet you did not scorn or despise me" (4:13-14). It seems that because he healed others and proclaimed the message of the gospel, they overlooked the small little detail that he did not heal himself (proof from God Almighty to them that he was not in fact Hermes)!

So both Acts and Galatians explains that the people thought Paul was one of the gods come down out of heaven and an angel of God. Where would they get such an idea? They get it from Genesis 6:1-4 (though it was surely part of their own mythology, as this is a universal story told on every continent). Genesis 6:1-4 explains that the "sons of God" took wives from among the children of men.[29] Keep the term "sons of God" in the back of your mind as we will return to this idea (see also the sermon "Sons of God" in the book). The only known interpretation of this passage at the time of Paul's writing (which includes 2 Peter 2:4-5 and Jude 6[30] and maybe Matt 24:37-38; Luke 17:26-27; 1 Cor 11:10, and

---

[26] From Hermes we derive the term *hermitic seal*. He was believed to possess a magic ability to seal treasure chests so that nothing could access their contents. Alchemy and hermeticism are two esoteric philosophic/religious traditions that are rooted in the magic healing of Hermes.

[27] From Hermes we derive *hermeneutics* or the art of interpretation of a text.

[28] The full thought reads, "you received me as an angel of God, as Christ Jesus." Hence, the idea that Jesus was an angel come out of heaven to be a man.

[29] The text does not say that the sons of *Seth* took wives from among the children of *Cain*. "Cain" does not equal "man," and "Seth" does not equal "God."

[30] Commentaries that take this view include This is the view of Peter and Jude include Richard J. Bauckham, *Jude 2 Peter*, Word Biblical Commentary (Waco, TX: Word Books, 1983), 50-53; Edwin A. Blum, *Jude*, The Expositors Bible Commentary Vol. 12 (Grand Rapids, MI: Zondervan, 1981), 390;, Peter H. Davids, *The Letters of 2 Peter and Jude*, Pillar New Testament Commentary (Grand Rapids, MI: Eerdmans, 2006), 48-51; Gene L. Green, *Jude & 2 Peter*, Baker Exegetical Commentary on the New Testament (Grand Rapids, MI: Baker Academic, 2008), 66-70; Michael Green, *2 Peter and Jude*, Tyndale New Testament Commentaries (Downers Grove, IL: InterVarsity, 1987), 191-92; Douglas J. Moo, *2 Peter, Jude,* NIV Application Commentary (Grand Rapids, MI: Zondervan, 1996), 241-42; Thomas R. Schreiner, *1, 2 Peter, Jude*, New American Commentary (Nashville, TN: Broadman & Holman, 2003), 447-51 and many others and many others.

1 Peter 3:18-20) was that this referred to heavenly beings taking wives from among human beings. The Hebrew equivalent of Hermes (Pênêmûe) was said to be one of these heavenly beings in Jewish tradition.[31] In other words, in ancient times, Hermes had once descended to earth in the form of a human being. The Galatians thought he was doing so again when Paul and Barnabas arrived.

The result of this forbidden union (they were not "according to their kind." Cf. Gen 1:12, 21, 24, 25; 6:20; 7:14) was that they had children called Nephilim. The word *nephilim* means "giant,"[32] as the Greek translation of the OT renders the word. This brings us full circle to the idea that "Galatia" may refer to an ethic group. These giants were destroyed in the Great Flood and their spirits were thought to have become the demons. After the Flood, more giants came upon the earth (perhaps through another rebellion of angels or through mixed DNA in someone on the Ark). This is a main reason for the battles of Joshua in the Promised Land, for when the spies returned they said, "There are giants in the land and they devour (i.e. eat) the people," something that is reported throughout the world when stories of giants come up. The point, again, is that the Galatians were intimately familiar with a worldview that we modern "enlightened" and "de-supernaturalized" people can scarcely imagine. It is a worldview that Paul explains in a good many verses in Galatians. With this as background, let's take a look at this hidden side of the letter, a side which you will see is not really all that "hidden" at all.

Paul begins by thanking God for giving us Christ who "gave himself for our sins to deliver us from the present *evil* age" (Gal 1:4). The present evil age is associated in the NT with both natural and *super*natural enemies. This is part of the burden of the letter to explain. A few verses later he says, "Even if we or *an angel from heaven* should preach to you a gospel contrary to the one we preached to you, let him be accursed" (1:8). Without the proper background, this sounds like a very strange thing to say. "An

---

[31] 1 Enoch 69:8-16.

[32] The word does not mean "to fall," but "giant." This is proven from Numbers 13:33 which spells the word two different ways (the second is an explanation of the first). The first way is the older *n-ph-l-m*. The second is *n-phy-l-m*, a word which in Aramaic means "giant." See Michael Heiser, *The Myth That Is True* (unpublished), 80-83.

angel from heaven" preaching to the Galatians? I've touched on how the Galatians believed Paul himself was a god sent from heaven in the form of Hermes and how this "sons of God" descended to earth in elder times in order to prepare you for this kind of language.

After this, for many verses the flow of Paul's thought seems to be exclusively natural. That is, he is dealing with Jewish teachers who have somehow duped the Galatians to return to the law and circumcision. Suddenly, in 3:1 he uses the word "bewitched" in the form of a question, "Who has bewitched you?" This has obvious connotations of the supernatural world. The word "bewitched" is *baskaino*, a very interesting word indeed. It means "to slander" or "to cast the evil eye" upon someone through magic and spells. The Greeks imagined that rays came out of the eyes, and had serpentine figures of their mythology such as the Gorgon, the Medusa, or the Basilisk (note the similarity to *baskaino*) that did just this. This word is a foretaste of stranger things to come.

The first of these strange things occurs when Paul says that the law was put into effect through angels by an intermediary. Actually, there are two strange things here. "Law" here refers to the Mosaic Law, including the Ten Commandments and its 600 plus applications of the civil and ceremonial case law. Acts 7:53[33] and Hebrews 2:2[34] both suggest this same idea, that angels put the law into effect. This comes from the Greek version (Septuagint) of Deuteronomy 33:2-4 which explains that ten thousands of holy ones came with the LORD upon Sinai and Moses received God's words.[35] The reason why angels would come with God at Mt. Sinai is explained by something Psalm 82:1 calls "the divine council" (ESV).

The divine council is, "A term used by Hebrew and Semitics scholars for the heavenly host, the pantheon of divine beings who administer the

---

[33] Stephen says here that the law was *diatagas* ("delivered by" or "ordained by," or "decrees given by," or "from the direction of") angels.

[34] This verse talks about "the message declared by angels that proved to be reliable."

[35] "The LORD came from Sinai and dawned from Seir upon us; he shone forth from Mount Paran; with ten thousands of [holy ones]; on his right hand were his angels with him. And he spared his people, and all his holy ones are under your hands; and they are under you; and he received of his words, the law which Moses charged us."

affairs of the cosmos."[36] Daniel 7:9-10 is a good place to see the function of this council. Here, thrones (plural) are positioned around God. Thousands upon thousands of holy heavenly beings are present. The heavenly court sits in judgment and the books are opened. Angels or "holy ones" are coming upon Mt. Sinai and giving the law to Moses because this is a chief function of their God-given authority as rulers and judges of the affairs of humanity. This may seem strange and foreign to contemporary ears, but it is the teaching of these passages.

Even stranger than the angelic decree of law, these angels have an intermediary between them and God. Many scholars who have no worldview to can contain such theology will insist that the "intermediary" here is Moses and that *he* is interceding between God (or angels) and *Israel*. If this were true, the next verse would be gibberish. It says, "An intermediary implies more than one, but God is one." This makes absolutely no sense as F.F. Bruce asks, "In what way does the affirmation that God is one form an antithesis to what is said about the mediator?"[37]

A better option is that the mediator is not human (between angels and men, a role the *demons* take in the ancient world![38]) but angelic, and that this angelic mediator mediates between the angels *and God*. In other words, He tells the angels what to write or say, or however it all worked out. Deuteronomy 9:9-10 says that when Moses went up the mountain to receive the tablets of stone, "The LORD gave me the two tablets of stone written with *the finger of God*, and on them were all the words that the LORD had spoken with you on the mountain out of the midst of the fire on the day of the assembly." The finger of God is not some nebulous anthropomorphism for the Father; it is descriptive language for God coming in visible form. Michael Heiser suggests that this mediator is none other than the Angel of the LORD.[39] This Angel is both a mediator *and God*, in

---

[36] Michael S. Heiser, "The Divine Council," in *Dictionary of the Old Testament: Wisdom, Poetry, and Writings* (Downers Grove, Ill: Intervarsity Press, 2008). This introduction to the council can be read online: http://www.thedivinecouncil.com/HeiserIVPDC.pdf.

[37] F. F. Bruce, *The Epistle to the Galatians : A Commentary on the Greek Text* (Grand Rapids, Mich.: W.B. Eerdmans Pub. Co., 1982), 178.

[38] Prophets play the role as mediators between God (as opposed to angels or the gods) and humanity.

[39] Heiser, *Myth*, p. 152-32. Heiser suggests that the angels are here as members of the divine council, a kind of heavenly court of beings who were created by God to rule over the affairs of heaven and earth.

other words Christ preincarnate. Thus, Paul's reference to "one God" makes perfect sense in the context. Even though a mediator implies more than one (i.e. three persons: Father, Son, and Holy Spirit), there is still only one God (i.e. one being: God). This is a proof-text of the Trinity!

Immediately after explaining that the law was giving through angels by an intermediary, Paul then begins to describe how Scripture imprisoned everything under sin (Gal 3:22). "Scripture" here is a word that encompasses the three forces that the Bible tells us are engaged against us: The world, the flesh, and the devil. It does not say this in so many words, but it is a helpful way of understanding the argument. Paul says that three main things have held us captive and imprisoned. The first is the law (Gal 3:23-24). He says that the Galatians were "held captive under the law, imprisoned. . ." and says that the law was our "guardian." The word "guardian" here is used in the ancient world of a slave who is set over the child of a father to superintend his life and morals until the child should grow to adulthood. The KJV famously renders it "a schoolmaster." The law was our slave-teacher and thus prison in the sense of showing us (and indeed increasing) our sin, thus our need for a savior and redemption (cf. Rom 3:19-20; 5:20; 7:5-13). As the "law" is being applied to Gentiles who did not have the Ten Commandments, it must refer to the moral part of the law that is written on our hearts by nature (cf. Rom 2:14-15). It is something that belongs to the whole world and as such I have tied it to "the world" for the sake of simplicity and understanding.

The second thing (actually the third) that relates to captivity is "the slave woman" (Gal 4:22-24). Paul uses OT history here allegorically. Abraham had a wife named Sarah. But he had a handmaiden named Hagar whom Sarah convinced to sleep with Abraham in order to give him a son since she was too old herself. Hagar gave Abraham a biological son, a child of the flesh but not the promise. Hence, I have linked this captivity to the flesh or the things in our nature that try to gain the promise through works rather than faith.

The third thing (actually second) that he says held us captive is "the elementary principles of the world" (ESV; Gal 4:3). This is the part I really want to focus upon. "Elementary principles" is actually a single word in Greek. The word is *stoicheia*. What are these *stoicheia*? Again, not having a supernatural worldview capable of handling the truth, many assume that it must refer to legalistic Jewish law-keeping. In fact, I first began to be suspicious of this view after hearing a pastor teach on Galatians 4:10-11, "You observe days and months and seasons and years! I am afraid I may have labored over you in vain." His argument was that Christians are no longer bound to keep the Sabbath because of this verse.

Judiasers, he said, were telling the Galatians they had to keep Jewish holy days. "Days" refers to refers to biblical OT days, the chief of which was the Sabbath. He then made the following startling claim, "False religions are headed up by demons and they are enslaving ... clearly the Jewish laws in view here are the old covenants (implying that OT Judaism was a false religion). To return to those, including the Sabbath, is to return to paganism. Therefore, Christians should not keep the Sabbath."[40] This is an astonishing—if not (unwittingly) blasphemous—claim. His point about demons comes from Galatians 4:8, "You were enslaved to those that by nature are not gods." He rightly points out that these "no gods" were enslaving people. He rightly calls them demons (see below). But his worldview is incapable of holding more than one enslaving principle in the ancient world. Yet, that is exactly what is going on. The *stoicheia* refers not to the Law (which was put into effect by angels, not demons), but to "those who are not gods." Note the "stoicheia sandwich" parallel in the following verses:

Vs. 3 You were enslaved to the *stoicheia* of the world.
Vs. 8 You were enslaved to those that by nature are not gods.
Vs. 9 How can you turn back to the weak and worthless *stoicheia* of the world, whose slaves you want to be once more?

Let me summarize before I explain. The *law* enslaved the Jewish Christians in Galatia prior to their conversion, while the *demons* enslaved the Gentile Christians in Galatia prior to their conversion. Both groups are present in the Galatians churches (the Gentiles are picked out by name in Gal 3:8, 9, 14) and both enslavers are here in this section of Galatians.

---

[40] http://www.youtube.com/watch?v=Ec1aTdFqVuk

To understand this, it is helpful to see where else Paul uses this kind of language and then turn to the OT source for his worldview.

First, note that in this passage, Paul does not call the *stoicheia* "demons," but "gods." In 1 Corinthians 8:5-6 he says, "Although there may be so-called gods in heaven or on earth—*as indeed there are many gods* and many lords—yet for us there is one God, the Father, from whom are all things and for whom we exist, and one Lord, Jesus Christ, through whom are all things and through whom we exist." Note, Paul does not deny the existence of other gods. In fact, he affirms it! Don't let that bother you. It is not a death-blow to monotheism. But you do need to let the text speak without silencing it yourself. What he says is that these "gods" are utterly inferior to the One God and to Jesus Christ who created them. God has self-existence, omnipotence, omniscience etc., but gods do not. (Note: the "gods" he has in mind here are personal entities, not merely the "god" of money or food etc). Who are these "gods?" There are two separate entities that are in view in the Bible.

The first entity can be seen in the same discussion to the Corinthians. Paul calls them "demons" (1 Cor 10:20-21). Demons are real beings, affirmed as far back as Deuteronomy 32:17 where they are equated with "gods." "They sacrificed <u>to demons</u>, not God, <u>to gods</u> they had never known, to new gods that had come recently, whom your fathers had never dreaded." These demons are the evil "spirits" of the Gospels which Jesus and the Disciples encountered on so many occasions. As I have already mentioned, they were thought in those days to be the spirits of the drown Nephilim, the giant offspring of the sons of God and daughters of men from Genesis 6:1-4.

This leads straight into a second class of being which the Bible often refers to as "gods." They are sometimes called the "sons of God," though they are also called the "heavenly host," "stars," and other things. The sons of God are heavenly beings who were present at the creation of the physical universe (Job 38:7), who came to present themselves with Satan to the LORD (Job 1:6; 2:1), and who took wives from the daughters of men and had gigantic wicked children who began to rule over men (Gen 6:1-4). They are real beings, as David affirms when he says, "I will You thanks with all my heart; I will sing praises to You before the gods" (Ps

138:1). Imagine if these gods were not real beings. It would be like saying, "I will praise you before the Justice League or the Smurfs."

Over and over again, Deuteronomy tells us that the whole world had been given over to and allotted heavenly beings to rule over them (cf. Deut 4:19-20; 17:3; 29:26; 32:7-9; 17). Psalm 82 particularly explains how these beings did not rule with justice and righteousness and will therefore be severely punished. Yet, as noted above, these gods are never equated with God or with Jesus Christ who created them. For example, in Colossians (the only other letter where the stoicheia appear; 2:8, 20) we learn up front that by Jesus Christ "all things were created, in <u>heaven</u> and on earth, visible and <u>invisible</u>, whether <u>thrones</u> or <u>dominions</u> or <u>rulers</u> or <u>authorities</u>—all things were created through him and for him" (Col 1:16). This verse is filled not only with natural creation, but with supernatural creation at the hands of Jesus. Notice that these supernatural beings are called thrones, dominions, rulers, and authorities. The NT sees heavenly beings as ruling beings. This is but the tip of the iceberg, but it is enough to affirm the existence of lesser beings (called gods) who are in no way equal to the Father, Son, or Holy Spirit. The magnificent truth Paul is giving to these Galatians (at this moment focusing on the Gentiles among them) is that in Christ through the gospel and by faith, they have been set free from the rule and authority of these beings who held them in captivity. He is now their master. Slavery to him is actually freedom for the very first time (see Gal 5:1ff).

"Sons of God" is a particularly important and relevant title given what Paul says throughout this section of Galatians. Sonship is perhaps the dominant theme of Galatians 3-4. Those who have faith in Christ are "<u>sons</u> of Abraham" (3:7). This sonship is not through the things of the world or the flesh, but comes about supernaturally by faith and adoption.

We are also "<u>sons</u> of God" (3:26). This sonship is rooted in the Sonship of Jesus Christ. "God sent forth his <u>Son</u>, born of woman, burn under law. . . so that we might receive adoption as <u>sons</u>" (Gal 4:4-5). In verse 6 "you are <u>sons</u>" and "God has sent the Spirit of his <u>Son</u> into your hearts." In verse 7 "you are no longer a slave, but a <u>son</u>." This change from slave to son is the topic that brings about the whole discussion of the *stoicheia*.

When it refers to Jesus as God's "son," this is the same yet different from the OT sons of God. It is the same in that Jesus in the OT was "The

Angel of the LORD." These other sons are also angelic or heavenly beings and Jesus was in this way like them. In as much as they were all sons of God, Jesus was their brother. Yet, Jesus is unlike all the other heavenly sons of God. For he is the *only begotten* son, that is the only unique son, the only uncreated son, the only omnipotent son etc. This is why it seems that any time the NT begins to talk about these heavenly beings, Jesus and his sovereign rule over them (because he both created them and defeated them at the cross and resurrection) is never far away.

It is fascinating that Paul should refer to us as sons of God too! In inheriting this title we are being lifted up to an exalted position held by the highest order of angelic beings. Yet, our position is greater than theirs. This is why it says, "Do you not know that we shall judge angels?" (1 Cor 6:3). As Jesus was fashioned in the womb of Mary "a little lower than the angels," he was also crowned with glory and honor so that now at the name of Jesus every knee will bow in heaven and on earth (Php 2:10). As a man, Jesus has lifted us up to his high estate in the world to come. He has set us free from the bondage and servitude of the demons and their fallen fathers. And if we have been set free, then we would never want again to return to the kind of slavery to them that we and our ancestors had before the gospel came and gave us new life. That is the supernatural worldview of Galatians. That is the significance of Galatians and the gods.

Works Cited

A Greek-English Lexicon of the New Testament and Other Early Christian Literature, 3rd ed. William Arndt, Frederick W. Danker, and Walter Bauer (eds). Chicago: University of Chicago Press, 2000.

Ambrosiaster, *Epistle to the Galatians* 3.17. In Edwards, M. J. *Galatians, Ephesians, Philippians*, Ancient Christian Commentary on Scripture NT 8. Downers Grove, Ill.: InterVarsity Press, 1999.

The Ancient Near East an Anthology of Texts and Pictures. Ed. James Bennett Pritchard. Princeton: Princeton University Press, 1958.

Anders, Max. *Galatians-Colossians*. Holman New Testament Commentary. Nashville, TN: Broadman & Holman Publishers, 1999.

Arichea, D. C. Jr., and Nida, E. A. *A Translator's Handbook on Paul's Letter to the Galatians*. Helps for Translators 18; Stuttgart, 1976.

Barclay, William. *Flesh and Spirit*. Grand Rapids, MI: Baker Books, 1962.

Barker, Dan. *Losing Faith*. Madison, WI: Freedom From Religion Foundation, 1992.

The Babylonian Talmud: A Translation and Commentary. Ed. Jacob Neusner. Peabody, MA: Hendrickson Publishers, 2011.

Baker Encyclopedia of the Bible. Ed. Walter A. Elwell and Barry J. Beitzel. Grand Rapids, Mich.: Baker Book House, 1988.

Betz, Hans Dieter. *Galatians : A Commentary on Paul's Letter to the Churches in Galatia*. Hermeneia--a critical and historical commentary on the Bible. Philadelphia: Fortress Press, 1979.

Black, David Alan. *It's Still Greek to Me*. Grand Rapids, MI: Baker Books, 1998.

Birkhan, Helmut. *The Celts*. Vienna, 1997.

Blaising Craig A., and Darrell L. Bock. *Progressive Dispensationalism*. Grand Rapids, MI: Baker Books, 1993.

Bruce, F. F. *The Epistle to the Galatians: A Commentary on the Greek Text.* Grand Rapids, MI: W.B. Eerdmans Pub. Co., 1982.

Burton, Ernest DeWitt. *A Critical and Exegetical Commentary on the Epistle to the Galatians.* New York: Charles Scribner's Sons, 1920.

Calvin, John. *Commentaries on the Catholic Epistles.* Trans. John Owen. Bellingham, WA: Logos Research Systems, Inc., 2010.

_____. *Commentaries on the Epistles of Paul to the Galatians and Ephesians.* Bellingham, WA: Logos Research Systems, Inc., 2010.

_____. *Institutes of the Christian Religion.* Ed. John T. McNeill. Louisville, KY: The Westminster Press, 1960.

Carson, D. A.; Moo, Douglas J.; Morris, Leon. *An Introduction to the New Testament.* Grand Rapids, MI: Zondervan, 1992.

Cassuto, Umberto. *A Commentary on the Book of Genesis: From Noah to Abraham.* Jerusalem: Magnes Press, 1964.

Chafer, Lewis Sperry. *Dispensationalism.* Dallas: Dallas Seminary Press, 1936.

The Christian Post. "C. J. Mahaney Takes Leave Over Charges of Pride." By Lillian Kwon. Monday July 11, 2011. http://www.christianpost.com/news/longtime-minister-takes-leave-to-reexamine-soul-52127/

Cole, R. Alan. *Galatians: An Introduction and Commentary.* Tyndale New Testament Commentaries. Downers Grove, IL: InterVarsity Press, 1989.

The Complete Word Study Dictionary: New Testament. Electronic edition. Ed. Spiros Zodhiates. Chattanooga, TN: AMG Publishers, 2000.

Cornwall, Judson. *The Exhaustive Dictionary of Bible Names* (North Brunswick, NJ: Bridge-Logos, 1998.

Dictionary of Deities and Demons in the Bible, 2nd extensively revised edition. Eds. van der Toorn, K., Becking, Bob, and van der Horst, Pieter Willem. Boston: Eerdmans, 1999.

Easton's Bible Dictionary. Oak Harbor, WA: Logos Research Systems, Inc., 1996.

Eerdmans Dictionary of the Bible. Grand Rapids, Mich.: W.B. Eerdmans, 2000.

ESV Study Bible. Wheaton, IL: Crossway Bibles, 2008.

Eusebius. *Ecclesiastical History.* Peabody, MA: Hendrickson Publishers, 1988.

Fuller, Daniel Payton. "The Hermeneutics of Dispensationalism." Unpublished Th.D. Dissertation. Northern Baptist Theological Seminary, Chicago, 1957.

Fung, Ronald Y. K. *The Epistle to the Galatians*. The New International Commentary on the New Testament. Grand Rapids, MI: Wm. B. Eerdmans Publishing Co., 1988.

Gaffin, Richard. *Resurrection and Redemption*. Phillipsburg, NJ: P&R, 1987.

George, Timothy. *Galatians*. The New American Commentary. Nashville: Broadman & Holman Publishers, 2001.

Gill, John. *Exposition of the Bible*. http://www.biblestudytools.com/commentaries/gills-exposition-of-the-bible/

Gordon, Cyrus. "אלהים in Its Reputed Meaning of *Rulers, Judges*." *Journal of Biblical Literature* 54 (1935): 139–144.

Groothuis, Rebecca Merrill. *Good News for Women*. Grand Rapids, MI: Baker Books, 1997.

_____. *Women Caught in the Conflict*. Eugene, OR: Wifp & Stock, 1997.

Heiser, Michael S. "Deuteronomy 32:8 and the Sons of God." *Bibliotheca Sacra* 158:629 (Jan-Mar, 2001): 52-74. http://www.thedivinecouncil.com/DT32BibSac.pdf

_____. "The Divine Council." In *Dictionary of the Old Testament: Wisdom, Poetry, and Writings*. Downers Grove, Ill: Intervarsity Press, 2008.

_____. *The Myth That Is True*. Unpublished.

_____. "The *stoicheia*/'Elements' or 'Elemental Spirits.'" *Behind the Façade* vol. 3, no. 10 (March 2005): 36-43.

_____. "You've Seen One *Elohim*, You've Seen Them All? A Critique of Mormonism's Use of Psalm 82." *FARMS Review* 19/1 (2007): 221–266.

Hendriksen, William and Kistemaker, Simon J. *Exposition of Galatians*. New Testament Commentary vol. 8. Grand Rapids: Baker Book House, 1953-2001.

Hill, Bob. *The Big Difference Between the Two Gospels*. Biblical Answers Ministries, 1999.

Hoehner, H. W. "The Duration of the Egyptian Bondage." *Bibliotheca Sacra Volume* 126:504 (1969): 306-16. http://faculty.gordon.edu/hu/bi/Ted_Hildebrandt/OTeSources/02-Exodus/Text/Articles/Hoehner-DurationEgypt-BSac.htm

Jerome. *Epistle to the Galatians* 2.3.15.

Jewish Encyclopedia. Ed. Isidore Singer and Cyrus Adler. New York: Funk and Wagnalls, 1912.

Galatians

Josephus, Flavius and Whiston, William. *The Works of Josephus: Complete and Unabridged.* Peabody: Hendrickson, 1996.

Kline, Meredith. *Kingdom Prologue.* Eugene, OR: Wipf and Stock, 2006.

Laertius, Diogenes. *Lives of Eminent Philosophers,* ed. R. D. Hicks. Kansas City Missouri: Harvard University Press, November 1, 2005.

Lightfoot, J. B. *The Epistle of St. Paul to the Galatians.* Grand Rapids, MI: Zondervan, 1957.

Longenecker, Richard N. *Galatians.* Word Biblical Commentary, vol. 41. Dallas: Word, Incorporated, 2002.

Luther, Martin. *Commentary on Galatians.* Grand Rapids, MI: Fleming H. Revell, 1988.

_____. *Lectures on Romans.* Louisville: Westminster John Knox Press, 2006.

_____. Vol. 26, *Luther's Works, Vol. 26 : Lectures on Galatians, 1535, Chapters 1-4.* Ed. Jaroslav Jan Pelikan, Hilton C. Oswald and Helmut T. Lehmann, Luther's Works. Saint Louis: Concordia Publishing House, 1999.

Matera, Frank J. *Galatians.* Collegeville, MN: Liturgical Press, 2007.

MacArthur, John. "Apostolic Commendation: Comments on Galatians 2:7." January 20, 1974. http://www.gty.org/Resources/Sermons/1654

Metzger Bruce M. and United Bible Societies. *A Textual Commentary on the Greek New Testament.* Second Edition a Companion Volume to the United Bible Societies' Greek New Testament, 4th Rev. Ed. London; New York: United Bible Societies, 1994.

Moo, Douglas J. *The Epistle to the Romans.* The New International Commentary on the New Testament. Grand Rapids, MI: Wm. B. Eerdmans Publishing Co., 1996.

Murray, Iain H. *Evangelicalism Divided.* Carlisle, PA: Banner of Truth, 2000.

Nickelsburg, George W. E. and Baltzer, Klaus. *1 Enoch : A Commentary on the Book of 1 Enoch.* Minneapolis, MN: Fortress, 2001.

O'Neill, J. C. *The Recovery of Paul's Letter to the Galatians* (London: S.P.C.K., 1972).

Osment, Emily. "Believe in Something." On the album *Fight or Flight.*

Owen, John. *The Works of John Owen.* London: Patenoster, 1826.

Pezron, Paul. *The Antiquities of Nations: More Particularly of the Celte or Gauls.* Mr. D. Jones, translator. London: R. Janeway, publisher, 1706.

Piper, John. "Did God Command Adam to Earn His Life." In *A Godward Life: Savoring the Supremacy of God in All Life*. Sisters, Or.: Multnomah Publishers, 1997.

_____. God is the Gospel: Meditations on God's Love as the Gift of Himself. Wheaton, IL: Crossway Books, 2005.

Philo of Alexandria. *The Works of Philo: Complete and Unabridged*. Ed. Charles Duke Yonge. Peabody: Hendrickson, 1996.

Rapa, Robert K. "Romans-Galatians." *Expositors Bible Commentary* revised edition. Ed. Tremper Longman II and David E. Garland. Grand Rapids, MI: Zondervan, 2005).

Reid, Daniel G. "Elements/Elemental Spirits of the World." In *Dictionary of Paul and His Letters*. Downers Grove, IL: InterVarsity Press, 1993: 229-33.

Ridderbos, Herman N. *The Epistle of Paul to the Churches of Galatia*. The New International Commentary on the Old and New Testament. Grand Rapids, MI: Wm. B. Eerdmans Publishing Co., 1953.

Riggs, J. R. "The Length of Israel's Sojourn in Egypt." *Grace Theological Journal* 12 (1971): 18-35. (http://faculty.gordon.edu/hu/bi/ted_hildebrandt/otesources/02-exodus/Text/Articles/Riggs-EgyptSojourn-GTJ.htm

Robertson, O. Palmer *The Books of Nahum, Habakkuk and Zephaniah*. The New International Commentary on the Old Testament. Grand Rapids, MI: Wm. B. Eerdmans Publishing Co., 1990.

Ross, Allen P. "Studies in the Book of Genesis - Part 2: The Table of Nations in Genesis 10 - its Structure," *BibSac* vol. 137: 548 (Oct-Dec 1980): 340-50.

Ryrie, Charles. *Dispensationalism Today*. Chicago: Moody Press, 1966.

Schleiermacher, Friedrich. *Life of Schleiermacher*. Trans. F. Rowan, vol. 1. London: Smith, Elder, and co., 1860.

Segal, Alan. *Two Powers in Heaven: Early Rabbinic Reports about Christianity and Gnosticism*. Boston, Brill Academic Pub, 2002.

Siculus, Diodorus. *Bibliotheca Historica (Library of History)* I. In Edwin Murphy, *The Antiquities of Egypt: A Translation, with Notes, of Book I of the Library of History of Diodorus Siculus*. New Brunswick: Transaction Publishers, 1990.

Stanford, Miles. "The Dispensational Gospels." http://withchrist.org/mjs/gospels.htm

Stott, John. *The Message of Galatians*. Downer's Grove, IL: IVP, 1986.

Taylor, Justin. "A Recently Discovered Letter of Critique Written to the Apostle Paul." http://thegospelcoalition.org/blogs/justintaylor/2011/03/25/a-recently-discovered-letter-of-critique-written-to-the-apostle-paul/

Theological Dictionary of the New Testament. Ed. Gerhard Kittel, Geoffrey W. Bromiley and Gerhard Friedrich, electronic ed. Grand Rapids, MI: Eerdmans, 1964-.

Till, Farrell. "The 210-Year 'Solution'." http://theskepticalreview.com/JFTHowLongInEgypt2.html

Tucker, Ruth. *Another Gospel*. Grand Rapids, MI: Zondervan, 1989.

Tuscaloosa News, USA. "72% Say Church is Full of Hypocrites." By Sarah Bruyn Jones. Jan 19, 2008. http://www.religionnewsblog.com/20397/survey

Wenham, Gordon J. *Genesis 1-15*. Word Biblical Commentary. Dallas: Word, Incorporated, 2002.

White, A. Blake. "Sabbath: Galatians 4:8-10." http://www.youtube.com/watch?v=Ec1aTdFqVuk

White Horse Inn. "A Survey of Christian Faith and Practice", 11-8-2009.

_____ "The Book of Galatians." 1-31-2010.

_____. "What Is Faith?" 9-2-2007.

Wise, Michael O. *The First Messiah: Investigating the Savior Before Christ*. HarperCollins, 1999.

Zondervan Illustrated Bible Backgrounds Commentary Volume 3: Romans to Philemon. Ed. Clinton E. Arnold. Grand Rapids, MI: Zondervan, 2002.

Zorn, Walter D. "The Faithfulness of Jesus the Messiah." Delivered at the Midwestern Region of *ETS*, March 17-17, 2007. http://www.lincolnchristian.edu/Documents/PE.Zorn.FaithfulnessofJesus.pdf

Names Index

Galatians

Scripture and Reference Index

Acts

Romans

1 Corinthians

Ephesians

Philippians

Colossians

1 Thessalonians

2 Thessalonians

1 Timothy

2 Timothy

Titus

Hebrews

GREEK MATERIAL

CHRISTIAN CONFESSIONS

Passage Index

Galatians

www.ingramcontent.com/pod-product-compliance
Lightning Source LLC
Chambersburg PA
CBHW032031090426
42733CB00029B/87